The Life and Times of Mary Musgrove

UNIVERSITY PRESS OF FLORIDA

Florida A&M University, Tallahassee
Florida Atlantic University, Boca Raton
Florida Gulf Coast University, Ft. Myers
Florida International University, Miami
Florida State University, Tallahassee
New College of Florida, Sarasota
University of Central Florida, Orlando
University of Florida, Gainesville
University of North Florida, Jacksonville
University of South Florida, Tampa
University of West Florida, Pensacola

The Life and Times
of
Mary Musgrove

STEVEN C. HAHN

UNIVERSITY PRESS OF FLORIDA

Gainesville/Tallahassee/Tampa/Boca Raton
Pensacola/Orlando/Miami/Jacksonville/Ft. Myers/Sarasota

17 16 15 14 13 12   6 5 4 3 2 1

Library of Congress Cataloging-in-Publication Data
Hahn, Steven C., 1968–
The life and times of Mary Musgrove / Steven C. Hahn.
p. cm.
Includes bibliographical references and index.
ISBN 978-0-8130-4221-3 (alk. paper)
1. Musgrove, Mary, 1700–1765. 2. Indians of North America—Mixed descent—
Georgia—Biography. 3. Creek Indians—Biography. 4. Women—Georgia—
Biography. 5. Land settlement—Georgia. 6. Creek Indians—Mixed descent.
7. Georgia—History—Colonial period, ca. 1600–1775. I. Title.
E99.C9M85 2012
970.004'97—dc23
[B]
2012018864

The University Press of Florida is the scholarly publishing agency for the State
University System of Florida, comprising Florida A&M University, Florida Atlantic
University, Florida Gulf Coast University, Florida International University, Florida
State University, New College of Florida, University of Central Florida, University of
Florida, University of North Florida, University of South Florida, and University of
West Florida.

University Press of Florida
15 Northwest 15th Street
Gainesville, FL 32611-2079
http://www.upf.com

Dedicated to the memory of my grandmothers

Dora Edith (Earnhart) Frey (1919–2009)
Nina D. (Mungle) Hahn (1909–2004)

Strong southern women

Contents

The Life and Times of Mary Musgrove

Introduction

Unearthing Mary Musgrove

ON THE BANKS OF the Savannah River there was once an inconspicuous patch of earth that jealously guarded many secrets of the past. Located four miles upstream from the Georgia city of that name, this tranquil place merely a decade ago was covered with jungle-thick brush interspersed among wise, old live oak trees dripping with Spanish moss—timeless symbols of the Southern Lowcountry. Somehow, through more than two centuries of urban development, this area remained undisturbed by the modern city that came to surround it. But, the ways of progress demand that tranquil places must eventually become useful in some way. By the mid-1990s the Georgia Port Authority, which manages the busy international port of Savannah, had begun hatching plans to ease its growing pains by developing this land. As I write, construction on the new Container Berth 8 is underway, and a fresh coat of pavement now covers that once-tranquil spot of ground. As you read, the retail giants Target and IKEA will be using that area as a temporary resting place for iPods and ready-to-assemble shelving units.[1]

Before construction began, however, the Georgia Port Authority (in compliance with historic preservation laws) hired a team of archaeologists to examine the site. Preliminary investigations conducted in the mid-1990s turned up physical evidence that suggested the presence of earlier settlements, both colonial and prehistoric. Not everyone was prepared, however, for the secrets this spot of ground would reveal in the summer of 2002, when a backhoe began to strip away the eighteen inches of topsoil that blanketed the site. In the exposed subsoil archaeologists found various stains—features—that suggested the presence of past dwellings and refuse pits. Shoveling and sifting through ancient soil, the archaeologists salvaged artifacts that collectively weighed over one ton and, in many cases,

New Bern

Georgetown

Pee Dee River

Charles Town

Catawbas

Santee River

Edisto River

Pon Pon

Savannah

Darien

Frederica

Ft. Prince William

St. Augustine

Ninety Six

Ft. Congaree

Ft. Moore

Savannah River

Ogeechee River

Ebenezer

Ft. Argyle

Altamaha River

Mt. Venture

St. Mary's River

St. Johns River

Seminoles

OVERHILL CHEROKEES

MIDDLE CHEROKEES

Chota

LOWER CHEROKEES

Keowee

Valley Cherokees

Augusta

Oconee River

Ocmulgee River

Coweta (1690–1715)

Flint River

Ft. St. Marks

Apalachicola River

Ostinaulah R.

Etowah R.

Oostinaulah R.

Chattahoochee River

Okfuskee

Coweta

LOWER CREEKS

Cumberland River

Tennessee River

CHICKASAWS

Talapoosa River

Coosa River

UPPER CREEKS

Ft. Toulouse

Tuckabatchee

Pensacola

Alabama River

CHOCTAWS

Ft. Tombigbee

Tombigbee River

Mobile

Mississippi River

New Orleans

Southeastern North America, ca. 1700–1763

(Adapted from John Juricek, *Colonial Georgia and the Creeks*, 15.)

dated to the early years of the Georgia colony. Most conspicuous among them was a collection of eight intact glass bottles, found in the remains of a cellar precisely as they had been left centuries ago. The bottles, long since emptied, had probably once served as receptacles for rum, at one time illegal—and therefore popular—in colonial Georgia. Here and there other objects of domestic life turned up: a large earthenware platter, a Bellarmine jar of German manufacture, a butter churn. Likewise, the discovery of a pit filled with the charred remains of roasted oysters offered some indication of the inhabitants' culinary preferences.

Interesting as these finds were, the unearthing of large quantities of items common to the Indian deerskin trade gave archaeologists important clues as to the manner of people that once lived there. One clue to the site's trading-post past was the 48-inch-long barrel of a gun typically used in the Indian trade. Other iron implements, ranging from gun parts to an intact, but rusted, pair of scissors used for cutting cloth revealed much about the consumer demands of both Indian men and women. Most intriguing, perhaps, was the discovery of whittled-down deer antlers that Indians had once attached to a kind of cape fashioned from deerskin, which Indian hunters draped over their heads in hopes of luring unsuspecting whitetail deer. Historians have long noted this hunting practice among Southeastern Indians in the documentary record, but not until then had its physical remains been discovered. The identity of the homestead's owners came tantalizingly into focus with the discovery of a decorative brass stamp bearing the likeness of the letter "M." Given what was known from the historical record, it became clear that this sheltered grove had once been home to none other than Mary Musgrove, one of colonial Georgia's most famous (and at times, infamous) residents.[2] The secrets she left in the soil are now ours to make of what we will.

What more is to be said about Mary Musgrove? I have had the pleasure (and pain) of confronting this question ever since I began my research for this book. After all, the chronicles of colonial Georgia, in which Mary Musgrove appears, are more than two centuries old. The basic plot of her life is, by now, fairly well known. Mary was born around 1700 in the Creek Indian town of Coweta, though some, both in her lifetime and in ours, have disputed the details of that claim. Her mother was a Creek Indian. Her father was an English deerskin trader, who brought her as a child to South Carolina to live and receive education from the English. She later married John Musgrove of South Carolina, who was himself half-Creek and worked in the deerskin trade. In 1732 Mary and her husband moved to Yamacraw Bluff, on the south side of the Savannah River, to open a trading post. The Musgroves, as is well known, were among the first to greet James Oglethorpe and his fellow colonists when they arrived at the same bluff to establish the colony of Georgia in 1733. Thanks to her connections to the nearby Creek Indians and her fluency in both the English and Creek languages, Mary served the Georgia colony during its first few years as a diplomat and interpreter. Widowed twice in the prime of her life, Mary's successive husbands, Jacob Mathewes and Thomas Bosomworth, were cunning, grasping men, who influenced their wife to claim (illegally, as British officials would have it) vast tracts of land in Georgia by virtue of her Indian heritage. For nearly twenty years the Bosomworth land case festered like an open sore, souring relations between Georgia officials and the Bosomworths, not to mention the colony's relations with the Creek Indians. Only toward the end of her life did Mary and Thomas reach a compromise with the Crown, whereby the Bosomworths relinquished many of their claims in lieu of a cash settlement and title to St. Catherine's Island, Georgia. Mary died sometime around 1764 and is presumed buried on the island, now a wildlife refuge.

Familiar as I was with the basic story line, I took up the subject of Mary Musgrove because I held a nagging suspicion that we still knew relatively little about her. For one thing, many accounts contradict one another on basic statements of fact, thereby casting doubt upon the accepted narrative of her life.[3] Nor was I convinced that we had explored the full scope of historical and social contexts that influenced her actions and shaped the content of her character. Perhaps the principal reason for my writing this book is that (with one exception) nobody has ever bothered to compose a book-length work dedicated to her life.[4] That task, rather unfortunately in my view, has engaged the pen of the novelist more frequently than it has the pen of the historian, the result being several fictionalized works that bear little resemblance to reality.[5]

Historians likewise shoulder some blame for our limited understanding of Mary. Most who have written about her have done so in reference only to the ways in which her actions promoted or threatened the development of the Georgia colony, rendering her exploits simply another "chapter" in Georgia history.[6] Mary's life, on its own terms, has thus far proven an unfit subject for in-depth analysis. Likewise, Mary's ill repute among the earliest generations of Georgia historians remains a troublesome burden.

Even a cursory glance at most works of Georgia history published in the nineteenth and early twentieth centuries makes evident Mary's status as a pariah, a status grounded principally in a chronic fixation on the nagging problem of her land claims and the unsavory reputations of her last two husbands.[7] While these are certainly pertinent topics to discuss (and discuss them I will), many such works devote undue attention to a series of uncomfortable, at times hostile, encounters between Mary and Georgia officials that occurred in Savannah in July and August 1749. By force of repetition, the image of Mary at her worst moments (as even her husband admitted) has been branded into the narrative of Georgia history, from which even writers sympathetic to her have found it difficult to disengage.[8] Conversely, there are others who have committed the opposite error of conveniently overlooking Mary's checkered relationship with Georgia officials in order to depict her as the peacemaking "Pocahontas of Georgia."[9]

While a few recent historical works have corrected some of these base assumptions, much about Mary remains mysterious. One commonly known fact that has not been explored in detail is that Mary spent the first half of her life in the Creek nation and in South Carolina. It stands to reason, then, that any understanding of Mary's later life in Georgia must devote considerable attention to the formative years she spent elsewhere and engaged in other activities—in childhood, in marriage, in giving birth, in managing a household, in learning the business of the deerskin trade, and in surviving sporadic episodes of frontier violence. Also pertinent are her acquisition of the English language, literacy, and Christianity, and her familiarity with the English system of laws and property. While all would acknowledge that these skills and attendant worldviews were an important part of Mary's being, most writers treat her acquisition of them with little or no comment, as if the task of cultural transformation was easily achieved. The copious volumes written about (and by) later generations of Indians who endured boarding schools and other institutions of assimilation should give us pause before making any such assumption. Moreover, as a historical figure, Mary appears primarily in her public persona—as interpreter, diplomat, or petitioner. While it is reasonable to devote significant attention to these subjects (and I will), Mary's private life likewise deserves investigation. Only by training our focus upon evidence that might be dismissed as mundane can we gain insight into the manner in which Mary might have worked, thought, loved, grieved, worshipped, or held grudges. And, as women tended to live their private lives independent of the functions of the state, it is incumbent upon anyone writing about female subjects to break free, at times, from the master narrative of political history, important as such a narrative may be in Mary's case.

It is not by accident that I have begun this story with a brief account of the archaeological investigation of Mary's trading post. As was the case with that edifice, Mary Musgrove has remained hidden virtually in plain sight, in the readily accessible paper trail she and her contemporaries left behind. Indeed, my own research has proceeded as a kind of excavation. By sifting carefully through the copious records of the South Carolina and Georgia colonies, small pieces of evidence pertaining to Mary's life—some new, some underutilized—began to turn up. Taken individually, these bits of information seemed to reveal little, but when viewed in relation to other written artifacts, they appeared as threads in the fabric of Mary's life. Gradually, I discovered that there was more to Mary Musgrove than I had previously known. Yes, the Mary Musgrove depicted in this book, as a trader, diplomat, and occasional thorn in the side of Georgia officials, remains much the same woman. But the Mary Musgrove I came to know lived a life riddled with contradictions, making her more complex—and therefore more fascinating—than I had first appreciated. I discovered a young girl who likely encountered as the first words she would read in the English language "Our Father, Who Art in Heaven"; a young wife in South Carolina whose closest neighbors were Creek Indians rather than English colonists; a mother whose children came into the world with the assistance of both Creek and English midwives; a mature woman who harbored young colonial girls who had conceived children out of wedlock; a grieving widow who turned to the Reverend John Wesley for comfort, yet who sought out her Creek relatives when Georgians turned on her; a "Princess" of the Creek nation who boasted of her ability to command thousands of warriors, but yet signed her name to legal documents that relegated her to the status of a feme covert. Much to my delight, I found a woman whose taste in literature compelled her to read historical accounts of European exploration in Florida, indicating that she shared her biographer's interest in the history of the southern frontier.

Eventually, I came to realize just how important these bits of evidence were to a much bigger story. Much more than a "chapter" of Georgia history, Mary's atypical life bears witness to broader trends in the history of the colonial Deep South. Her mixed ancestry, itself a product of the frontier deerskin trade, affirms the presence of colonial America's "hidden" population of *mestizos*, who, as the historian Gary Nash writes, "conducted their lives, formed families, raised children, and created their own identities in ways that defied the official racial ideology," which relegated persons of color to the lowest social orders.[10] Mary's life was not, however, simply one of defiance, for in many respects she conformed to the ways of the colonists; she enslaved both Indians and Africans, married an Anglican minister predisposed to orthodoxy, and died a plantation mistress, making her not unlike many of her peers of British ancestry.

In the pages that follow I will attempt to untangle these seemingly contradictory aspects of Mary's in-between life. Suffice it to say here that I believe her unique background required her to display the outward trappings of conformity that she might avoid the stigma of being branded racially or culturally alien. This balancing act became even more important in her adult years, as the colonies of Georgia and South Carolina matured into plantation societies, which eventually supplanted her Creek relatives' way of life, not to mention certain aspects of that of her fur-trading father. If Mary could have had it her way, I imagine that she would have preferred to live in a world that did not force her to take sides, or to decide if she was "Creek" or "English." As Michael Green puts it, "just as no internal boundaries separated Coosaponakeesa and Mary, no rigid frontier needed to demarcate the Creek nation and Georgia. Her life represented a distinct vision for the future of the English in America, a future that was never realized."[11] In seeking to build that future, Mary drew upon past experiences, and I argue here that a consistency of purpose to make Georgia in the image of the frontier communities in which she resided as a younger woman—Coweta, Pon Pon, South Carolina, and Yamacraw Bluff—underlay her activities in Georgia, as both peacemaker and troublemaker.

While it is true that Mary Musgrove devoted much energy to bridging the differences between her parents' peoples, I do not think her actions can be explained as a function of an abstract reverence for multiculturalism. Rather, Mary promoted the development of a multicultural Georgia for practical and often self-serving reasons. Writing about certain "culture brokers" on the Pennsylvania frontier, the historian David Preston observes that many of these men were "hardly neutral" in their dealings with Native Americans, as the pursuit of economic self-interest often influenced their negotiations with local tribes.[12] While the fact that she was half Creek and female undoubtedly informed her outlook on Indian affairs, I nevertheless believe that Preston's observation holds true for Mary. As the following pages will attest, Mary possessed an uncanny ability to conflate her own self-interest with that of the Creek nation and the Georgia colony, and we must come to grips with that fact in order to understand her willingness to promote both harmony and discord.

Having broached the subject of biography, I wish to take a moment here to justify my chosen medium of historical presentation and to offer a few more words of disclaimer.[13] First of all, this work has taken the form of biography partly to satisfy my own whims but also in answer to Carol Berkin's call to "write more biography" of Southern women.[14] Precious few such biographies exist (the same is true for male subjects in the colonial Deep South) and the biographical medium offers a momentary escape from traditional narratives that overshadow the lives of ordinary (and extraordinary) women. As I have found that biographers tend to err on the side of praise for their subjects, my goal is to be frank about Mary's life. Readers will find plenty about her to praise, but at times, Mary swore too much, let her temper get the best of her, manipulated her own relatives, and held fellow human beings in bondage. Uncomfortable as these facts may be, to sanitize her life would in my mind be an injustice to her memory.

Let me be clear: Mary left relatively few of her own words behind and what we know about her comes largely from the scribbling of others. Consequently, to fill the gaps I routinely extrapolate from indirect evidence and ethnohistorical sources. So, this book should also be thought of as a "life and times" work, exploring one life in order to reflect generally upon a region's history. Moreover, much of what we know about Mary comes from men, some of whom were openly hostile to her. This fact requires that we read the evidence "against the grain" to untangle Mary from the pens her male antagonists have wielded. Being of the male variety myself, that untangling process must begin with me. I do not claim to have overcome all these problems in this book, but if it is true that the past is "like a foreign country," then any historian, of any gender, operates under similar constraints as they seek to solve the riddles of the past. Better to work within these limitations than to leave a story as exceptional as Mary's lying dormant in undisturbed soil.

1 🖋 Creek Beginnings

Your memorialist was born at the Cowetaw Town on
the Oakmulgee River, which is a branch of the Altamaha
and the Chief Town of the Creek Indian Nation.

Mary Bosomworth, 1747

How IT CAME TO PASS that Mary could claim such a beginning is something of a story in itself.

The infant girl who would one day become Mary Musgrove first drew
breath in the Creek Indian town of Coweta, and like most Indians she was
never exactly sure when she was born, at least as the English reckoned it
on their calendars. But given what we know of Mary and the Cowetas, the
year 1700 seems, to most historians, a reasonable guess. Although we have
come to know her as "Mary," Creek relatives likely addressed her using
kinship terms, later bestowing upon her a name expressive of her temper, physical appearance, or the circumstances of her birth. As she never
revealed that name in writing, it is unknowable to us, and we will address
her as most others did in her lifetime, as Mary.

Mary probably came into the world like any Creek newborn. Her
mother, feeling the first pangs of childbirth, would have first isolated herself in a special hut built outside of town. There, she endured labor alone
or with the help of a few female relatives, who brought victuals and water
and served as midwives. Such behavior was rooted not only in practical
considerations, but also reflected the Creeks' deeply beliefs about the order
of their universe and the respective roles men and women played in it. The
Creek Indians regarded men and women as complementary but distinct
halves of human creation, an order that was reflected in their speech, dress,
spiritual beliefs, and ceremonies. Right living demanded constant attendance to the purity of those gender distinctions, a purity they achieved by

ritually separating men from women. This ritual separation was particularly observed at those moments in life when masculine and feminine traits were most prominently on display. Menstruation and childbirth constituted two such special occasions for Creek women.[1]

As Creek women traditionally remained secluded after childbirth for a period ranging from four days to four months, Mary's mother would have been primarily, if not solely, responsible for introducing her daughter to the sensations of the world outside the womb. Creek women were known to bathe their children shortly after birth, and we might imagine Mary's mother trudging down to a nearby stream to wash the amniotic fluid and colostrum off of her. Cleanliness, though, was only one consideration, as there was a ritual quality to bathing among the Creeks, who believed that a daily (usually morning) plunge into the cold waters promoted hardiness in lives young and old. A hard lesson in hardiness, perhaps, but one thought necessary in a world that required physical fortitude.[2]

Lessons in fortitude only complemented the tender care that Creek women provided their newborns. Creek women typically breastfed their babies in excess of one year, which delayed the onset of ovulation and enabled them to space the birth of their children two to three years apart. Creek women sometimes prepared their newborns for suckling by dipping a finger or twig in water, and then sprinkling it on the infant's tongue. Mothers used a similar technique to feed their newborns a watery concoction of herbs and roots to make the newborn strong. Between feedings, Mary's mother probably laid her down on the soft skin of a fawn or a buffalo calf, a way of invoking those animals' shy behavior, which the Creeks regarded as proper for young females. As, by the turn of the eighteenth century, Creek women had begun using English cloth, chances are that the infant girl became accustomed to the feel of wool or linen against her tender skin.[3]

Eventually, Mary's mother would have decided that enough time had passed to allow her new baby to be seen in public. To eradicate any lingering traces of the pollution of childbirth, she would have bathed in the river, washing her clothes, dishes, and other personal effects as thoroughly as her body. The pair would then have left the birthing hut, finally giving the new mother the opportunity to introduce her baby girl to the people known as Cowetas.

If in some outward aspects the event of Mary's birth was ordinary, the Creek town she called home for the first few years of her life was anything but. By the year 1700 Coweta already experienced an eventful past and had become, in Mary's words, "the chief town in the Creek Indian nation."[4] Its political reputation, as well as its geographical situation, though, owed much to the forces of colonialism, that tangle of mercantile relationships, imperial rivalries, and movements of people and goods that formed the broader context for Coweta's rise to power. As a site of trade and diplomacy, Coweta likewise served as a bridge between the Indian and English worlds, the first of several such communities that Mary would call home during her lifetime.

From their original homelands in the Mississippi River basin, the Cowetas over several centuries had gradually drifted east, arriving on the Chattahoochee River just as English colonists began settling in South Carolina, which was established in 1670. Spurning Spanish Florida's repeated offers of alliance, the Cowetas turned their attention to the English and the burgeoning deerskin trade emanating out of Charles Town, South Carolina. In 1685, the Cowetas welcomed the first English traders into their territory. This move incurred the wrath of Florida officials, who in 1686 sent soldiers to burn Coweta to the ground and in December 1689 built a fort in the vicinity of its ashes. The following spring, the Cowetas led a mass Indian evacuation of the Chattahoochee River in order to gain a better vantage point for trade. For the next quarter century, the Cowetas served as South Carolina's most reliable trade partners and their most prolific military allies.[5]

Coweta-on-the-Ocmulgee was just one of at least ten Indian towns that came into being on that river and its tributaries in what is today the Georgia piedmont. We do not know for certain its precise location, but evidence indicates that the Cowetas lived about thirty miles upstream from present-day Macon, Georgia.[6] While physical evidence of Coweta-on-the-Ocmulgee is currently lacking, we may still make a few educated guesses about life there based on historical and archaeological evidence. Coweta appears to have been modest in size, perhaps with as few as thirty "gun men" (that is, men capable of fighting wars) and a total of no more than two hundred individuals.[7] Like most Creek towns, Coweta-on-the-Ocmulgee probably featured a well-swept public square, which would have been surrounded by four buildings—shed-like structures festooned with ritual paraphernalia and painted with sacred symbols—used for ceremonial gatherings. Cowetas also would have prepared a so-called "chunky yard" or ball ground, a clear, level area that the Creeks used for their favorite games.[8]

Beyond the public spaces, Creek families built their homes, typically rectangular structures made from young trees sunk into the ground, interwoven with river cane and saplings, and daubed with mud to keep out the elements. The Creeks modeled the arrangement of their houses on the town square, and it is thought that the buildings comprising these domestic compounds each had a specific use, perhaps for storing grain and deerskins, for cooking, or for sleeping.

Archaeological evidence likewise suggests that the Cowetas consumed a wide range of the Ocmulgee watershed's natural resources, ranging from white-tailed deer (their principal source of protein) to freshwater mussels and hickory nuts. As for domesticated plants, corn had probably been their staple for centuries, but the Cowetas grew fond of at least one species the Spanish introduced into the area, the peach tree, as is evident from the multitude of peach pits found at some sites.

Ocmulgee River sites also contain an array of goods manufactured in Europe. Glass beads, pendants, and buttons appear to have been the most commonly sought items. Also common, though in lesser quantities, were decorative items such as iron bracelets and bells. While ornamentation was important, English trade goods also had a utilitarian appeal, as the rusted remnants of iron gun parts, hatchets, hoes, axes, and knives confirm. In addition to these artifacts, the documentary record attests to a brisk trade in cloth, principally woolens and linens from England. Spanish majolica (a type of dinnerware) and olive jars provide lasting evidence of the Creeks' plunder of the Florida missions around the turn of the eighteenth century.[9]

The assemblage of artifacts found on the Ocmulgee River sites can therefore be attributed to the trade between the colony of South Carolina and its Indian neighbors. Initially, the Proprietors of South Carolina (the eight men in whose name the colony's charter was originally granted in 1663) established a trade monopoly with the Indians, and it was under this scheme that the deerskin trade operated for a few years, until enterprising men from Carolina, seeking their own fortunes in deerskins, began violating proprietary rules. By 1690 a virtually open and unregulated trade with the Indians of the interior ensued, attracting men from high and low into the business, as merchants, traders, and lesser employees such as pack-horsemen. By the end of the century, Carolina merchants were exporting tens of thousands of deerskins annually, in excess of sixty-four thousand in 1699 alone (a bumper year).[10]

While the ability to furnish new and useful goods gave the traders some leverage over the Indians, the fact is that the Indians still held the balance of power and thus were able to control the social context of their interactions. Traders seeking to peddle their wares in Indian communities had to overcome some important disadvantages. Most English traders presumably did not at first know how to speak Muskogee or other Indian languages, making bargaining, not to mention social interaction, difficult. These early traders must also have been a socially awkward lot, not knowing the proper way to smoke tobacco from a pipe, to greet a friend, to show respect to the elderly, or to treat the ladies with propriety.

It was, of course, in the Indians' own interest to help the awkward Englishmen overcome these potential impediments to friendly social intercourse and trade. The principal means by which the Indians helped to bridge the cultural divide was by offering the hands of their women in marriage. From the Indians' perspective, this practice had the advantage of creating kinship alliances with rootless strangers who had no previous ties to the community. By seeking out such alliances, Creek families gained a measure of control over the traders, imposing upon them local rules of kinship reciprocity. Moreover, the Creek brides of the English traders served as important cultural intermediaries. In quiet hours, Indian women had the opportunity to teach their husbands the rudiments of the language and the social customs of their people. Also, by way of their husbands, Indian women gained privileged access to happenings in the colonies, which revealed potentially valuable information that could be shared with town leaders.[11]

As the Cowetas claimed to have been "the first" to open the trading path to Carolina, it should come as no surprise that theirs is the first Creek town on record to have offered one of its women to an English trader.[12] In 1685, Quiair, the chief of Coweta, gave the hand of his "niece" in marriage to the "leader" of an English trade delegation, no doubt the South Carolina trader and explorer Henry Woodward, who led the English trade delegation that arrived in Coweta that summer.[13] The match was short-lived due to his untimely death the following year, but Woodward blazed a trail that other Englishmen would be obliged to follow. It is likely that many unions between English traders and Indian women were never documented, but traders who worked around the turn of the eighteenth century—men such as John Musgrove, Thomas Jones, Thomas Graves, Thomas Welch, William Steads, Phillip Gilliard, and Alexander Nicholas—all had Indian mistresses or wives. Among these men was a trader of modest means named Edward Griffin, who found companionship with a Coweta woman. The intertwining of their lives and, more specifically, their genes, explains how Mary came into being in the first place.

The Courtship of Mary's Father

The identity of Mary's mother remains a matter of speculation. The woman's name is not recorded, but, as an adult, Mary avowed that her mother was "sister to the old Emperor," Brims of Coweta. Known also by his war title "Hoboyetly," Brims had emerged as the leader of the Cowetas by 1705 and remained so until his death in late 1732. Likewise Mary claimed to be "of the same blood" as the "mico's and chief's" who ruled Coweta in the 1740s, including Brims's "son" Malatchi and his brother Chigelli. Based upon these assertions, it seems that Mary's mother was closely related to Coweta's chiefs, granting her infant girl, by birthright, a privileged place in Coweta society.[14]

We know more about Mary's father. His name was Edward Griffin, and he probably came to South Carolina in the 1690s, as indicated by the arrivals of several other men by that surname, possibly relatives, before 1700. Some of the Griffins prospered and went on to become respectable planters, weavers, and ship captains.[15] Mary's father, Edward, however, never rose to the ranks of the landholding class and never held public office or a rank in the militia. Instead, he worked all his adult life in the Indian trade, spending much of his time, we may presume, among his Indian clients.

For much of his career as a trader, Griffin worked in the employ of Colonel Thomas Broughton, one of several great planters who dominated South Carolina's Indian trade. Having ready access to credit and political influence, men such as Broughton used hirelings like Griffin to conduct trade on their behalf in the Indian nations. Broughton's circumstances, in particular, were favorable due not only to his wealth but also to the colony's governor, Nathaniel Johnson, who was Broughton's father-in-law. Favorably located near trading paths connecting it to the frontier,

Broughton's Mulberry Plantation was a common destination for many a trader venturing to and from Indian country. An aggressive businessman, Broughton may have been guilty (as others charged) of having his traders enslave members of Indian nations allied with South Carolina—a violation of the colony's laws. Broughton also appears to have pressured his father-in-law to oppose regulations to the Indian trade that might have circumscribed his activities.[16] For these and other reasons, Edward Griffin may have found Broughton a good employer. Griffin, for his part, seems to have been a devoted employee.

Judging by the few times he surfaces in the public record, Edward appears to have been a contentious man, possessing a sharp tongue and a willingness to stir controversy, traits he may have passed on to his daughter. In 1703, Griffin ran afoul of the law by uttering "several contemelous and reflecting words" against Dr. Charles Burnham of Charles Town, a member of the Commons House of Assembly. Griffin's indelicate speech earned him a night in jail, and he was able to earn his release only after writing a petition to the assembly and agreeing to pay ten shillings to cover the cost of his confinement.[17]

Four years later Griffin waded into political controversy over the regulation of the Indian trade. In 1707 the South Carolina Assembly passed a much-needed law regulating the trade, a law Thomas Broughton and Governor Johnson opposed. When the law went into effect later that year, the experienced trader and frontiersman Thomas Nairne, a proponent of regulation, was named as the first Indian agent.[18] Nairne began work in his official capacity as an agent that fall, when he was directed to spend several months traveling through Indian villages. Not long after Nairne's agency commenced, Thomas Broughton received two letters from eyewitnesses who had observed Nairne in action, both of which Broughton submitted to the assembly to peruse. Edward Griffin may have penned at least one of the letters, which castigated Nairne for giving a speech before the Indian traders that "degraded his honor the governor" by calling him a "foolish old man." The letter also charged that Nairne arbitrarily confiscated Indian slaves and selectively denied unlicensed traders the opportunity to sell their goods.[19] When Nairne returned to Charles Town the next summer, Edward Griffin and another Broughton employee, John Dickson, were on hand to testify that they had overheard Nairne in a tavern speaking treasonously against Queen Anne. Nairne was arrested two days later on charges of treason and languished in jail for the next five months.

Many have assumed that Edward Griffin and John Dickson were little more than naive dupes, whom the government used to trump up false charges against an innocent man.[20] Nairne wrote contemptuously of them as well, calling Dickson a "perfect villain" and Griffin a "meer lunatick."[21] Nairne's supposed treasonous talk about Queen Anne might have been a fabrication. But Edward Griffin was neither a lunatic nor a dupe. Nairne's attempts to regulate the trade directly threatened Edward Griffin's trade activities, and, by association, the financial interest of his employer. Griffin and Dickson's indictment against Nairne, then, was a politic, rather than lunatic, response to the trading act (and the man responsible for enforcing it) that they appear to have opposed.[22]

In spite of his opposition to Nairne, Griffin evidently adapted to the new regulations and continued working in the Indian trade. Extant records indicate that Griffin was, at best, only modestly successful in his chosen profession. Griffin formed a partnership with Charles Peirce and another man who went by the last name of Holford. In compliance with the Indian trading act, they posted bond for a trading license in March 1711 and appear to have continued in business together for the next three years.[23] Griffin may have profited somewhat while in partnership with those men, as he posted bond for a license in his own name in 1714, which suggests that he had accumulated enough capital to trade on his own.[24]

But the life of an Indian trader, if sometimes rewarding, could be a risky one. Sometimes, those risks came from the Indians, who were known to murder the occasional trader and plunder his goods. At other times, risk came at the hands of South Carolina's own Indian agents, who enforced the rules of the trade arbitrarily to enrich themselves or perhaps to reward their friends. On one occasion, Edward Griffin rather unfortunately experienced the wrath of the Indian agent John Wright, who in the fall of 1713 seized a pack of skins from "Charles Pearce &c," no doubt a reference to the partnership of Holford, Peirce, and Griffin. In addition to seizing their skins, the agent forced them "to pay double pay" to their Indian burdeners, thus cutting into their profit margin. And though Wright's actions were brought to the attention of the Commissioners of the Indian Trade (the Indian trade's regulatory body) in November 1713, there is no evidence to indicate that Wright was ordered to compensate Griffin's company.[25]

Any drain on profits could be a serious matter, as many traders lived just a few steps ahead of their creditors. The Indian trade, in fact, might best be thought of as a chain of credit connecting London mercantile firms to merchants in Charles Town, who in turn furnished goods on credit to the traders. In many cases hard money, which was difficult to come by, never passed hands, and even the most successful traders were what today we would call "cash poor." Edward Griffin was among these cash poor and, as a consequence, occasionally ran into debt. In the years 1712 and 1713, Griffin borrowed ninety-one pounds from three different men, all Indian traders. Although he owed a relatively modest sum, Griffin was unable to pay, and about a year later the three creditors filed debt lawsuits against Griffin in the Court of Common Pleas.[26] Griffin, however, chose not to appear in court, and we do not know if he ever made good on his debts.

So, if Edward Griffin might be judged as a sometimes indebted, sharp-tongued contrarian, compared to many of his peers he nevertheless appears to have been a generally decent man. In contrast to many traders, who were infamous for their drunkenness, violence toward the Indians, and scurrilous business practices, not once was Edward Griffin charged with any of the infractions for which so many other traders stood accused before the colony's board of Indian Commissioners. As the Creek Indians never once complained about him, we might imagine that his Creek acquaintances thought well of him, well enough, that is, to accept him as an in-law.

While bicultural marriages occurred often enough, it is generally assumed that Southeastern Indians were ambivalent about marriage with English men. On the one hand, a young woman's marriage to an English trader had its advantages, as the trader's self-interest could converge with that of his wife's people.[27] On the other hand, Indians had good reason to view English traders as potentially poor spouse material. Having been raised in a foreign culture, most traders presumably lacked many of the important skills that defined Indian manhood. For example, Indian men were expected to provide food for their families, and traders unaccustomed to tracking, shooting, and processing wild game would have had difficulty fulfilling their obligations to feed their wives and other dependents. English traders also would have lacked the requisite knowledge to participate in Indian ceremonial life, and they lacked kinship connections that were essential to a person's identity. It is plausible, then, that Edward Griffin, regardless of his attractive qualities, had much to prove before any Indian woman would have him.

Although Creeks exercised considerable personal autonomy in choosing their spouses, Creek marriages were nevertheless communal affairs requiring the tacit approval of their clan-kin. Typically, a Creek man proposed marriage indirectly, by sending his mother, sister, or another female relative to speak on his behalf to the maternal relatives of his bride-to-be. The prospective bride's maternal relatives would then discuss the matter among themselves to evaluate the proposed match. A ceremony solemnizing the marriage usually followed. Creek marriage rituals, however, adhered to no standardized form, and the written record documents a variety of practices.[28] Some rituals were relatively simple, involving an exchange of gifts.[29] Many other Southeastern Indian wedding ceremonies, though, appear to have been more involved and drawn out, in which onus was placed on the man to "prove himself a brave warrior, and a cunning, industrious hunter." Male ritual activity in marriage therefore typically involved symbolic demonstrations of prowess in these realms of activity.[30]

The young suitor Edward Griffin, then, was probably on his best behavior whenever he was among the Cowetas, as he attempted to win Mary's mother in marriage. To win his future in-laws approval, Griffin may have given them cloth, ammunition, guns, or iron knives, anxiously hoping that he could somehow keep his creditors at bay and cover their cost himself. As the family pondered his marriage offer, Griffin might have spent time in the field learning how to track deer or practicing his marksmanship in hopes of bringing his bride a handsome gift of venison. It is also possible that Griffin made some show of loyalty to Brims and his family, agreeing, perhaps reluctantly, to join his warriors in a skirmish against another Indian tribe or assisting them in an attack on a mission village in Florida.

The character of Mary's father's courtship of her mother, of course, is unknown. But we do know that Griffin established a relatively durable relationship with his Indian wife. Griffin's Coweta wife bore him at least two children, a boy who went by the name Edward Griffin, and the daughter, who became Mary Musgrove. It is probable that Edward was the older of the two, and given the tendency among Creek women to space the birth of their children by at least two years, we can infer that Griffin and his Coweta wife remained a couple for at least that amount of time.[31] Although there is reason to suspect that Griffin was a rather attentive father, business would have required him, like most traders, to spend considerable time back in the colony, making his residence in Coweta intermittent. And while Griffin's contributions as a parent later became manifest, Mary was very much her mother's daughter as she grew from an infant into a young girl.

Mary's early childhood was probably similar, if not identical, to that of other female Indian children. As the daughter of a Coweta woman, the townspeople would have recognized her not as an individual bearing "mixed-blood," but as a member of her mother's Creek clan. Reckoned through the female line, clan membership conferred an essentially "Indian" identity upon any individual so belonging, regardless of the father's origin, as the Creek Indians held that children "belonged" to their mothers. This was no less true—and possibly more—for children born to European fathers, who sometimes complained of their Creek wives exercising "sole direction of the children."[32]

Mary's mother nevertheless would not have labored alone in caring for her and Edward. Child rearing was instead a collective effort, usually involving the mother's female clan-kin. While not directly responsible for the hands-on care of young children, Mary's male clan-kin would have also doted on her as one of their own. By their example, she would have received repeated, sometimes subtle reminders of her clan's expectations for proper behavior. As the Creek Indians—and for that matter all Indians—conceived it, mastering the rules of kinship was the quintessence of the socialization process; to be a good kinsman was, in effect, to be "civilized."

Central to those rules was generosity, the demonstration of which was considered obligatory and which bound members of the entire clan to each other. Mary would have witnessed the spirit of kinship generosity each time a male clan member returned home bearing meat, giving some to the elderly who were too blind or lame to hunt. She would have observed the same ethic at work among her female relatives, as they worked themselves into the ground attending to the sick and dying, cared for her while her mother worked, or shared food with a hungry relative, even if they had very little to eat themselves. Although we can hardly expect her to have mastered all the rules of kinship as a young child, Mary nevertheless may have learned her lessons well. As an adult Mary Musgrove spent much of her life indebted, due partly to the fact that she was generous to a fault toward her English and Indian neighbors, and gave freely, asking for nothing in return.

Mary's early childhood among her Creek kin might have been a relatively indulgent one, at least compared to that of a young English girl.

While English parents took punitive measures to "break" the independent wills of their children, and expected them to behave more or less like miniature adults, Creek parents had a considerably different outlook on youth and development.[33] As the Creeks understood it, childhood was a time when the individual's ability to reason and to control his or her passions was underdeveloped; these abilities, it was thought, took a lifetime to achieve, hence the Creeks' reverence for old age. As a consequence, Creek parents expected their children to be demanding, to act before thinking, and to make mistakes. Creek parents therefore tolerated the follies of youth more easily than did their European counterparts, who commented frequently on the Indians' unwillingness to mete out corporal punishment. Persuasion and mild ridicule instead were the Indians' primary tools for instilling proper behavior in their young people.[34] Moreover, the Creeks tended to expect very little work from their children, in the belief that their constitutions were ill suited to the rigors of manual labor. And although a Creek childhood was not entirely undisciplined, Mary's early years among the Cowetas prepared her very little for the rigors of rote learning, of catechismal indoctrination, or of the routines of plantation life to which she later had to adapt when she came to live among the colonists.

Unlike English children, who were encouraged to walk at an early age, Mary was probably allowed to crawl with relative freedom during her first year of life and learned to walk at her own pace, with the occasional assistance of female clan-kin.[35] As she grew into a toddler, Mary most likely continued to suckle occasionally at her mother's breast, as it was common for children to decide for themselves when to stop nursing, sometimes as late as seven years of age.[36] As with nursing, Mary probably toilet trained on her own accord, rather than being subjected to an arbitrary regimen established by her parents. Southeastern Indian children typically wore little clothing, particularly in the summer months, which made it easy for them to relieve themselves when (and where) nature called. As Mary gained more control over her excretory functions, her relatives would have gradually expected her to show more modesty and relieve herself in the woods or elsewhere out of sight.

Unless Mary was endowed with an exceptional memory, it is unlikely that she was able to recall many of these early life experiences. Still, it stands to reason that she retained at least a fleeting memory of her early childhood, and a comparison can be made with Native American women writers from the nineteenth and twentieth centuries, whose life experiences mirrored Mary's in some ways. Women such as Gertrude Bonnin (Lakota), Sarah Winnemucca (Paiute), and Ella Deloria (Dakota) all grew up in the Indian manner among their own people, acquired formal education among whites, and later bridged both worlds as writers and activists. Taking up the pen as adults, each of these writers drew inspiration from their childhood experiences, and all reveal the unmistakable influence of their mothers, their female clan-kin, as well as the daily work routines of Indian women. It is thus likely that the gender-specific experiences of Creek women had a profound, perhaps lasting, impact on Mary, whose first impressions would have been formed at her mother's side. Accordingly, long before she had ever learned to read, sign legal documents, or engage in diplomacy, Mary learned what it meant to be a Coweta woman, an identity that she would never entirely shed.

Regarding the work routines of Indian women, suffice it to say that most European observers believed that women bore the brunt of life's drudgery, while the men idled away their time with the aristocratic pursuits of politics, hunting, and warfare.[37] To the untrained eye, this may have appeared to be true, but such an observer would have failed to understand the complexity of the gendered division of labor among Indians, in which men and women played separate, but complementary roles. The world of Indian women—labor intensive as it was—was not all drudgery; indeed, women worked collectively at their own pace, and took time out to converse or attend to their children. While Creek gender conventions granted them only a secondary role in politics, Creek women nevertheless exercised considerable economic independence and claimed ownership of their homes and property.[38] Important to Creek economic life, the work of Creek women varied from season to season and required a diverse set of skills that all young Creek girls were expected to master by the time they had reached adulthood. Mary probably left Coweta long before she had mastered these skills, but time spent among her female relatives must have left an indelible mark on her expectations for womanhood.

As young girls tended to learn by imitating their mothers, Mary would have spent considerable time at her mother's side as she engaged in agricultural pursuits, the most important of which was the communal, festive cultivation of maize. Every spring, Mary's mother would have joined other female relatives in making regular trips to a plot of cleared land that their clan had claimed by ancient right. Mary would have observed how they hoed the soil, working up rows of small mounds arranged several feet apart. The youngster likewise must have noticed how others following close behind used a sharpened digging stick to make a small hole at the summit of each mound and dropped a few corn kernels into each hole.[39] And although she was too small to be very helpful, it is plausible that Mary trailed close behind, and on occasion awkwardly imitated her elders by trying her hand at the hoe, making errant holes with a digging stick, or by dropping a few corn kernels in place.

As with agriculture, Mary likely helped her mother gather wild plants, fruits, seeds, and firewood, quite possibly the first chores she was entrusted as a young child.[40] In addition to gathering the fruits of the earth, Creek women bore primary responsibility for cooking, and Mary likewise would have spent considerable time watching her female relatives prepare Creek culinary favorites, such as *sofke*, a soup-like dish made of cracked corn hominy.[41] Although there is evidence to suggest that the introduction of English trade goods eroded the Creeks' skill at making handicrafts, Mary would have nevertheless observed that her female relatives continued to make earthen pottery more or less the old-fashioned way. Some might have preferred earthen vessels to the traders' brass kettles; others might have been loath to give up the old ways because they considered pottery-making a form of artistic expression that defined them as women of a particular clan. Mary, then, would have had ample opportunity to accompany her mother on trips to the banks of a local stream to search for clays with the proper consistency. She would have noticed how her mother hunched over to wind the clay into coils and assemble them into the form of a vessel, which would later be smoothed, decorated, and fired.[42]

Creek women also invested considerable effort in the manufacture of clothing. Around her mother's house, the subject of clothing must have generated a considerable amount of conversation, given that the current generation of Creeks had begun to dress in a manner significantly different from that of their grandparents. Mary might have heard from her grandmother that their people had once dressed almost exclusively in skins, cloth made out of woven mulberry fibers, or mantles constructed from bird feathers. She likely heard her female relatives discuss the merits of the dizzying array of English fabrics now available to them and wax fondly about how easily cloth could be cut with English scissors, how metal awls enabled them to punch holes effortlessly, or how steel needles enabled them to sew with greater precision.

What enabled Coweta women to obtain cloth and sewing implements was the truck in deerskins that had, in part, caused them to relocate to the Ocmulgee River in the first place. Most scholars recognize that the Southeastern Indians had prepared deerskins for centuries and that these skins had served as instruments of tribute and exchange long before Europeans set foot in the region. The establishment of the trade in Charles Town, South Carolina, however, made deerskins a commodity, which expanded the scope and volume of hunting. For the men, this meant more intensive and lengthier hunting seasons. Women, too, felt the effects of intensified commercial hunting, as it was their traditional role to transform the raw deer hides into supple, durable—and thus marketable—skins. Mary's mother, then, probably spent far more time working with hides than did her grandmothers.[43]

As much as these tasks might have occupied her female relatives, all would not have been work for the young Mary, for play was an equally important part of a Creek childhood. Foot races, for example, were a common diversion for children of both sexes, and we may surmise that Mary occasionally lined up with other children in the *chunkee* yard ready to test her feet, running hard when the signal was given. In addition to these athletic endeavors, children—like their elders—enjoyed playing games of skill or chance. In one popular game, called "rolling the stone," contestants rolled a small ball or disc along a shallow trench, at the end of which several small holes had been dug. The goal was to roll the ball such that it came to rest in one of the holes, points being rewarded according to the level of difficulty.[44]

Creek children also spent much of their leisure time listening to stories told by their elders. It is conceivable that as a young girl Mary spent many a night by the hearth, listening as an elderly relative spun tales intended to impart knowledge of the past, teach moral lessons, or simply to amuse. In these small moments we find the transmission of Creek culture from generation to generation. We should not presume, however, that a child of seven years could become a walking repository of all its diverse aspects. Much of the knowledge that constituted Creek culture was specialized, requiring years of training and the accumulation of experience.[45] Children, then, most likely were not exposed to the more sophisticated Creek storytelling traditions, but instead listened to simpler tales of animals and mythological creatures. While entertaining on one level, these stories provided children with models for proper behavior and oriented them in the natural and spiritual worlds.[46]

For example, Mary would have learned that the patchwork design on a turtle's shell derived from a punishment he received (the smashing of his shell) for verbally abusing a woman while she was pounding corn, a subtle reminder that words should be chosen carefully and uttered deliberately. She also would have been familiar with Thunder, a mythological hunter who dwelt in the sky, caused thunder and lightning, and, if venerated properly, assisted Creek hunters in the pursuit of game. More ominous, though, were the Tie-snakes, serpent-like creatures that inhabited bodies of water and were central characters in many Creek tales. We might imagine a young Mary captivated by stories of how, by eating a concoction of squirrel brains, a man transformed himself into the first Tie-Snake, and how Tie-Snakes would occasionally kidnap unsuspecting persons that ventured too close to watery places.[47]

More generally, Mary's early exposure to these types of myths would have instilled in her a rudimentary understanding of Creek spirituality, which differed drastically from the Christianity she professed as an adult. Most fundamental was the difference between Christianity's monotheism and the Creek belief in a diverse spiritual universe. As a child, Mary might have heard occasional talk of a being her mother's people called *Ibofanga* or "The Master of Breath," which they associated with the sun. Although the Creeks honored this deity every time they smoked tobacco, they did not believe that it held a monopoly on spiritual powers. Nor was *Ibofanga* the chief object of Creek theological or philosophical speculation. Rather, the Creeks devoted much of their attention to lesser spiritual beings, each with distinct characteristics and abilities, such as the Tie-Snakes and Thunder.

Another key distinction between Christianity and Creek spirituality lay in their respective treatments of gender. Stories relating the origin of corn, for instance, posit that it derived from the blood of women and that its generation was a mystical, secretive process requiring solitude. Because the Creeks sanctified corn, their tendency to associate women with its origin bestowed upon them an elevated status. This origin story differs markedly from the Judeo-Christian story of the Biblical Eve—who discovered fruit in a different manner—and her association with original sin. Young Mary would have thus understood that female blood was a powerful thing, capable of generating human life and the fruits of the earth that sustained it. So powerful was female blood, in fact, that it had to be protected jealously from the men, which might have helped Mary understand why her menstruating female relatives disappeared for a few days each month, hiding away in huts built in the woods for that purpose. Perhaps she came to understand why the women brought their children into the world in similar isolation, knowing that she must do the same when her turn for motherhood came.[48]

Child of War

If, in the above approximation of her early childhood, Mary's life should appear tranquil, it is important to recognize that she was also a child of war, born at a time of increasing hostility between the Creeks and the Spanish mission Indians in Florida. Buttressed by English arms and ammunition, the Creeks played an important role in destroying much of La Florida. In the process of reducing the missions, Creek warriors regularly took live Indian captives and sold them to slave merchants in Charles Town, making the Creeks an integral part of colonial America's most robust trade in Indian slaves. Exalted in victory and enriched by the trade in slaves and skins, Creek military success nevertheless came at a price, as the South Carolina government increasingly pressured Creek warriors to enlarge the scope of their efforts, encouraging far-flung contests against Spanish and French outposts on the gulf coast and against distant Indian nations.

Meanwhile, the tendency among traders to extend credit liberally to the Indians incrementally increased Creek debts to the English. The inability of Creek hunters to make good on their debts, combined with the increasing bellicosity of the English traders, set both parties at odds with each other, souring what had once seemed a mutually beneficial relationship. Mary may have been too young to understand or to notice, but the brewing antagonism between the Creeks and the traders cast an ominous pall on the Ocmulgee River, foreshadowing the eventual breach between the two that was just a few years off.

Creek wars of attrition against Spanish mission Indian villages commenced not long after the exodus of the Chattahoochee River towns to the Ocmulgee River. The first attacks came in 1691, and in 1702, Spain and England officially declared war. Due to the efforts of Carolina's Indian allies, the end came rather swiftly for the Florida mission villages. In May 1702 English-allied Indians burned and looted the Timucuan mission of Santa Fe, taking many of its residents prisoner. In October of that year, a war party led by the South Carolina militiaman Anthony Dodsworth confronted a joint Spanish-Apalachee war party sent to check their advance on the Flint River.[49] Dodsworth's men made quick work of the Apalachees, and more than a year later, Colonel James Moore struck what was for all intents and purposes the deathblow, when in January 1704 he led a party consisting of fifty white men and one thousand Indians into Apalachee. There, Moore and his warriors assaulted and captured the mission village of Ayubale, and later forced the fortified town of San Luis into submission. In the wake of Moore's raid, only two Apalachee villages were left standing, both of which fell when Creek war parties returned that summer. A Creek raid on the lone remaining Timucua outpost of Abosaya in the summer of 1705 completed the conquest of North Florida, leaving the Creeks and other Indians allied with the English as masters of that territory.[50]

While young and near her mother's side in Coweta, Mary nevertheless would have felt the second-hand effects of her people's wars. Visiting delegations of South Carolina officials, for example, likely caused Coweta to stir with excitement as they fanned the flames of war. As a toddling two-year-old, Mary was probably present when Anthony Dodsworth visited Coweta in the summer of 1702 to deliver a war message from the governor of South Carolina urging the Creeks to "depopulate" the Spanish mission provinces. Shouts of approval may have punctuated Dodsworth's speech, as he encouraged them to "carry off the women" and have the Christian Indians "exterminated from these parts." While the war was regarded as offensive, Dodsworth's speech also seems to have spurred the Cowetas to make defensive preparations, including the construction of a "palisade" to defend the women and children back in town.[51]

A more conspicuous gathering occurred in Coweta just three years later, when a large delegation of Indians and three Englishmen arrived there to ratify the first of many Anglo-Creek treaties. Conducted at the "Coweta Court" in August 1705, the ceremony drew a range of Coweta's Indian allies from far and wide. Among them were their neighbors from just downstream, led by the headmen of Ocmulgee and Cussita. Others, however, came from culturally affiliated peoples who lived to the west, the Abicas, Tallapoosas, and Alabamas of north-central Alabama.[52]

While the men gathered to declare their "hearty alliance" with the Crown of England and made promises to "give total rout" to the French and Spanish, the women would have busied themselves making Coweta habitable for the throng of visitors, putting their domestic skills to much-needed use in extending hospitality. Mary would have noticed how many families cleared their cabins to make room for weary guests to sleep, perhaps causing her to reside temporarily in the house of a relative, sleeping and eating in cramped quarters that had been filled—temporarily, one hoped—past capacity. Food preparation was likewise essential, for the visitors probably traveled with just enough victuals to reach their destination. Coweta women, then, would have been extra busy making *sofke* or bread from corn, boiling venison, and fetching water. The three English visitors would have grabbed the attention of the Cowetas and likewise expected hospitable treatment. Little did Mary know that one of the men sent to interpret on that occasion was John Musgrove, the South Carolina trader who was to become her father-in-law.

War manifested in village life in other ways, particularly in the ritualistic manner by which the Cowetas prepared for it. Mary probably noticed, for example, the change that overcame the able-bodied men as they readied themselves for military actions. She would have sensed their aloofness as they withdrew from intimate contact with women, refusing to eat with them during the day or to lie with them at night. She might likewise have noticed the warriors' tendency to wear little clothing, painting their upper bodies in red and black, and that they spent much of their time in the council house whooping and hallowing to the beat of a drum. Men also purified themselves for battle on such occasions, but their methods of fasting and of drinking beverages made of consecrated roots and herbs would have remained mysterious to all the women in Coweta.[53]

The return of victorious war parties was a festive occasion as well, featuring choreographed ceremonies that Mary would have had ample opportunity to witness. Typically, a runner sent by a returning war party informed the villagers of their good luck in vanquishing their foes, prompting the women to sweep their homes, bathe, and dress in their finery. Upon the warriors' return, the Cowetas would have gathered to watch the victors dance around the town's "war pole," usually the trunk of a tree that had been painted red and festooned with war implements and trophies of human hair. After parading these scalps around publicly, it was common for a war captain to affix some of them to the tops of the homes of families that had recently lost loved ones in battle, a symbol of the vengeance that was finally theirs. Although warfare was a man's business, female relatives of the avenged would have celebrated victory as well, perhaps staying up the whole night dancing and singing.[54]

As is the case in any war, however, some men inevitably fell in battle, and rituals of mourning would have tempered the Cowetas' victory celebrations. Chief among the mourners of a deceased warrior were his female clan-kin and his widow, who, in particular, would have been conspicuous enough for a child to notice. Mary was therefore probably acquainted with at least a few families that spent their waking hours crying and wailing for days on end. She likewise must have noticed widows who had divested themselves of all "gay apparel" by casting off beads, brooches, and necklaces, and allowing their unkempt hair to fall haphazardly upon their shoulders.[55]

Rather frequently, perhaps, Mary would have witnessed groups of Indian captives being led, tied together by the neck with leather straps, into Coweta to await their uncertain fates. Responding to the pressures of the market, the warriors might have claimed rights to some of the prisoners, who they sold to English traders to cover their debts. Other prisoners, however, met a different fate, determined by centuries-old Creek traditions. As the rules of kinship required vengeance for lost clan members, the matrilineal system of the Creeks endowed women with the primary responsibility for determining the fate of prisoners. Creek women in mourning might choose to adopt a prisoner as a way of replacing their beloved family member. Those adopted were usually young children, who grew up to assume the full rights, responsibilities, and loyalties of their adoptive clan—in effect, becoming fully "Creek" from the perspective of culture and kinship. Other prisoners, in contrast, became slaves, perpetual outsiders who spent their lifetimes working the fields and fetching water for their Indian masters. Others still were singled out for execution as a means of avenging the death of a relative killed in war.[56]

It should be pointed out that Creek women figured prominently in the dispatch of condemned prisoners. Mary therefore would have had opportunity to witness this more violent side of feminine behavior, perhaps even sharing in the delight of her mother and female clan-kin as they stripped and verbally abused a captive condemned to the pyre. She would have seen how Creek women tortured staked prisoners, beating them with sticks or burning them with firebrands, sometimes for hours, even days, before they mercifully committed the condemned to the flames. Within the proper bounds of warfare and the torture of prisoners, the rules of blood vengeance gave cultural sanction to any member of Coweta society to commit violence on occasion, and Mary probably accepted it as a fact of life.[57]

In time, and with a little prodding by their English allies, the Cowetas remembered the wars against the Florida missions as a period of conquest, and they claimed vast tracts of vacated land on the Georgia coast and in north Florida on the basis of the "heaps" of enemy bones left there.[58] Still, there were disturbing signs that the violence directed toward their enemies might come home to roost among the Creeks. Creek hunters increasingly struggled to overcome their indebtedness to English traders, who were resorting more frequently to violent means of enforcing payment. Creek warriors, meanwhile, had difficulty finding enough slaves to compensate traders for the ammunition and guns advanced to them. After the destruction of the Florida missions, they had to roam far and wide to find prospective captives, leading them south to the Florida Keys and as far west as the Mississippi River. If they managed to capture numerous slaves, Creek men often found themselves drawn into disputes between bickering traders vying for their share of the spoils. Desperate to satisfy creditors back in Charles Town, traders resorted to enslaving former captives whom the Creeks had adopted, striking a blow to Creek families and to the clan system itself.

While Indians of all gender and age distinctions suffered at the hands English traders, women seem to have suffered disproportionately from violence. Traders, for example, were known to force women into marriage and to whip and even murder them.[59] Traders also seem to have targeted free Indian women for enslavement, and even Creek men were known to use adoptive women as bargaining chips to satisfy English creditors.[60] The position of Indian women in Creek society, then, may have been somewhat precarious at that time, a fact that must also be reckoned with when considering the historical context of Coweta womanhood in the early eighteenth century.[61] At the time that Mary lived in Coweta-on-the-Ocmulgee, the signs of these disturbing trends were already present. But worse was yet to come. Little wonder, then, that Indians in the region soon began entertaining the idea of wresting a measure of independence from the English by killing the traders and establishing trade relationships with the Spanish and French.

Given Mary's tender age, it might at first seem that the tumult of the eighteenth century's first decade did little to shape the subsequent course of her life. But there are striking continuities between Mary's Indian girlhood and her adulthood. First of all, the frontier warfare that consumed the region remained a constant presence, and as an adult Mary would be on both the giving and receiving end of skirmishes involving Indian allies of La Florida. Likewise, the Cowetas' animosity toward the Florida mission Indians seems to have had a lasting impact; in adulthood Mary would recruit Creek warriors to fight against La Florida and its Yamasee allies, her willingness to do so perhaps intensified by the prejudices she developed in youth. Much like her Coweta relatives, who were complicit in Carolina's Indian slave trade, Mary Musgrove seems never to have questioned the practice of buying and selling human beings, as she was a slave owner for much of her adult life. And finally, her birthplace of Coweta was in fact a displaced community that was increasingly being integrated into an Atlantic world system. As such, it was subject to forces—people, markets, imperial ambitions, and cultures—that were external to it. So, too, was the young girl of our story, whose English father would soon remove her to South Carolina, where she would be transformed into a colonial youth named Mary Griffin.

2 ⚘ The Reeducation of Mary Griffin

> . . . your Memorialist about the Age of 7 years, was brought
> Down by her Father from the Indian Nation, to Ponponne in
> South Carolina; There baptized, Educated and bred up in the
> Principles of Christianity. . . . That She was in South Carolina
> when the Indian War broke out in the year 1715.
>
> *Mary Bosomworth, 1747*

PENNED MANY YEARS AFTER the events it relates, the above epigraph
is all that remains in Mary's own words of her assumption of a new life in
South Carolina. In fact, this passage constitutes the only direct evidence
relating to her obscure childhood. Given its brevity, it might appear that
Mary's adjustment to English living was uneventful—a quick and easy
process of acculturation. As it stands, the tale of her childhood persists as
but a footnote to her eventful life. Mary came to South Carolina, learned
how to read, and became a Christian. End of story.

But there is much more to Mary's cursory reflections than at first meets
the eye. We might begin by observing that Mary specifies her residence as
"Ponponne" (Pon Pon), a frontier community in Colleton County where
English and Indian people blended with regularity—a likely home for a
person who was a living testament to that process. Moreover, that Mary
mentions being educated and converted to Christianity in one breath indicates that her schooling was similar to that of her English contemporaries, for whom instruction in literacy and church dogma were insepa-
rable. Education likewise seems to have affected the means by which Mary
oriented herself in time, a subtle indicator of the depth of her cultural
transformation. Mary initially asserts that she arrived in the colony "about
the Age of 7 years," reflecting the imprecision with which Indian people
counted their age. Yet, when recalling the outbreak of the "Indian War,"

Mary matter-of-factly refers to "the year 1715," demonstrating her acquired ability to reckon the past in European calendrical terms. Mary's words may even offer us a window onto her feelings about her childhood. Tellingly, she uses passive verb constructions ("brought down by her father") that seem to minimize her own volition and ascribe her cultural transformation to the agency of others. Become an educated Christian she did, but perhaps under conditions not of her own choosing.

Importantly, Mary's allusion to the Yamasee War, a pan-Indian revolt against the South Carolina trade regime that began in April 1715, hints at the formative role that war played in shaping her outlook on Anglo-Indian relations. As it did for many colonists, the war brought misery to Mary's life, inflicting terror and material want. But Mary's pain must have been exceptionally acute, as her father was among the many traders who lost their lives during the conflict. Forced to flee and orphaned by Indians, Mary came to identify strongly with the English and their ambitions. However, Mary's sympathies for the English never diminished her concern for her mother's people; nor did she seek to distance herself from them entirely. Caught between two warring peoples at an impressionable young age, it becomes clear why Mary spent much of the rest of her life trying to avoid another "Indian War." Mary's childhood years in South Carolina, then, were hardly a footnote to her life but rather the crucible for many of her adult sensibilities. We turn to them now because they deserve closer scrutiny and reflection, more perhaps than Mary herself was willing to engage in.

Pon Pon

By the turn of the eighteenth century, the offspring of English traders and Indian women constituted a small but growing element within the orbit of South Carolina. Often referred to as "mustees" (an English corruption of the Spanish word *mestizo*), they were almost exclusively the offspring of European men and Indian women. Most numerous among them, perhaps, were the children of Indian slave women and their white masters.[1] Others came into the colony as servants who were then educated, taught a trade, and freed.[2] Others still were the progeny of English deerskin traders who had somehow managed to bring them into the colony for religious instruction.[3] While the mustee children of deerskin traders might be found in any of the colony's parishes, an unusually high concentration of them lived in the frontier parish of St. Bartholomew's, on the southwest side of the Edisto River, an area Mary called home for a quarter century.

The Edisto River begins over two hundred miles from the South Carolina coast and is fed along the way by several swampy tributaries that contribute to the murky appearance of its water.[4] The Edisto and nearby rivers support an ecologically diverse environment of swampy lowlands, deciduous forest, pine barrens, and treeless grasslands—"savannahs," as the Carolinians called them—that punctuate the lands between the Edisto and other nearby river basins.[5] The account of an anonymous "Gentleman" who passed through the area in 1734 gives us a glimpse of what the countryside looked like and how English colonists adapted to living in it. At the Edisto River, the Gentleman observed "fine Cyprus swamps, which they count the best for rice, which, if it was well settled, would be very valuable." Crossing the Ashepoo River, one of the Edisto's southern tributaries, he came upon a large "savannah," which he described as "a large spot of clear land, where there never was any timber grew, and nothing but grass." These grasslands, the writer continued, are "exceeding good for a stock of cattle, and on which they frequently settle their cow-pens." Although good for bovines, the Gentleman observed that the savannahs' boggy terrain made human travel difficult.[6]

Whereas the settlement of South Carolina commenced in April 1670 at Ashley River (several miles upstream from present-day Charleston), development of the colony's southern frontier did not begin in any meaningful way until a decade or more later.[7,8] A frontier community at its inception, its first inhabitants pursued occupations that ensured that Colleton County would retain much of its frontier character. Given the abundance of Indian traders, it should come as no surprise that the deerskin trade was among the most important economic endeavors in which Colleton County's first residents engaged. Some traders, like Mary's father, employed themselves exclusively in that business and identified themselves professionally as "Indian traders" throughout their lives. Many persons, though, entered the deerskin trade with the intention of diversifying into other economic activities, notably agriculture. Colleton's residents, like settlers elsewhere in the colony, probably experimented with a variety of agricultural products during those first decades. The cultivation of rice, however, caught on around 1700 and soon became the colony's most important staple crop. Rice grew well in Colleton County, as it did elsewhere, along the swampy lower courses of the Edisto, Combahe, and Ashepoo Rivers, and on Edisto Island. The profits to be derived from rice were enough to lure many traders into the more settled ways of plantation life—the Musgroves, as we shall see, were no exception.[9]

In addition to rice, Colleton County's forests allowed for the harvesting of wood and the manufacture of timber products. Shingles and planks made from the durable cypress and cedar trees, for example, were among the most popular trade items in early Carolina. Likewise, a bounty system enacted by Parliament in 1704 promoted the manufacture of naval stores—chiefly pitch, tar, and turpentine made from local pine trees. Most importantly, Colleton County's grasslands—savannahs—proved to be an excellent environment for the increase of the colony's herds of cattle and other livestock, whose meat was much in demand among South Carolina's Caribbean trading partners. Cattle ranching therefore became the most important economic pursuit of the area's residents, making Colleton County the epicenter of livestock production.[10]

From the beginning Colleton County's ecclesiastical composition was, like its economic and environmental profiles, diverse. At the colony's inception, the Carolina Proprietors adhered to a policy of religious toleration, which guaranteed that settlers could worship as their consciences dictated and participate in civic life regardless of their religious preferences. Consequently, the colony attracted large numbers of non-Anglicans, or Dissenters, as they were referred to pejoratively. And while Dissenters could be found throughout the colony, Colleton County seems to have attracted a disproportionate number of them.[11] Most numerous were the Presbyterians, many of them of Scottish or Irish extraction. Baptists were also conspicuous, and a small but noticeable number of Quakers settled in Colleton County. According to one estimate, by 1715 roughly one third of the families living in St. Bartholomew's Parish worshipped in accordance with one of these Dissenting traditions.[12]

The presence of Dissenters had a corresponding effect on the county's politics, which became rancorous and factional as Dissenters clashed with Anglican officials in Charles Town over the colony's governing policies. Harmonious for a time, the Colleton Dissenters' breach with the Anglicans began after the installation of James Moore as governor in 1700. Moore, a staunch Anglican, was the first of his religious persuasion to hold the position of governor in a decade and (as some charged) a reckless proponent of South Carolina's military expansion. Dissenters first clashed with Governor Moore in 1701, when he proposed attacking the Spanish at

St. Augustine, and later rioted in the streets when a heavily Anglican assembly controlled by Moore passed tax legislation to fund that expedition. Dissenters would fare no better under Moore's successor, Nathaniel Johnson, also an Anglican. In 1704 Governor Johnson called the assembly into an emergency session and convinced its members to hastily pass an Act of Exclusion barring Dissenters from holding public office. Around the same time, the Johnson-controlled Assembly pushed through a Church Act establishing the Church of England as the colony's official institution of worship, thereby reversing proprietary church policy.[13]

Colleton Dissenters protested these measures by petitioning government officials in England and by hiring Daniel Defoe (later of *Robinson Crusoe* and *Moll Flanders* fame) to write a scathing pamphlet against Anglican "Party Tyranny" in South Carolina.[14] Dissenter protests eventually led to the repeal of the noxious laws, which allowed Dissenters back into government. Anglicans did, however, get much of what they wished for with the passage of a new Church Act that established ten Anglican parishes in the colony, three of which were to be laid out in Colleton County.[15] Although it would take several years for church institutions to take root there, one of the parishes established in the 1706 Church Act was St. Bartholomew's, encompassing territory to the south and west of the Edisto River. Pon Pon, which was soon to be Mary's new home, lay within its borders.

If at first it seems that South Carolina's squabbles over church and state were incidental to the life of young Mary Griffin, it is important to realize that the creation of the Anglican parish of St. Bartholomew's likely played a role in her father's decision to bring her into the colony, as well as in the timing of this decision. Circumstantial evidence suggests that Edward Griffin was Anglican.[16] Griffin therefore may have sensed an opportunity when he learned of the establishment of St. Bartholomew's Parish, anticipating the erection of a church, the arrival of a minister, and the founding of a school—institutions that Griffin considered requisite for the proper instruction of an English youth, which is what Edward Griffin hoped his daughter would one day be.

Reeducation

Mary began what can only be described as an intensive process of cultural immersion, arriving at Pon Pon around the time her father was busy tormenting the Indian agent Thomas Nairne. Although Mary was glib about it, her arrival at Pon Pon was in reality a most improbable event. Given that most of the Indian traders' offspring lived out their lives in Indian communities, something extraordinary must have happened to enable Edward Griffin to remove his daughter from Coweta. Several explanations are possible, though only one seems probable: that Mary's mother had died. Knowing the temperament of Creek women in matters relating to their kin, it would have been highly unlikely for any living Indian woman to willingly give her daughter over to her English spouse. We might also speculate that Mary lacked other female Creek relatives who were willing or able to care for the young girl. Out of necessity, then, the Cowetas may have reluctantly agreed to allow Griffin to bring his children into the colony. If this was indeed the case, Mary's transition to colonial life would have been doubly traumatic, marked by mourning the loss of her cultural moorings, as well as of her mother. Mary's removal to Pon Pon, then, was most likely not a joyous event.

Softening the blow of her adjustment to life in St. Bartholomew's Parish, however, was the presence of several other mustee youths, who, like Mary, were the offspring of local Indian traders. These individuals probably came to the colony at roughly the same time, lived in relative proximity to one another, and experienced together many of the formative experiences of youth, including schooling and baptism. While we do not know precisely whom this group comprised, circumstantial evidence allows us to hazard a few informed guesses as to their identities. Most probably it included Mary's brother, Edward Griffin, who appears to have been baptized (hence his Christian name), spoke at least some English, and probably lived within the colony's borders as a young adult. Another was Thomas "Tommy" Jones, the son of an Indian trader by that name. Like the Griffin siblings, Jones was half-Creek and related to them by blood. Added to their number was James Welch and his unnamed brother, the "half breed" sons of the trader and explorer Thomas Welch, who pioneered South Carolina's trade with the Chickasaws around the turn of the century.[17] Close in age if not blood relations, these individuals remained on intimate terms throughout their lives, testifying to their common backgrounds and to the bonds forged in a youth spent among strangers.

As for the material circumstances in which Mary found herself, the fact that her father owned no land and was sometimes in debt seems to indicate that the Griffin family's means were modest at best, a rather common condition in the raw environment of St. Bartholomew's.[18] Griffin and his children may have squatted on vacant land and therefore had a home to call their own, but it is perhaps more likely that the family rented land or boarded in the homes of more prosperous Indian traders. Regardless of who owned it, Mary's Pon Pon home would have been a simple one- or two-room "earthfast" cabin, an impermanent structure erected on a hastily constructed frame made of wood posts driven directly into the ground (thereby lacking a proper foundation or cellar and being more vulnerable to rot or infestation). Most earthfast homes were modest in scale, usually measuring fifteen by twenty feet and one-and-a-half stories high. The entire first floor typically constituted a single room that served many purposes, such as cooking, sleeping, eating, and entertaining guests.[19] Assuming that Griffin and his kids boarded with another family, their home must have been crowded, allowing for little privacy.

As with the modest size of their home, the Griffins also must have owned relatively little in the way of personal possessions. As a young girl, Mary, like most children, would not have been familiar with the concept of a "toy." We may presume that she grew up eating with pewter, rather than silver, cutlery, and was served meals in red earthenware containers, wood bowls, or on pewter plates, rather than on the expensive wares from continental Europe or the china that graced the finer homes in Charles Town. Mary's modest home also would have lacked decorative items; most things lying around the house would have been purely functional—wood tables and chairs, an old storage chest, straw mattresses, a few iron or copper cooking pans, and an axe for chopping firewood. As it seems Griffin was a literate man and was eager to have his daughter educated, one assumes that a worn copy of the Bible was also on hand—quite possibly the only book Griffin owned.

The move to Pon Pon must have been disorienting at first. Having lived her life to that point in Coweta, Mary would have been used to sleeping and eating in an airy Creek cabin, drawing comfort from the din of conversation that flowed from the nearby homes of neighbors and kin, the sound of women pounding corn, or the occasional bark of a dog. At sparsely settled Pon Pon, however, Mary's nearest neighbors were most likely out of her direct sight, while split rail "worm" fences laid out in zigzag fashion kept wild and domestic animals out of their garden plots, dividing the land in ways the Creek Indians could not yet conceive of. Living in a part of the colony that was disproportionately endowed with livestock, Mary would likely have heard the rustle of cattle as they plodded unattended through fields and forests. As the South Carolina colony's enslaved African population was then on the cusp of outnumbering its European inhabitants, it stands to reason that Mary might have occasionally glimpsed slaves working in rice fields, or, in what was then a more common employment, riding horseback through the forests and savannahs "hunting" their owners' stray cattle.[20] At night or on Sundays, she might have heard echoes of slaves singing or chanting in strange tongues to the beat of a drum played much as it would have been in West and Central Africa.[21]

The adjustment to a new physical and sensory environment included becoming accustomed to a new style of clothing. As a very young girl, Mary probably wore very little and would have thought nothing about seeing older women walking around with exposed breasts. In the English settlements, however, modesty demanded covering more skin than Mary was accustomed to doing, and it is tempting to imagine that hers scratched a bit when for the first time she put on an ankle-length petticoat with sleeves that extended to the wrist and fastened a cap tightly around her chin. English shoes made with hard leather soles likewise would have crimped her feet, and Mary probably at times wished for a good pair of comfortable Indian moccasins. Sexual modesty, though, only partly explains why colonial women and girls dressed in ample and sometimes confining clothing. As the historian Karin Calvert explains, colonial-era costume reveals underlying concerns about "power, autonomy, and independence." The petticoat and cap, she argues, symbolized submissiveness and dependency by covering and restricting movement, which is why women and children of both sexes wore them.[22]

Assuming that she had no mother, how Mary learned the feminine domestic arts (as practiced by the English) is anyone's guess. Because of the colony's high mortality rate, many South Carolina households were composite in nature, often consisting of remarried spouses, half-siblings, and the children of relatives and friends.[23] As the historian Darcy Fryer observes, these demographic realities caused South Carolina families to adopt an "extensive" parenting strategy, whereby parents routinely sent their children to work in the homes of relatives or friends. Extensive parenting had the advantage of enabling youths to acquire skills needed in adulthood and also allowed them to establish personal networks, upon which success in business or in finding a spouse was often founded.[24] As business would have required Edward Griffin to spend a considerable amount of time away from Pon Pon, it is likely that he too employed "extensive" parenting techniques with his own children. Mary therefore probably learned the rudiments of English housewifery in the company of a neighbor, by participating and observing the rounds of daily life as experienced by the mistress of the house and her daughters.

On one level, adjusting to feminine work routines at Pon Pon probably wasn't all that difficult. There were many similarities between the respective roles of women in Creek and English society. Like their Creek counterparts, English women did the cooking, cleaned the house, and assumed most of the day-to-day childcare responsibilities. Moreover, the work routines of South Carolina women were largely determined by the seasonal demands of the agricultural economy. So, English women would have tended vegetables in the garden during the spring and summer, harvested and preserved them in the fall, and salted down meat after the autumn butchering to avoid spoilage. Given Colleton County's abundance of livestock and its pastoralist economy, English women also would have spent much of their time milking cows, churning cream into butter, or feeding the animals when they were penned in the spring and fall for birthing and slaughtering.[25]

On other levels, however, the vast differences between Creek and English gender concepts and practices may have made the adjustment quite difficult. Whereas agriculture was principally a female occupation in Creek society, this was not the case among the English, who regarded it as the male's duty to work the fields. Likewise, English society was patriarchal and therefore differed sharply from the matrilineal practices of the Creeks, in which clan identity and property were vested in women. Married English women, by way of contrast, were rendered politically and economically invisible because of the prevailing ideology of *coverture*. As defined by William Blackstone, *coverture* established husband and wife as "one person in law," meaning that the "very being or legal existence of the woman is suspended" and that her legal identity becomes "incorporated and consolidated into that of the husband."[26] In theory, then, women could not enter into separate contracts, buy or sell property, sue or be sued for debts, and most certainly could not engage in politics.

However tidy it appeared in theory, in practice the rules of *coverture* were circumvented with some frequency in the colonies, where improvisation was needed to assure a family's economic viability. Observing the behavior of people around her, Mary might have noticed that South Carolina women did in fact engage regularly in economic endeavors. For example, women participated vigorously in local informal economies of exchange, in which neighbors bartered milk, butter, herbs, eggs, or garden vegetables with other female neighbors.[27] Many wives likewise became knowledgeable about business practices and kept themselves abreast of family finances in preparation for widowhood. The colony's high mortality rate virtually assured that women would spend at least part of their lives in a widowed state, requiring that they step in as "deputy husbands" to execute wills and assume responsibilities as heads of household.[28] Nor did *coverture* render married women entirely invisible. Married women in South Carolina sometimes exercised control over valuable dowry property by virtue of written prenuptial contracts, while others were given power of attorney by their husbands, which enabled them to buy, sell, and make contracts in the husband's absence. As surviving property records indicate, women in Colleton County routinely bought, sold, and bequeathed property, wrote wills, and witnessed property transactions. Married or not, women were far from invisible in the economic realm, and Mary must have expected the same for herself as she approached adulthood.[29]

While nearby women may have served as role models for Mary, it is also true that the move to Pon Pon placed her more intimately in the company of men. One colony-wide population estimate, taken in 1708, suggests that there were about 1.5 free white men in the colony for every free white woman. The sexual imbalance among African slaves was slightly greater, and it is probable that the gender imbalance was even more pronounced in outlying communities such as Pon Pon.[30] As for how these colony-wide trends impacted Mary, we can be reasonably sure that men dominated her closest social and familial networks. Because she moved in male circles regularly and dexterously later in life, we might suspect that this early exposure to male company gave her this ability, be it in the role of trader, Oglethorpe's interpreter, or petitioner before the British Board of Trade.

In the course of acclimating to Pon Pon, Mary acquired the English language, one of the most important cultural adjustments required of her. Although Mary may have made it look easy, becoming bilingual in Muskogee and English was no simple task, as the two languages had dissimilar grammatical structures and no cognates. It would therefore be much more difficult for an individual to become fluent in these two languages than for a native Spanish speaker to learn a bit of Italian, or for a Choctaw speaker to understand a few Muskogee words.

The differences between English and Muskogee are manifold, as evidenced by their varying systems of pronunciation. English, for example, is considered a "stress" language, in which the syllables of words are distinguished from one another by placing greater emphasis on the pronunciation of one or more of them. Muskogee, by contrast, is considered a "tonal accent" language, in which speakers vary their pronunciation by speaking in a high or low pitch, subtle changes that sometimes give vastly different meanings to words that sound similar to non-native speakers.[31] While English and Muskogee share many of the same vowel sounds, Muskogee consonant sounds vary greatly from those found in English. For instance, the Muskogee language lacks the sound for the English letter "r." Imagine, then, the difficulty of pronouncing her Christian name "Mary" for the first time, or her father's surname "Griffin." Moreover, many Muskogee consonants are spoken in an unaspirated manner—that is, without the puff of air English speakers add to the beginning of stressed syllables. As a result, Muskogee speakers do not differentiate between consonant sounds such as "p" and "b." Likewise, Muskogee features consonant sounds not found in English. The most notable of these is a voiceless lateral fricative (spoken with the tongue on the roof of the mouth, with the air passing over the sides of the tongue) that resembles the "thl" sound in the English word "fifthly."[32]

Muskogee grammar is likewise markedly different from that of English. Muskogee verbs, for example, follow their objects, just as Muskogee nouns precede the adjectives that modify them—exactly the opposite of the standard order used in English. The Muskogee language is also a heavily affixed one, in which suffixes, prefixes, and infixes (an affix inserted into the middle of a word) function much the way possessive pronouns and prepositions do in English.[33] Verb conjugation is also a tricky matter; the Muskogee language includes several verb tenses with no English equivalents. For example, Muskogee verbs include tenses that differentiate between complete and incomplete action, and distinguish between the recent and the remote past.[34] Some Muskogee verbs may be conjugated to distinguish not simply between the singular and plural, but also a third, "dual" category when the action relates specifically to two things. Other verb tenses even distinguish between deliberate and accidental actions.[35]

That Mary eventually overcame these and other obstacles and became fluent in English and Muskogee is well documented in the historical record.

But what, exactly, does it mean to be "bilingual"? Linguists acknowledge that the term can connote many different things, but they have nevertheless developed a good working vocabulary that can characterize Mary's linguistic capabilities.[36] It seems she was what linguists call a "balanced bilingual," attributable to those persons who have a roughly equivalent mastery of two languages. Likewise, "receptive" bilinguals have markedly different abilities than do "productive" bilinguals. Receptive bilinguals, as they are defined, may understand the written or spoken form of a language, but they cannot produce it themselves. Productive bilinguals, in contrast, have the ability to do both. Mary undoubtedly falls into the latter of these two categories. Mary may also be described as an "additive" bilingual, meaning that her acquisition of a second language did not come at the expense of her first (as is the case for so-called "subtractive" bilinguals).[37]

That Mary was an additive bilingual is of particular importance in her case, because people tend to achieve this kind of proficiency only under certain social conditions. Additive bilingualism typically occurs when both languages are "valued in the society in which they reside."[38] Subtractive bilingualism, in contrast, is found in situations where one language "is valued more than the other, where one dominates the other, [or] where one is on the ascendant and the other is waning."[39] It follows that there must have been a critical mass of people living at Pon Pon who spoke Muskogee. Many of Pon Pon's English deerskin traders spoke the language, but the core of the Muskogee-speaking community must have consisted of Mary and her peers. It is not difficult to imagine that Mary spoke her native tongue with some regularity in the presence of her brother Edward and other of Pon Pon's mustee youths. That Mary remained fluent in Muskogee suggests, moreover, that she spent her adult years in a society, here, South Carolina, in which her native tongue remained "useful and valuable," a subject that will be taken up in the next chapter.[40]

It was also probably an inadvertent stroke of good fortune that Mary's father brought her to the colony for instruction "about the Age of 7 years." Linguists have long demonstrated that the human capacity to learn multiple languages diminishes after a certain critical period has passed, with estimates ranging from between five and ten years of age.[41] Modern research in language development in children therefore suggests that Mary may have been exposed to English before her move to South Carolina and subsequent schooling there. It is hard to believe that Griffin—functionally bilingual himself—would not have introduced his daughter to at least a few English words. Also, as Carolina military leaders and traders made regular stops in Coweta, Mary would have heard the English tongue spoken when her father addressed other English visitors. This exposure to English, albeit limited, did allow some of her Creek contemporaries to gain passing familiarity with it.[42] In other words, Mary probably already knew some English before she moved to South Carolina and was well prepared to enhance her bilingual skills.

Mary, though, owed much of her linguistic dexterity to the formal schooling she received at Pon Pon. In this way she was the beneficiary not only of the Anglican Church's rise in South Carolina, but also the missionary zeal that gripped the colony around the turn of the century. During the first three decades of its existence, the colony lacked a formal Anglican establishment, and a clerical manpower shortage left much of the backcountry unchurched. To combat the forces of heathenism in South Carolina and elsewhere, in 1701 Anglican clergymen established a missionary society called the Society for the Propagation of the Gospel in Foreign Parts (SPG). In 1702 the society sent Rev. Samuel Thomas as its first minister to South Carolina, ushering in a new era of Anglican evangelicalism. Following the passage of the Church Act of 1706, the society began sending ministers to fill the vacant parishes it had established. The SPG likewise donated Bibles, religious tracts, and educational materials to the colony, and over the next decade the Anglican Church began to take shape as an institution in South Carolina.[43]

When it began work in South Carolina, the society directed much of its missionary zeal and intellectual energy toward the conversion of Indians and the colony's enslaved Africans.[44] Some SPG ministers, for example, wrote tracts defending the humanity of slaves and Indians, as well as their capacity to receive the gospel. Others took halting steps to learn the Indian languages that would enable them to evangelize effectively, and one SPG official toyed with the idea of establishing a college for Indians. SPG ministers even sent a Yamasee youth known as "Prince George" to England for schooling, ultimately hoping that he would return as an evangelist to his people.

What is striking about the period under consideration is the optimism that characterized SPG missionaries, and, to a limited extent, the Indians themselves, for the Christian education of Indian youth. As it turned out, the underlying optimism that sparked missionary activity prior to 1715 constituted a window of opportunity that made possible the education of so-called mustee youths such as the Griffin, Jones, and Welch children. In time, however, missionaries lost interest in converting Indians and came to prefer the settled comforts of parish life to the travails of frontier living. Indians, increasingly wary of the demands the colonists placed upon them, also seem to have lost interest. As a consequence, the educational opportunities open to Mary and her peers were closed to subsequent generations, making theirs unique in the world of colonial South Carolina race relations.

In many ways, though, the parish of St. Bartholomew's was an unlikely place for educational opportunity to present itself. Many of the traders who resided there were disinclined to attend church and were thought little better than heathens, and thus poor role models for their children. More importantly, St. Bartholomew's Parish was hardly a parish at all, for it lacked not only a church, but also a school, a parsonage, and glebe land to support the priest's work; in fact, the parish did not begin to take shape institutionally in any real sense until the mid-1720s and was still in an unfinished state nearly a decade later. St. Bartholomew's also went without a priest for its first eight years of existence. Not until 1713 did the parish welcome its first resident priest, the ill-fated Nathaniel Osborn.[45]

In spite of the underdeveloped state of the parish, the opportunity to receive an education presented itself to Mary Griffin in a roundabout way, most probably through the agency of one Ross Reynolds. Although we know relatively little about him, Reynolds arrived in the colony around 1709 and worked as a schoolmaster in the remoter parts of St. Bartholomew's Parish for a few years afterward. Reynolds was noted for his willingness to teach Indian youths and was once recommended to the SPG as a potential missionary to the Yamasees.[46] However, local SPG officials seem to have been only dimly aware of the schoolmaster's work, and Commissary Johnston interviewed Reynolds in 1712 to learn what he was up to. During that interview, Reynolds revealed that he had "taught three Indian traders [children] some gotten on Indian Women to read a little and to Speak English, for which he was paid according to contract."[47] Mary Griffin most likely was one of the children who frequented his school.

Mary's education probably progressed even further under the tutelage of Rev. Nathaniel Osborn, St. Bartholomew's first parish priest. Osborn arrived in the colony in March 1713 and was sent to the vacant parish of St. Bartholomew's, where he continued until the Yamasee attacks of April 1715 forced him to flee to Charles Town. He died there in July of that year.

Unfortunately for the historian, Nathaniel Osborn was not as prolific

with the pen as were some of his Anglican contemporaries serving elsewhere in South Carolina. Consequently, we know very little about his missionary efforts in St. Bartholomew's. What we do know suggests that Osborn faced a daunting task ministering to the population scattered about
the thirty-by-forty-mile parish, which required him to conduct services in
"four or five" different places, each week, and at times to ride more than
twenty miles to reach his parishioners.[48] For the most part denied ministerial services, St. Bartholomew's Anglican residents welcomed the priest
and appear to have been eager to partake in church rites of passage. In the
space of nine months, Osborn baptized over seventy persons, a considerable number for a parish with only one hundred and twenty families.
Tellingly, Osborn related that most of the recently baptized were children,
including five "molatto Children, being those of our Indian Traders, by
Indian women during their abode amongst them."[49] The trader Edward
Griffin's daughter was probably among those baptized, and thus she came
to officially receive her Christian name, Mary.

Clearly, by the time Mary was baptized between May 1714 and March
1715, she had come a long way from her Coweta roots. As a child of "a riper
age," no Anglican priest would have baptized her had she not understood
basic elements of the Anglican faith.[50] How she acquired that faith invites
questions concerning her prebaptismal education: How did she learn to
read religious texts? How did she learn the articles of faith? As religious
instruction and literacy education were intertwined, Ross Reynolds and
Nathaniel Osborn each would have played a role in remaking Mary into a
literate Christian.

Recent scholarly work on child literacy in colonial America gives us a
fairly good idea of the kind of methods Ross Reynolds likely employed to
educate Mary Griffin. Most children at that time followed what John Locke
called the "ordinary road" of literacy education, consisting of, in order, the
Horn-book, Primer, Psalter, Testament, and Bible. Mary would have progressed gradually from learning her alphabet with the Horn-book, to the
more complicated texts, all of which, even those most dedicated to skill
development, were religiously inspired. In Mary's time, school masters
employed what is known as the "syllabic" method of reading instruction,
in which children, after memorizing the alphabet, learned first to combine
vowel and consonant sounds (e.g., *hi, hid, him*). Once they had learned
those fundamental skills, they learned to pronounce words by dividing
them into their constituent parts—syllables—which acted like building

blocks for the pronunciation of longer, more complicated words. By starting with basic short syllables, young scholars soon learned to read words, short verse, and then moved on to full sentences and longer passages. Instruction in writing, and sometimes in elementary math, followed only after the child had become a competent reader.[51]

Once a child had mastered the rudiments of reading, he or she then moved on to formal schooling, which typically involved the primer.[52] Although its main purpose was to develop reading skills, primers also were religious books. Because of their attentiveness to orthodoxy, however, church officials approved for school use only those primers that conformed to Anglican principles. Fortunately, the surviving correspondence of SPG ministers and schoolmasters enables us to guess with reasonable certitude which texts Mary encountered during the course of her education. Easily the most popular, and most readily available, primer in the colonies outside of New England (where the famous *New England Primer* reigned supreme) was Edmund Coote's *The English School-master*.[53] Originally published in England in 1598, Coote's work was reprinted countless times, and one edition published in 1700 was likely similar to the one Ross Reynolds used to teach Mary.[54]

Mastery of the primer pointed the way to the eventual study of the Psalter, Bible, and other advanced texts. To prepare students for advanced reading and for baptism, clergymen relied upon church catechisms, single-volume works that presented an abridged version of Church teachings. By the time Mary began her education, Congregationalist New Englanders had already published several versions in Boston and Connecticut. Anglican clergymen stationed in the colonies, however, used only those catechisms that conformed to Anglican Church teachings, and typically imported them from England. Clergy had any number of such catechisms to choose from, but seem to have relied almost exclusively on a newer work, John Lewis' *Church Catechism Explained*, which was first published in 1700 and quickly became a favorite among SPG missionaries.[55] Lewis' work was familiar to South Carolina's clergy; in fact it was the main religious instructional text in use at Benjamin Dennis' school in Goose Creek Parish at the precise time Mary prepared for baptism.[56] Given that Mr. Dennis' school served as a model within the colony for the instruction of youth, we may reasonably conclude that Nathaniel Osborn and Mary Griffin were intimately acquainted with *Church Catechism Explained*.[57]

Anglican clergy adopted Lewis' text because its "brief and plain" style was well suited for "the younger sort" of parishioner.[58] Like most catechisms, *Church Catechism Explained* consists of a multitude of questions pertaining to the tenets and practices of the Christian faith. Following each question is a (theologically correct) response, with scripture passages offered as "proof." In preparation for baptism, catechists would have been required to commit the church catechism to memory in its entirety—no simple task. Learning typically entailed rote memorization, the goal being to recite, publicly and aloud, verbatim responses to the questions printed in the catechism. Benjamin Dennis, the Goose Creek schoolmaster, appears to have employed this method of instruction, reporting that he would "catechize twice a day" with his students, adding that he had them "twice each week expound out of Mr. Lewis' Catechise by heart." Difficult as that may seem, some of his students appear to have been equal to the task, causing Dennis to boast proudly "some have proceeded a great way therein."[59]

Given that Mary became a Christian and could read, write, and perhaps do some elementary math, it would appear that her education was better than average, especially considering that most girls at that time were illiterate. Mary's abilities imply that she dedicated much of her time—perhaps a disproportionate amount relative to her peers—to schoolwork, making it plausible that young Mary became a bookish sort of child capable of exercising the self-discipline required for scholarly tasks.

Presuming that Mary spent many an hour with furrowed brow combing through these texts, it stands to reason that she would have come to internalize the subtexts embedded within them. In addition to their more transparent functions of teaching literacy and the rudiments of Christianity, each book also reinforces the values held by their English authors—instilling, in effect, "Englishness" in their readers. Coote's *English Schoolmaster*, originally penned in 1598 when William Shakespeare was nearing the height of his creative powers and the English nation was on the cusp of becoming a great economic empire, seems to fixate on what might be described as bourgeois values related to commerce, hard work, and the pursuit of economic respectability. For instance, one sample paragraph tells the story of a horse seller who appears caught between his desire for profit and his fear of divine retribution if he were to deal dishonestly with his customers.[60] By echoing the theme of divine retribution, Coote links abstract notions of sin with contractual obligations, thereby equating morality with honest dealings in commerce. He spoke, in other words, in a language that resonated among his commercially oriented readers.

In addition to instilling the value of honesty in business, Coote's *English School-master* offers a Western understanding of time and history, which would have supplanted any Creek understanding of the past that Mary might have acquired during her early childhood. In a short section on arithmetic, Coote includes a historical chronology rooted in the Biblical, Greek, and Roman pasts, beginning with Adam and Eve and ending with the fall of Rome. Highlights included the "Universal Flood," the erection of the first temple in Jerusalem, the bard Homer, the Roman Republic, and for good measure "when England received the Gospel," in the year AD 187.[61] Coote formats this chronology as a sequential list spanning five pages, with each entry bearing a date, followed by an important historical figure or event. That Coote chose this format is itself significant, for its linear progression instills a linear notion of time common to Europeans.[62]

John Lewis' *Church Catechism Explained* likewise reflects the English worldview of its writer but in a very different way. As E. Jennifer Monaghan explains, Anglican texts were a component "of a rigidly hierarchical structure, in which Christian belief was mediated by the clergy of a formal religious establishment with a strong liturgical tradition."[63] As intended, Lewis' work reinforces notions of obedience, duty, and hierarchy common not just to High Church Anglicans but also throughout rigidly class-based English society. Young readers, then, were to come away with due respect for Church, King, and their social superiors.

For example, the format of the catechism affirms the Church's mediation of spirituality. By posing preselected questions to the reader, the catechism enables the Church to direct the readers' attention toward aspects of the faith it deems important. In a similar fashion, the prescribed answers to each question allow for little to no independent initiative on the part of the catechist to interpret scripture or question the articles of faith. Catechists "got religion" so to speak, not so much by reading the Bible themselves, or through their own direct experiences with the divine, but by memorizing that which the Anglican Church deemed necessary for them to know. By imparting religious doctrine on a need-to-know basis, Anglican priests reinforced both spiritual and temporal power as it was understood in the early modern English world.

The figure of Jesus Christ might appear to inspire little devotion to temporal powers, as Jesus claimed none for himself during his life on earth. Anglicans, however, transformed Christ into an office holder who wielded earthly, as well as spiritual, power, styling him as "King, Priest, and Prophet" who "governs and protects his Church."[64] The Anglican catechism also had a way of presenting the Ten Commandments as divine decrees for social stratification and hierarchy. A favorite was the Fifth Commandment ("to honour thy father and thy mother"), which was presented in a manner designed to humble the individual before the power of the state, then conceived of as an extension of the family. In particular, the Eighth Commandment ("thou shalt not steal") and the Tenth Commandment ("thou shalt not covet thy neighbor . . .") encouraged catechists to accept the economic and social hierarchy and to be content with "that state of life unto which it shall please God to call you." Most English Protestants would have agreed, but the Anglican catechism clearly had manual laborers in mind when they demanded they be "content" in their present work. Hence the inclusion of Ephesians 4:28: "Rather let him labour, working with his hands the thing which is good," as well as two like passages from Thessalonians. In summarizing the Christian's duty to his neighbor, Lewis ends with a general admonition to "honour and obey the King, and all that are put in authority under him; to submit [thyself] to [thy] Governors, Teachers, and spiritual Pastors and Masters; to order [thyself] lowley and reverently to all [thy] Betters."[65]

As the preceding discussion indicates, being "Educated, and bred up in the Principles of Christianity" meant imbibing a constellation of beliefs particular to English people of Mary's generation. Through baptism, and by spending long hours with church catechism and primer in hand, she was able to partake of rites of passage common among English children, thereby giving her a frame of reference for a childhood similar to that of the colonial population. If it is true that Mary was her mother's daughter before the age of seven, it is right to say that by the spring of 1715 she had become very much a daddy's girl. Now baptized, Mary may have looked forward to proving herself a good Christian by giving up something for Lent. With Easter approaching, she might have found that her hard work in committing the catechism to memory had given her a new appreciation of the mysteries of Christ's crucifixion and resurrection. Little could she have known, however, that her Creek relatives were among those who had begun hatching plans to turn her world upside down by rendering South Carolina a latter-day Golgotha and making martyrs of South Carolina's traders.

Holy Week 1715 was a time of rising anxiety in South Carolina. Swirling rumors of an Indian uprising had set the colony's leadership on edge. The rumors proved all too prophetic when on Good Friday the Yamasee and Creek Indians began killing Indian agents and traders at the Yamasee town of Pocatalico and later directed their wrath at the English settlements. Among the living witnesses was a factor for a London mercantile firm named Charles Rodd, who penned one of the earliest (and most often cited) accounts of the outbreak of the "Indian War." Rodd conceded that South Carolina's residents had been entertaining rumors of an Indian uprising for about a week, but that many dismissed them as being "ill-founded." Governing officials didn't take those rumors seriously until two traders, Sam Warner and William Bray, arrived in the colony to warn them that the Indians would take up arms unless the governor addressed certain grievances.

In the hopes of heading off a potential attack, Governor Charles Craven sent Bray and Warner to the Yamasee town of Pocatalico, where Yamasee and Creek Indian leaders had been gathering to discuss their plans. Indian agents John Wright and Thomas Nairne also arrived, and all parties sat down together the night of April 14 to exchange diplomatic gestures. The English delegation expressed to the Indians the governor's condolences, as well as guarantees of "satisfaction" for any wrongs that had been done to them. The Indians, appearing "satisfied" with the offer, "shook hands in a token of friendship," and shared drinks as men do. Thinking all was "as usual," Nairne and the rest of the English delegation retired for the evening and fell asleep not knowing that it would be their last day on earth.

The killing began in the predawn hours of April 15, Good Friday, as painted warriors "resembling devils come out of hell" sounded the blood-curdling war whoop and began firing their guns "without distinction" on their white visitors. The lucky ones died quickly in the first barrage of gunfire; others succumbed slowly to torture, as was the case for the agent Thomas Nairne, who perished in a slow-burning pyre that prolonged his agony for "several days." After the killing at Pocatalico was finished, bands of Indian warriors proceeded into the colonial settlements, killing, plundering, and burning their way to Port Royal, forcing its residents to seek refuge in a ship anchored in the harbor. For several weeks thereafter,

Indian war parties continued to ravage the frontiers of the colony, driving its inhabitants into the safer confines of Charles Town.[66]

From one perspective, Rodd's account chronicles the final, violent collapse of a thirty-year relationship between two mutually irreconcilable peoples. The tendency to draw sharp distinctions between "us" and "them" and to fixate upon acts of violence is perhaps understandable when chronicling a war. But postbellum perspectives on the conflict tend to obscure an antebellum reality that was much more complicated.[67] Indeed, Rodd's account may be read in alternative ways that indicate the degree of intimacy and cultural accommodation that had made the alliance possible in the first place. For example, the Carolinians' tendency to dismiss the rumors of an Indian uprising suggests the degree of trust they had placed in their Indian allies. Most importantly, the Indians' deception at Pocatalico would not have been possible had they not already been on intimate and familiar terms. By sharing drinks and talking together, the agents and Indian leaders behaved much they had done in the past. Business "as usual," as Rodd would have it.

Indeed, reading Rodd's account backward rather than forward in time exposes a world that was lost on South Carolina's southern frontier, one defined by the intimacy between, rather than the separation of, Indian and English peoples.[68] Predictably, the Indian War brought much of that world to an end by enforcing a degree of separation, welcome on both sides, between the two groups. But that fact should not lead us to assume that such an outcome was inevitable, because many individuals on the southern frontier—Mary Griffin included—lived lives that hinted at different, though unrealized, possibilities for the future.

The boundary between colonial and Indian lands, for example, was porous from the very beginning. Indians living on the colony's southern borders, particularly the Yamasees, frequently crossed into the settlements, perhaps to hunt, fish, or trade, or to meet with the governor in Charles Town. The porousness of the southern frontier, though, cut both ways. English traders and Indian agents frequented Indian country regularly, and there were also settlers who lived more or less permanently on Indian lands (admittedly sometimes to the Indians' chagrin). Some of them were traders or agents, such as Thomas Nairne and William Bray, each of whom took up tracts of Yamasee lands adjacent to Granville County and were, quite literally, living among the Yamasee when the war began.[69]

Given the physical proximity of many of South Carolina's English and Indian frontier inhabitants, it is not surprising that their respective cultures tended to rub off on one another. John Norris, a resident of St. Bartholomew's Parish, for example, indicates that Indians often worked for their English neighbors as commercial hunters, while others hint at the Indians' accommodation to European-style agriculture and animal husbandry. Conversely, colonists integrated Indian corn, peas, and "twenty sorts" of Indian beans into their diets and came to regard highly the flesh of the white-tailed deer. In particular, military service drew English and Indian men into tight company, and there emerged a shared culture of convivial drinking, made evident by the erection of a "punch house" at Port Royal that attracted an Indian clientele.[70]

This is not to say that the relationship between Indians and English colonists on the southern frontier was universally amicable. As the outbreak of war attests, that was far from the case. Yet, even when parsing through the journals of the South Carolina Indian commissioners, which record the myriad complaints of Indians against the traders and white neighbors, one cannot help but notice the degree of intimacy between them that provided the context for their complaints. The traders' chronic physical abuse of the Indians, for instance, is symptomatic of familiarity rather than strangeness. Indian complaints against the traders could likewise assume a familial dimension, as when the traders abused their Indian spouses, divorced them, or tried to make wives of unwilling women. On other occasions, Indians and traders appear as the squabbling business partners they were, haggling over accrued debts or the sale of a slave. The Yamasee War, then, can be attributed to the Indians' fear of the growing power of the South Carolina trade regime, but it should not be assumed that the two cultures simply misunderstood each other and could not bridge their cultural differences.

While it is true that by 1715 many Yamasee and other Indians held the South Carolinians in contempt, it should be noted that this viewpoint was not universal among the Indians. Many at Pocatalico beat the drums of war, but there were a number of individuals who tried to minimize its effects or avoid bloodshed altogether. Some presumably did so for strategic reasons, as many Indians already knew and feared the capabilities of the South Carolina war machine. But Indians sought to limit or avoid the war, it seems, for emotional reasons also, stemming from their personal attachments to particular colonists they considered to be friends. Some

Indians likewise had relatives, "mixed blood" or not, living within the Carolina settlements, and wished to spare them the violence that was about to be unleashed. A few tried to warn their English friends ahead of time of the imminent danger they were in.[71] Others sat out the war entirely, while more still protected male and female hostages whom the Indians considered to be "good" people.

Only in retrospect, then, does the Anglo-Indian relationship that preceded the war assume the character of a black-and-white confrontation between irreconcilable foes. Memory of the war has obscured the varying shades of gray that constituted the cultural and social matrix for many a frontier life, Mary Griffin's among them. We therefore find it hard to imagine a world in which Indians learned to speak English and, conversely, in which English farmers learned to plant and eat Indian foods. Theirs was a world in which Indian and English people called each other neighbors, and learned to befriend, to cooperate, to hate, or even to love one another, as neighbors tend to do. Mary Griffin, one of the mustee youths then living at Pon Pon, was the living embodiment of these processes. That the Indian War brought this world to an abrupt end, causing people caught in the middle to choose sides, must have been, for her, a bitter pill to swallow.

As for Mary Griffin's own war experience, it happened that St. Bartholomew's Parish bore the brunt of the Indians' attacks. Following the massacre at Pocatalico, two parties of Yamasee Indians directed their efforts toward the colony itself; one headed toward Port Royal to lay waste to St. Helena's parish, while the other steered into the heart of St. Bartholomew's. Luckily for Mary and others in her parish, a lone Yamasee Indian man, who "had lived chiefly among the English, having a wife & children in the settlements," gave notice to St. Bartholomew's residents of the impending attacks. The alarm, noted Rev. Nathaniel Osborn, "came so very seasonably & providentially that the greater part of my Parish escaped with their lives." Osborn, like others in his parish, was "forced to run away with nothing but the very cloaths upon my back." Given that Mary survived the conflict, we must presume that she was among those who fled with Osborn in haste to Charles Town. Writing just five weeks later, Osborn related that the parish of St. Bartholomew's had been "intirely deserted" and that their houses had been "either burnt or spoiled" by the enemy. All that remained was a "small garrison" that manned a hastily constructed fort at Willtown.[72] In the months that followed, the emptied parish suffered yet another startling attack by a Creek war party led by Mary Griffin's uncle Chigelly. In late July, Creek warriors crossed the bridge at Pon Pon, laid waste to plantations as far as the Stono River, and then on their retreat burned the bridge to slow the pursuit of the South Carolina militia.[73]

Mary's father, meanwhile, must have been among the estimated ninety to one-hundred traders who died during the conflict. We don't know precisely under what circumstances Edward Griffin met his end, but the historian Stephen Oatis shrewdly observes that the Indians likely did not implement their plans to execute the traders "as swift, smooth, or sudden as accounts have often implied."[74] Writing sixty years later, the naturalist William Bartram recounted a story told to him by a veteran Creek trader explaining how almost all the traders were massacred in Apalachicola, where they had fled for protection. Bartram wrote that they had gone there hoping to find asylum and met together in a house "under the avowed protection of the chiefs of the town." While the chiefs assembled in council to determine their fate, "Indians in multitudes surrounded the house and set fire to it; they all to the number of 18 or 20 perished with the house in the flames."[75] Griffin, then, may have died in this manner, after spending several weeks in fear for his life. Never again did his name surface in the historical record, making it almost certain that Mary never heard from him again.

By the summer of 1715, after spending roughly eight years among her father's people, Mary had come to share their fate as a victim of the so-called Indian War. It is reasonable to think that she spent several weeks, if not months, living in Charles Town homes that had been set aside for refugees. Mary probably waited anxiously for word of her father, giving him up for dead as the weeks, months, and then years passed with no sign of him. Having lost her mother years earlier, Mary Griffin was now an orphan of racially ambiguous origins who probably owned nothing more than the clothes on her back. Picking up the pieces of her life must have seemed a daunting task for a fifteen-year-old girl in these circumstances. Fortuitously, the means of recovery came to her in the form of John Musgrove (also half Creek), and together they would return to Pon Pon to reconstitute their lives as married adults.

3 ✳ *Mary Musgrove*

Between Creek Nation and Colleton County

... that after she was married to Mr. John Musgrove she was settled in Carolina upwards of seven years till June 1732.

Mary Bosomworth, 1747

... about the year 1716 your petitioner's first husband, John Musgrove, made an absolute purchase of the said 650 acres of land [in Colleton County, South Carolina] ... the petitioner and her husband had been 14 or 15 years in undisturbed possession of the said tract and improvements.

Mary Bosomworth, 1753

Soon after the Indian war, the said Mary Bosomworth married her first husband John Musgrove ... that soon after their marriage the said John Musgrove made an absolute purchase of the said tract of land [in South Carolina] ... that she delivered the said Mary Bosomworth (then Musgrove) of a child upon that very tract of land.

Elizabeth Hunt, 1753

[Mary] was born in the [Creek] Nation, lived there till ten years of age, afterwards Carolina, where her relatives and friends frequently visited her; again went to the Nation, where she was delivered of her first child. And in short [Mary] was as well known there before the settlement of this Province [Georgia] as she is now.

Thomas Bosomworth, 1756

Piecing together the details of Mary Musgrove's life before her arrival in Georgia is a complicated task that has left many a researcher (this one included) scratching his head. No two writers, it seems, are in agreement as to when Mary wed her first husband, John Musgrove, how much time the couple spent in South Carolina, or exactly how they made a life and livelihood for themselves.[1] Little wonder. As the preceding statements illustrate, the paper trail offers several contradictory scenarios, leaving one to ask: wherein lies the truth?

The truth is that Mary's whereabouts at given times between 1715 and 1732 aren't always clear, although I will make several educated guesses in the pages that follow. That said, the evidence can be reconciled to reveal two trends that characterized Mary's life as a young adult. The first trend is the enduring racial fluidity of South Carolina's southern frontier. While leaders of both the South Carolina colony and the Creek nation tried to erect barriers between their respective peoples following the Yamasee War, Mary's life assumed a pattern at odds with official policy. Mary's presumable return to the Creek nation to deliver her first child suggests that Mary did in fact visit her Creek kin for extended periods of time, perhaps causing her to estimate that she had lived in South Carolina only "upwards of seven years" before moving to Georgia. Just as the Musgroves made occasional treks to Creek country, Thomas Bosomworth hints that their Creek relatives returned the favor by visiting their home in South Carolina. More compelling, however, is evidence confirming the existence of a small Creek community, composed in part of Mary's relatives, that took up residence on John Musgrove's Colleton County lands in 1717. Dubbed the "Pon Pon Indians" by the locals, their presence endowed the Musgrove estate with a multicultural character that defied the colony's emerging ethic of racial separation.

The second trend is that the Musgroves appear to have planted themselves ever more firmly in the colonists' world as time passed. Their process of assimilation, commenced in childhood, intensified following John's purchase of land in St. Bartholomew's Parish in 1717. Commonly remembered as a "trader," John's principal economic endeavor may have been raising livestock. By 1731 John was also harvesting modest quantities of rice and began identifying himself as a planter, leading one to surmise that Mary assumed the outward appearance of a planter's wife. Tellingly, that Mary appears to have given birth to a child in South Carolina, slept on a featherbed, and submitted to *coverture* may reflect her growing tendency to regard Colleton County as "home." By all accounts, then, the Musgroves had assumed many of the trappings of "Englishness," enough it seems to have convinced their neighbors (and perhaps themselves) of their status as upright South Carolinians.

Keeping open the path between Colleton County and the Creek nation demanded that the Musgroves retain the trappings of "Creekness," while their aspirations for economic and social respectability required that they generally act like English colonists. For the Musgroves, reconciling their bicultural heritage was by no means an easy task, as they confronted not only racial prejudice but also repeated Yamasee Indian attacks in the vicinity of their Colleton County home. Somehow, the Musgroves carved for themselves a niche that placed them somewhere between these two societies. Their personal successes, moreover, enabled them to imagine a world characterized by Anglo-Creek mutual dependence and cultural accommodation. Hence we see the importance of this period in the life of Mary Musgrove. More than simply a footnote to the more public life she later lived in Georgia, this earlier period bears witness to the making of a woman who expected to succeed in colonial society without dispensing entirely with her Creek relatives or the part of her that was Creek.

John Musgrove

Over the course of her life, Mary wed three times. Her choice of marital partners suggests certain patterns that may reveal something of the woman herself. While we cannot know the inner workings of Mary's heart, it is nevertheless true that each of her husbands came from a higher rank in colonial society than had the one before. Although their backgrounds differed, these men resembled one another in their ambitions to rise above the humble stations to which they were born—and to some extent, each of them did. While this may have been accidental, Mary's attraction to this type of man may suggest that she harbored like ambitions to rise above her own humble roots, and may even reveal a growing accommodation to the half of herself that was English.

To understand how the couple came together in marriage, it is first worth noting that Mary and John Musgrove shared strikingly similar biographies that made them a likely match. Like Mary, John was half-Indian, born to a Creek mother and a colonist father, John Musgrove of South Carolina. John was probably a few years older than Mary; his purchase of land in 1717 suggests that he had reached the age of majority by that time.[2] Like most children of mixed ancestry, young Musgrove probably spent the first few years of life with his mother's people, in a rather obscure Creek community called Tuckesaw located on the Savannah River just upstream from Apalachicola town. Colonists later built a boat landing at the site, but recalled the area's Indian past by naming it Tuckasee King Landing.[3]

Whereas Mary's father was poor and rather obscure, John's father, Captain John Musgrove, was a somewhat prominent figure in turn-of-the-century South Carolina. Captain Musgrove was English or possibly Barbadian by birth and probably came to the colony in the 1690s, after which he embarked on a successful career as an Indian trader and planter. Upwardly mobile in business, John Sr. was also upwardly mobile as a citizen, serving the colony as a militia captain (later, colonel), a member of the Commons House of Assembly, and a member of the Indian Trade Commission. That John Sr. prospered in the Indian trade indicates as well that he was a shrewd businessman, perhaps verging on the unethical. Musgrove was, in fact, among the most chastised Indian traders of his generation and was known to enslave free Indians to cover his debts and to use strong-arm tactics to compel his Indian clients to go to war. It is hard to say exactly in what manner John Sr. influenced his half-Indian son, but it is reasonable to suspect that Captain Musgrove's rise in South Carolina society served as a model for young John, who might have anticipated capitalizing on his father's name and wealth and who likewise saw nothing wrong with enslaving human beings of various hues.[4]

How the young John Musgrove came to South Carolina remains a mystery, for he left no written account of his life as Mary did. A curious incident, however, suggests that John's father might have forcibly removed him from his Indian village. As the story goes, in December 1706 the Commons House of Assembly accused John Musgrove of seven different improprieties, one of which involved a man known as the "Tuckesaw Indian King." According to one story, Musgrove "threatened the lives of the Tuckesaw King and another [Indian]," demanding four Indian slaves. Musgrove wanted the slaves as compensation for his Indian wife, who the Tuckesaw King (his wife's uncle, perhaps) had taken away. The Tuckesaw King, however, saw things differently, complaining that Musgrove and another trader "had turn'd away their said wives on purpose."[5] In the end, Musgrove and the Tuckesaw King reached a compromise by which Musgrove received in lieu of his estranged wife three Indian slaves, all of whom had been designated "free." (The charges against Musgrove were drawn up, and he was detained briefly, but he was never prosecuted for his alleged malfeasance.)

Regardless of who was at fault, it is clear that Musgrove and his Indian wife experienced a hostile separation and never resumed life as a couple. What, then, was the source of the irreparable strife between them? Given the timing of their separation, it is plausible that the source was their son John, who found himself caught in a tug-of-war between his parents, and between two family systems—one matrilineal and the other patrilineal. As a member of a matrilineal people, John's Indian mother undoubtedly would have preferred to raise him as an Indian, as would have John's male clan-kin, who would have assumed responsibility for shaping his development into manhood. The patrilineal culture into which John Sr. was born, however, reserved such responsibilities for biological fathers. So, it seems likely that John Musgrove came to South Carolina against his mother's (but not necessarily his own) will.

As the historian Rodney Baine suggests, John likely spent the subsequent years of his youth on his father's Berkeley County estate learning the tricks of the cattle ranching trade.[6] That John developed a high level of expertise in animal husbandry (a point I discuss in detail below) indicates that his father played an important role in his development; perhaps the two even developed some degree of mutual affection. Yet, other circumstances suggest that John may have lived with the stigma of illegitimacy (as well as of his racial ambiguity) while in his father's care. After dispensing with his Indian wife, Captain Musgrove married a white woman named Margaret, who gave birth to a son around 1712. Improbably, Margaret and John named the infant "John," as if they intended him to replace his older, half-Indian brother. Tellingly, while his will no longer exists, when John Sr. died in 1719 it is clear that the English John Musgrove became the primary beneficiary of his father's estate and during his minority was placed under the guardianship of his father's in-laws and friends.[7] After reaching the age of majority, he was granted several tracts of land in Craven County, totaling more than a thousand acres.[8] English John later inherited, and then sold, a few of his widowed mother's slaves, and his ability to sign bills confirming their sale in his own hand indicates that he was literate and received at least some of the formal schooling that his half-Indian brother lacked.[9] English John later expanded his estate to include a tract of land on the Saluda River, and he survived at least to the year 1756.[10] His descendants, who continued to inhabit that part of the colony, may have included surveyor Edward Musgrove and his daughter, also named Mary, a Revolutionary War heroine.

Indian John's course in life was different from that of his English half-brother, as his mixed ancestry and illegitimate origins made him an out-sider. That at least some white South Carolinians considered him so is evident in the impersonal manner by which they referred to him. Not only does one of the earliest documentary references to John add the derisive qualifier "half breed or mustee," but his contemporaries also omitted his first name, referring to him simply as "Musgrove" or "Young Musgrove."[11] In addition, it appears that not once did John's white neighbors ever call on him to endorse a will, serve as executor of an estate, or grant him power of attorney.

John's status as an outsider therefore invites questions about the de-gree of his assimilation to English culture. For one thing, Musgrove never learned to sign his own name, indicating his lack of formal education. Nor was John entirely fluent in English. In 1725 the South Carolina In-dian agent Tobias Fitch described Musgrove as "as good a Linguister as any" but added that he "wants some English."[12] In this he differed from his wife, Mary, whose competence as an interpreter many praised without qualification.

John also appears to have been more comfortable fighting as an Indian warrior than as a colonial militiaman. When, for example, John set out to attack Yamasees living near St. Augustine in 1719, he did so with a group of fifty Creek Indians, all under the command of Whitlemico, John's uncle from Apalachicola.[13] Nearly a decade later, Musgrove volunteered again to fight the Yamasees living near St. Augustine. Rather than joining the main expeditionary force commanded by John Palmer, however, Musgrove was appointed jointly with another Creek Indian to lead a party of thirty to forty warriors.[14] Given that John fought alongside Creek Indians on these occasions, it is possible that he fought in the manner of a Creek Indian: fasting in the days before battle, singing war songs in the company of his fellow warriors, searching for providential signs of success, or painting his face in the fear-inducing colors of war.

Yet, even if we may call into question Musgrove's degree of "English-ness," he seems nevertheless to have gradually adjusted to life among the Carolinians as he matured. Although he never became literate, John came to appreciate the power of the written word. He learned, for example, how to write his initials; the few extant documents bearing his name are in-scribed with "IM," written in block letters ("I" being the Latin form of "J").[15] His letter strokes are bold and his lines straight, with a gentle tilt to the right that suggests he was right-handed. John likewise used the initial of his last name to mark his horses, which he branded with a script "M."[16]

On a practical level, John's ability to inscribe his initials on paper and in flesh enabled him to establish a presence in civil society and in business. John's branding mark first proved useful in 1717, when he successfully sued his father's neighbor, Alexander Skene, for a white mare that Skene had detained from him and that was identifiable because of its brand. Four years later, John witnessed a promissory note for ninety-six pounds made out by Thomas Jones (an Indian trader) to Thomas Jones (a planter by the same name). Whether he knew it at the time, Musgrove must have eventually discerned the importance of that act, as planter Jones later pre-sented the same note to the Court of Common Pleas when he sued trader Jones for the money still owed him. By 1732, John Musgrove was marking legal documents pertaining to his own business dealings, such as a bill of sale that committed a substantial portion of his estate to Daniel Green of Charles Town.[17]

On a deeper level, however, these initialed documents offer insight into John's cultural orientation. For instance, John's use of his English patronymic may indicate that he came to identify more with his English father than with his Creek mother. More specifically, the act of making one's mark typically occurred in the context of property transactions, and thereby John learned to associate his patronymic with property that could be bought, sold, and, most importantly, bequeathed. Hence we may as-sume that John's adoption of the Musgrove name betrays his orientation toward the English system of patrilineal inheritance. Not incidentally, John passed on the Musgrove name, as well as a portion of his estate, to his two sons in his will, drafted in 1734.[18]

How John and Mary met and eventually wed is best left to the imagina-tion. Suffice it to say here, however, that the two would have had ample opportunity to cross paths both before and after the Yamasee War, as their Indian-trader fathers shared many mutual acquaintances and had overlapping social and business networks. Although establishing the cir-cumstances of John and Mary's marriage is difficult, the documentary evi-dence consistently suggests that they wed in a Christian ceremony. Both Mary and John publicly identified themselves as Christians, and given that each of Mary's subsequent unions took place before a minister, we have little reason to think that her first marriage to John was any exception. Moreover, South Carolina authorities recognized the legality of their union under English common law.[19] Evidently, their wedding took place shortly before February 1717, when John Musgrove purchased his Colleton County lands. Elizabeth Hunt, Mary's neighbor and midwife, recalled that Musgrove made this purchase "soon after their wedding," indicating that Mary and John were newlyweds at the time.[20]

Mary and John therefore did not intentionally wed to promote peace between the Carolinians and Creek Indians, but rather did so on their own terms. Still, it is evident that South Carolina officials knew of the Musgrove marriage and sensed an opportunity to capitalize on it politically. Shortly after Creek messengers began floating peace proposals that spring, the Commons House of Assembly agreed, on May 25, 1717, to send a peace delegation to the Creeks, intending to end the war and resume trading. Not by coincidence did the Commons House appoint Captain John Musgrove, John's father, to lead that delegation, as House minutes indicate that they were aware of unspecified circumstances that gave him unique leverage over the Creeks. In justifying their decision to appoint him, the Commons House explained that "as we understand that the said Musgrove is much respected among the Creek Indians, we have reason to believe he may have some influence over them, and perswade some of their head men to come to the Ponds [at the head of the Ashley River] to make proposals for a Peace."[21]

Bearing in mind these circumstances, it seems likely that John and Mary accompanied Captain Musgrove that summer to Coweta, where they arrived in late July bearing gifts and words of peace from the South Carolina government. Mary seems to have remembered that event well, as if it were an integral part of her life story, and recounted some of its details years later in a memorial she composed to defend her land claims in Georgia.[22] Moreover, the Spanish Lieutenant Diego Peña, who arrived in Creek territory that August, provides more direct evidence of Mary and John's presence in Coweta and the positive effect their marriage had on the peace negotiations. Peña relates first the exuberance of a certain "Chieftainess Qua" of Coweta, who "opened her arms" to embrace the party "and with wailing and sighs celebrated their arrival," possibly to welcome her long-lost kinswoman.[23] Peña later reported that "the leader of the English (was given) the daughter of the chief as wife" and noted an exchange of presents that took place between Brims and Captain Musgrove. Although the Spaniard misunderstood the exact details of the marriage arrangement (John the younger was the bridegroom, not the Captain, and Mary was not Brims' daughter), his comment nevertheless may indicate that the couple had a second marriage ceremony in Coweta in accordance with Creek customs, as a way of validating their Christian ceremony.

What exactly happened to John and Mary in the months after Captain Musgrove's famed visit to Coweta remains a matter of speculation. It is tempting to think that the couple returned to South Carolina with the captain that October, escorting a group of ten Creek Indians, led by Brims' "son" Ouletta, to Charles Town, where the peace talks continued. More probable, however, is that Mary and John stayed behind in Coweta with the trader Theophilus Hastings, who with a party of "three or four white men besides women and children was left amongst the Enemie Indians [Creeks] as a pledge of the safe passage of their people" until April 1718.[24] Perhaps in the meantime Mary gave birth to that "first child" to which Thomas Bosomworth referred many years later. Within a year, however, the couple appears to have returned to Musgrove's recently purchased land in St. Bartholomew's Parish, where they and a few of their Creek relatives established a homestead that was probably like no other in the colony.

"Planters"

In the wake of the Yamasee War, leaders from both South Carolina and the Creek nation took decisive measures to eliminate the familiarity that had characterized their prewar relationship. South Carolinians, still reeling from the attacks that wiped out two parishes, established a ring of forts on the colony's borders to defend themselves against future incursions of Indians and their Spanish and French allies.[25] Meanwhile, the Creek Indians took steps to create a buffer between themselves and the colonists. Anticipating English reprisals, the Creek towns scattered along the Ocmulgee, Oconee, and Savannah Rivers relocated in 1716 to their former territory on the Chattahoochee.[26] More than a year later, the Creeks and Carolinians agreed to a peace treaty that established the Savannah River as the boundary between them. The treaty prohibited the Creeks from crossing to the river's north bank, while it forbade the South Carolinians from settling south of the river, and from bringing their livestock there.[27]

These various measures reflect more than just a preoccupation with defense. They also reflect a heightened sensitivity to race, particularly among white South Carolinians, who increasingly came to view both Indians and Africans as a fifth column that threatened the colony's internal stability. Much has been written on the subject of race as it applies to white Carolinians' "mounting anxiety" about their African slaves, who by around 1710 had outpopulated whites.[28] But whereas that story is well known, significantly less has been written about the status of Indians within the colony and the degree to which this "anxiety" among whites was a product of their interaction with them. Recently, the historian William Ramsey has argued persuasively that the Yamasee War was an important catalyst for white South Carolinians' racial attitudes. Ramsey notes that anti-Indian rhetoric became more pervasive among Carolinians, and that the practice of enslaving Indians declined precipitously over the next decade.[29] As a further indication of this mounting racial anxiety, the South Carolina Assembly passed various measures to promote the growth of the white population, including a law mandating the importation of white servants, and a 1717 act that limited political participation to any "white man, and no other."[30]

Together, the growth of the colony's black majority and the protections devised to grow the white minority and buttress its legal status contributed to a process we might call the "whitening and blackening" of South Carolina. This process left little room for Indians, who, it was imagined, would have little to no role in the new order of plantation agriculture. Yet, the colony was not in a position to entirely dispense with local Indian allies, who continued to serve the colony as scouts, messengers, and most importantly as a fighting force to oppose Spanish and Yamasee invasions or to capture runaway slaves. Thus, South Carolina's emerging racial order of black and white left just enough wiggle room for Indians. However, the need to distinguish between the colony's friends and foes subjected all Indians to the scrutiny of whites, a process William Ramsey describes as "an early exercise in 'racial profiling,'" in which South Carolina became "a testing ground for new racial definitions, boundaries, and policies that set the tone for the colony's plantation regime."[31]

In some important ways St. Bartholomew's Parish was a likely testing ground for the colony's emerging racial order. For one thing, the parish's total destruction during the Indian war had returned it to frontier conditions. Death and migration among the settlers reduced the parish's population essentially to zero, and Yamasee attacks there persisted for more than a decade after the war's so-called end in 1717, making it a dangerous place to live.[32] As a consequence, even in 1721 only 47 "free" heads of household (along with 144 slaves) lived in St. Bartholomew's, scattered thinly over the more than thirty-six-thousand acres of the parish's taxable land.[33] St. Bartholomew's, then, may have welcomed (or at least tolerated) Indians because of its defense needs, and the dearth of white inhabitants lent the Indians a measure of invisibility.

Importantly, John and Mary's move to St. Bartholomew's Parish coincided with the influx of other mestizos who had lived at Pon Pon before the war. Along with the Musgroves, Thomas Jones, Mary's brother, Edward, and the Welch brothers established in St. Bartholomew's a mestizo enclave on the southwest side of the Edisto River. In turn, their presence attracted small bands of Creek and Yamasee Indians who lived more or less permanently on or near the Musgroves' lands. Among them was John Musgrove's uncle from Apalachicola, Whitlemico, who moved to Pon Pon shortly after John's purchase. Following Whitlemico to St. Bartholomew's was a Creek warrior named Oweeka, who earned praise from the South Carolina government on several occasions for his exploits against the Yamasees. Circumstantial evidence suggests that these men attracted a handful of followers over the years, most of whom were Creek, but others, like a man named "Wehomee," who were Yamasee. Assuming that at least a few women and children followed them, even a conservative estimate of their numbers—say, twenty-five—would indicate a substantial presence in a parish that at one time had only 47 free heads of household.

Dubbed "the Indians that live about Pon Pon," this immigrant community had a complicated relationship with their white neighbors. Occasionally, Oweeka and Whitlemico provided South Carolinians with welcome military assistance, including three important forays into Spanish Florida. At other times, however, the Pon Pon Indians engaged in activities that threatened the colony and its rising plantation system. Most conspicuously, the Indians at Pon Pon sheltered mobile predatory bands of Yamasees and Creeks and were thus witting or unwitting accomplices to the occasional murders and thefts of property (including slaves) that occurred in the vicinity of Port Royal. In addition to the infractions their guests committed, Pon Pon Indians themselves committed various "disturbances," such as killing livestock and the occasional English settler, at least according to South Carolina officials. Nor did Pon Pon's seemingly loyal mestizos evade scrutiny, for it was well known that bilingual go-betweens such as

Tommy Jones and John Musgrove occasionally spread rumors detrimental to South Carolina traders and Indian agents.[34]

So, on one level, the Pon Pon Indian community provides a laboratory for the study of cross-cultural interaction at an important moment in South Carolina's history. The substantial number of Indians living near the Musgroves also may help to explain how Mary and John managed to retain the trappings of "Creekness." For example, it is likely that the Muskogee tongue remained in use at Pon Pon, requiring Mary and John to speak—and therefore retain—their native language. In addition to providing a social context for additive bilingualism, the Musgroves' estate likely also supported certain aspects of Creek ritual life, as well as Creek oral traditions and culinary and medicinal practices. So, it is plausible to assume that Mary and John had ample opportunity to partake of the culture into which they were born.

The ticklish point, however, was that the demands of business, and the art of getting along with their white neighbors, required Mary and John to present themselves more or less as English. As South Carolinians were in the habit of scrutinizing the behavior of the Pon Pon Indians, Mary and John's association with them may have made it doubly important for the Musgroves to brandish their "English-ness." One means John employed to accomplish this was by serving the colony zealously in various quasi-military capacities, including spy, diplomat, Indian agent's assistant, and warrior against the Yamasees. Whether this type of service was a conscious assimilation strategy or a true reflection of the Musgroves' interests as victims of Yamasee attacks, it is clear that South Carolina's governing officials placed considerable trust in John, and his services may have "whitened" him in the eyes of his English neighbors.

Another strategy Mary and John employed to overcome the scrutiny of their neighbors was to succeed at the South Carolinians' own game as upwardly mobile planters. Much of the existing Musgrove lore depicts John Musgrove as an "Indian trader," a likely calling given his bicultural background and his father's success in that occupation. However, this characterization of John—and, by association, Mary—is incomplete, as it fails to consider evidence of John's other enterprises and his response to new economic opportunities. A new characterization therefore is in order, one that focuses on the Musgroves' homestead in St. Bartholomew's rather than on the far-flung trade networks of the southern frontier. From that vantage point, we come to appreciate John Musgrove's diversified economic pursuits, which included the raising and selling of livestock, service to the government, and even the cultivation of rice. Importantly, our characterization of John Musgrove must also take into account his view of himself. By 1731 John had claimed the title "planter," indicating his aspiration for the trappings of gentility conferred by that identity. In the context of John's aspirations, we may also appreciate those of Mary, who was a planter's wife before she emerged in history as the famed interpreter and diplomat for the Georgia colony.

As land was the foundation of the planter's livelihood and status, we begin with the story of how John acquired his property in St. Bartholomew's. The record shows that John first joined the ranks of the propertied on February 4, 1717, by entering into a "lease and release" agreement with Thomas Jones, a shoemaker in St. Bartholomew's Parish, and his wife, Elizabeth, for lands described as "being situate lying and being in the Parish of St. Bartholomews on the South west side of Ponpon River, Colleton County . . . containing about five hundred acres more or less."[35] That John made an "absolute purchase" (a sum of 250 pounds) of his St. Bartholomew's property seems to have been a source of pride for the Musgroves. Mary insisted on the point years later, adding that her husband had paid his taxes "quickly" and that he had improved the estate during the fifteen years they lived there.[36]

The Musgrove property located on the southwest side of Pon Pon River may be more precisely identified as lying at the "Round O Savannah," roughly equidistant between present-day Walterboro and Cottageville, South Carolina.[37] More precisely still, the Musgroves' land can be traced to the intersection between State Secondary Road 45 and Jacksonborough Road near the hamlet of "Iron Crossroads" and about eight miles north of the ruins of the old Pon Pon Chapel. Secondary Road 45 at first appears to terminate at this intersection, but a small, unpaved path referred to by the locals as the "old Round O Road" continues in a convoluted way east and southeast, all the way to the former site of Parker's Ferry. Somewhere along this sandy, secluded (and somewhat eerie) path once lived the Musgroves and the Pon Pon Indians. Today the area has mostly returned to nature, and stands silent to the buzz of human activity that once filled the air.[38]

Of the area's English social geography, certain patterns are discernible within the roughly triangular area formed between Jacksonborough, Parker's Ferry, and the Round O. For one thing, the prime real estate seems to have been located in that triangle's southern point, where John Jackson and some of the more eminent members of the community owned property. Most of the parish's public officeholders also seem to have been drawn from this area, with members of the locally respectable Melvin, Dedcott, and Martin families serving as members of grand juries, or as church wardens. Speaking of churches, Jackson's land was but a mile or two from both the Anglican chapel and the Bethel Presbyterian church in St. Bartholomew's Parish, which is surely indicative of the concentration and quality of the area's population. Prime real estate also seems to have been concentrated near the Edisto River, which had marshes well suited for rice cultivation and was more accessible to markets centered in Charles Town.

Turning to the northwest point of this triangle, the Round O, by way of contrast, was roughly five to eight miles west of the Edisto River, and a full eight miles north of the St. Bartholomew's chapel. Good roads do not seem to have connected the place to the river, or to the more concentrated settlements farther south, until the 1730s. Its relative lack of proximity to river passages and institutions such as the church therefore made the Round O somewhat of a hinterland, at least back in 1717, before the region's population began to flourish. In terms of topography, the Round O was then a flat, relatively high area of land where pine trees flourished, punctuated by the occasional swamp and a few creeks. Grasslands or "savannah" dominated the Round O, which earned a reputation for its suitability for livestock.[39] John Musgrove therefore probably opted to settle at Round O because he knew it to be an ideal location for his herds.

The Musgroves' land seems to conform to the area's prevailing tendencies. Judging by extant land plats, their estate was entirely landlocked and situated upon on relatively high, dry ground punctuated with pine barrens. Accordingly, the couple would not have had privileged access to the Edisto River and would thus have lacked a convenient means by which to trade with Charles Town merchants. Moreover, the dry uplands were not ideally suited for rice cultivation, making it likely that the Musgroves made their living by other means, be it the Indian trade or the raising of livestock.

Of the Musgroves and their immediate white neighbors, we may cautiously assert that they were modestly prosperous by parish standards. Therefore, we should not regard Mary and John as "poor." For example, the Musgroves' neighbors on the west and southwest, respectively, were William Singleton and Bryan Kelley, whose landed estates roughly approximated theirs in size.[40] Also, many of the area's residents, including Alexander Clark and Moses Martin, who lived opposite of Bryan Kelley, owned at least a few slaves.[41] And, though no comprehensive attempt has been made here to calculate precisely the financial worth of the area's inhabitants, suffice it to say that many were able to build respectable estates. On the low end we find individuals like Ebenezer Walcott, whose 350 pounds of personal property was modest but sufficient for him to achieve a minimal degree of economic competence. On the high end were members of the local elite, such as John Jackson, whose personal estate was valued at just over 3,200 pounds at the time of his death. In the middling sort we might include Matthew Smallwood and John Edwards, who each owned roughly one thousand pounds of personal property.[42]

Returning to John Musgrove's economic activity, what is at first striking is the relative lack of evidence for his work in the Indian trade, which may indicate that he dabbled in it only sporadically. In part, the colony's restrictions on the trade may explain why John did not routinely engage in it. The colony's 1716 Indian Trading Act, for example, reorganized the trade by creating a public monopoly that forbade private enterprise. In 1719, the colony passed a new Indian Trading Act that allowed private traders to operate among the Indian nations, provided they did not trade within a twenty-mile radius of the colony's forts.[43] John Musgrove seems to have taken advantage of the new law and commenced trading some time before February 1723. Trading proved a headache for Musgrove, however, as Fort Moore's commander Gerard Monger confiscated his stock of deerskins, citing some unspecified violation of the trading act. Monger later exonerated him, but the experience might have caused John to shy away from the Indian trade and devote his energies elsewhere.[44]

In addition to the arbitrary threats of fort commanders, structural conditions made the Indian trade a difficult one by which to profit, and this might also have caused Musgrove to avoid it. At that time, a handful of "pet" merchants dominated the public trade and also served as the private traders' main suppliers and sources of credit. Quite a few of the traders met with difficulty when it came time to cover their debts to these pet merchants. Among them was a friend of the Musgrove family, Thomas Jones, who in three years' time could not cover a debt contracted in 1718 with Thomas Dymes and Roger Saunders, the heads of one of the government's pet merchant houses.[45] Jones was not alone in facing the wrath of the merchants. In fact, the Court of Common Pleas sessions for the year

1720 are noteworthy for the frequency by which merchants sued traders for debts contracted two years earlier.

In response to merchant grumbling, and perhaps pressure from aspiring traders, the colony revised its Indian trade policies yet again in 1723, instituting reforms that restored entirely the system of private enterprise, albeit in regulated form. Musgrove may have taken advantage of the opportunity the 1723 act offered. In August 1725, the Indian agent Tobias Fitch happened upon Musgrove in Cussita, perhaps indicating that Musgrove had returned to the Creek nation to trade.[46] On February 2, 1726, Musgrove paid thirty pounds for a trading license, making it likely that he traded with the Creek nation that year as well.[47] Beyond that time, however, the record is silent as to John Musgrove's trade activities, suggesting only limited engagement in that occupation until he established his trading post at Yamacraw Bluff in 1732.

How, then, did the Musgroves earn their keep, if not by the Indian trade? One source of income seems to have derived from what might be called the colony's "frontier defense complex." As the historian Verner Crane noted long ago, postwar South Carolina's principal budget items were those earmarked for Indian management and defense.[48] Such expenses included the construction of the colony's various forts, and the salaries paid to officers, enlisted men, and Indian agents. While these were the primary beneficiaries, the frontier defense complex also generated a secondary level of economic opportunity for those who provided food and tools for the garrisons, or who worked on an ad hoc basis, as messengers, guides, boat pilots, or interpreters. A person could not get rich by this type of employment, but government remuneration was predictable and lucrative enough to provide a nice boost to one's annual income. Individuals who had the goods or skills the colony needed for defense were wise to partake of government largesse.

Like many of the men he knew, John Musgrove took advantage of the opportunity to supplement his income by serving the government, typically in activities belonging to the realm of Indian affairs. The first recorded instance dates to February 1724, when John charged the government more than forty-five pounds for "dieting" a party of Creek Indians, presumably that of Chigelly and Ouletta, who had come to Charles Town the previous autumn. More than three years later, Musgrove again worked on the government's behalf, this time going to the forks of the Altamaha River in August 1727 to investigate the rumor of Matthew Smallwood's murder. The government paid Musgrove fifty pounds for services rendered on September 30, a few days after he returned to Charles Town. About a month later, Musgrove accepted a twenty-pound-per-month salary to work for Charlesworth Glover during his agency to the Creeks, during which time Musgrove recruited and later commanded a party of Indians that attacked the Yamasees at St. Augustine. Shortly after the destruction of the Yamasees, Musgrove led a delegation of Creek chiefs that included Brims, one of his unnamed "sons," and Chigelly to Port Royal to receive gifts. Musgrove began his salaried position on November 1 and remained in Glover's official employ until June 1, 1728, upon which he collected the one-hundred and forty pounds that were his due.[49]

Whereas service of this kind might account for a small portion of the Musgroves' income, most of it probably came from livestock. Cattle ranching had been a foundation of the colony's economy since its inception, with Colleton County emerging, in particular, as the epicenter of beef production prior to the Yamasee War. Although an internal market for beef existed within South Carolina, the main demand came from the British West Indies. Archaeological evidence and probate records indicate, too, that horses, as well as swine, a popular source of meat, were great in number. Indeed, it is tempting to conclude that rather than a "black majority," the colony boasted a majority that walked on four, rather than two, legs.[50]

That the Musgroves invested heavily in livestock we may discern first by inference. John's late father, Captain Musgrove, owned 230 head of cattle when his estate was appraised in 1723, more than enough for a few animals to have accompanied his son to St. Bartholomew's Parish. Moreover, Mary indicates that livestock constituted a considerable part of her estate at the time she and John moved to Georgia. In her 1747 memorial, for instance, Mary claimed that they moved there with "all their goods, cattle, and other effects," and boasted of their "considerable" estate, which she described as consisting of "Horses, Cattle, etc."[51] Indeed, the Musgroves' home in Georgia was known as "The Cowpen," indicating everyone's perception of its main function.[52]

To this we add some direct evidence. In March 1732, for the considerable sum of five-hundred pounds, John Musgrove sold off a portion of his personal property to Daniel Green of Charles Town, including "thirty head of cattle," "twelve hoggs," and eleven horses.[53] Even if this sale constituted John's entire holdings in livestock (and we have reason to believe it did not), his estate compares favorably to the holdings of the area's middling planters and even to some of the local gentry's.[54] To put it another way, by 1732 John Musgrove had acquired enough land and perhaps enough personal property to qualify as a member of the Commons House of Assembly.[55] No small success, indeed.

Moreover, the same bill of sale indicates that the Musgroves owned at least two slaves at that time, a "negro man named Lewis" and an Indian by the name of "Justice," most certainly the same man who later joined the Musgroves in Georgia. As with their livestock, the Musgroves' ownership of two slaves compares favorably with their contemporaries. At that time, more than eighty-one percent of all South Carolinians owned at least one slave, and nearly thirty-two percent of South Carolinians owned between one and five slaves. Factoring in the nineteen percent of estates that owned none, we can assert that the Musgroves owned as many or more slaves than half of all South Carolinians.[56]

To understand how the Musgrove estate functioned, we must turn first to the business of cattle ranching, which would have dictated the daily and seasonal rhythms of life on the estate. The Musgroves, like virtually all South Carolinians, would have practiced an "open range" style of ranching, in which cattle roamed to graze freely through the savannahs and pine barrens for much of the year. As a typical herd of two hundred cattle needed at least three thousand acres of land to survive, it was common for cattle to stray far beyond their owners' property, often grazing on the unfenced land of neighbors. Cattle marks seared into the flanks of the animals enabled their owners to identify them. Only at certain times of the year, however, did ranchers pen their cattle, typically in the spring, to allow pregnant cows to deliver and nurse their calves, and again in the fall, the beginning of the butchering season. Herding the animals into the pens usually required their owners and slaves to track them down in the woods on horseback. The open range method, though sometimes characterized as a "lazy" form of animal husbandry, was advantageous in that it required less labor, and cattlemen did not accrue the additional expense of feeding their animals.[57]

Another distinguishing feature of backcountry cattle ranches was their "largely undifferentiated" pattern of social relations.[58] Day-to-day interaction tended to be integrated, as masters and slaves often worked and ate alongside one another and sometimes slept under the same roof. At the same time, a gendered division of labor delegated to household members of each sex distinct but complementary responsibilities. Men performed much of the labor involved in cattle ranching. It is therefore easy to imagine John Musgrove setting out into the woods on horseback, along with Lewis and Justice, to herd the cattle back onto their property in the spring for birthing, branding the young calves, and setting out again in the fall to bring animals in for butchering. Dairying, in contrast, was a responsibility that typically fell to the women. Mary, perhaps with the assistance of a female servant, would have been responsible for identifying lactating cows each spring, milking them, and churning cream into butter, a precious commodity. The cattle business, then, required the input of the entire household, masters and slaves, men and women.

John's 1732 bill of sale hints at not only the nature of his livestock operation, but also some of the family's consumer habits. Although most eighteenth-century cattle homesteads were modest, the archaeologists Mark Groover and Richard Brooks have noted what they call "a noticeable level of formative consumerism" among the cowpen homesteads they excavated.[59] The Musgroves likewise appear to have accumulated consumer goods. Among them were two "feather beds," which were more comfortable and expensive than straw-filled mattresses and were status symbols for colonial Americans. John also parted with a wood table and a set of twelve spoons, six pewter plates, and two "dishes," which may indicate the Musgroves' preference for choice cuts of roasted meat, rather than stews that were commonly eaten in bowls. Some of the items, of course, were utilitarian and work-related, such as the two hoes, two axes, and three fishhooks he sold to Green. Nevertheless, on the working assumption that this single transaction represented only a portion of their personal effects, it seems likely that the Musgroves, like many upwardly mobile colonists, were seekers of material comfort.[60]

The Musgroves likewise sought respectability. Perhaps the most important feature of John's bill of sale is the manner by which he identifies himself: "John Musgrove of Colleton County in the Province of South Carolina planter." John could justify characterizing himself in this way because he had, in fact, begun planting rice on his property, and sold to Green "one hundred bushels [of] rough rice" as part of the transaction mentioned above. This is a telling statement, and one that may reveal John's struggle to break into the rice market. Because roughly one-third of his estate consisted of "barren" land, John may have tried his hand at dry planting, as did many early colonists, or perhaps built earthworks around what low lying areas he had on his property to collect rainwater. John's search for land that could be manipulated into good rice fields may even explain why the size of his estate seems miraculously to have grown over time, from the original "five hundred acres more or less" to in excess of 650 acres.[61] The small size of John's labor force also may have kept output low. Studies of eighteenth-century rice production indicate that a single slave could produce annually about forty-nine bushels of rice, which required about one to three acres per field hand. Musgrove's hundred bushels, then, could have been produced by two slaves working about four acres of land, which was a modest level of output at best.

John's relatively small labor force also determined the quality of rice he produced, which was described as "rough." The production of "rough rice," as it was called, was a relatively simple process whereby slaves would thrash bundles of dry stalks by hitting them with a stick, easily removing the grain. Rough rice production was not labor intensive, unlike the production of white rice, which required several more stages of milling and "polishing." Rough rice has the disadvantage of spoiling easily, so it could not be exported but was often used as seed and sold locally to other planters.[62]

Finally, the badge of "planter" implied dignity and respect. Planters by definition owned land, making them independent and eligible to participate in politics. Regardless of the size of their estates, planters also claimed the right to exercise mastery over their homesteads and their dependents—wives, children, and slaves. This conception of mastery also extended to mastery over nature, as South Carolina planters took great pride in wresting a profitable farmstead from the area's wild terrain.[63] Most importantly, John's embrace of an identity rooted in agriculture directly contradicts the beliefs of Creek men, who regarded agriculture as women's work. As a planter, then, John Musgrove seems to have come a long way from the warlike "half breed or mustee" he was depicted as in 1719. Why, then, having achieved a degree of respectability, did John and Mary leave all this behind to start over at a place called Yamacraw Bluff?

Yamacraw

With the benefit of hindsight, it is clear that the Musgroves' move to Yamacraw Bluff in June 1732 was one of the seminal events in Georgia history. But to understand the event in their time, we must instead consider their move in the context of South Carolina's expansion, which accelerated in the 1730s. The Musgroves, then, formed part of the vanguard of South

Carolinians who turned their attention to the Savannah River, which was then attracting new settlements and an orgy of land speculation. Moreover, their relocation was not an exodus from South Carolina; not only did the colony claim jurisdiction over the new settlements on the Savannah River, but the Musgroves never relinquished their St. Bartholomew's properties. They remained, in effect, South Carolinians, and only later did they find themselves swept up in the creation of the new colony that was to become Georgia.

Since the days of Thomas Nairne, imperialist-minded South Carolinians had dreamed of expanding the colony to the south and west. Even after the devastation of the Yamasee War, expansionists such as Robert Montgomery and John Barnwell continued to offer proposals for English settlement beyond South Carolina's border at the Savannah River. None of these proposals ever amounted to much, however, due to conditions within the colony that checked the expansionist impulses of those few dreamers. For one thing, the continued threat of Yamasee and Spanish invasions made South Carolina's settler population wary of venturing farther south. Political unrest was also to blame. In 1719, South Carolinians instigated a revolution that ousted the proprietary regime and in 1721 led to the installation of the colony's first provisional royal government. The Lords Proprietors, however, did not go down without a fight and continued to lobby for a restoration of their governing rights. In the tumultuous decade that followed the 1719 revolution, the South Carolina land office remained closed, making it impossible for prospective settlers to obtain new land grants. The proprietors' continued intermeddling essentially left the colony in a state of limbo, and its interregnum government could do little to make it attractive to settlers.

By the late 1720s, however, conditions for the colony's southward expansion had begun to improve dramatically. In 1728, John Palmer's overwhelming attacks near St. Augustine largely ended the Yamasee threat, making the colony's southern border more secure. A year later the recalcitrant proprietors finally sold their remaining charter rights to the Crown, which then assumed undisputed governance of the colony. Most important, perhaps, was the arrival in 1730 of the colony's new royal governor, Robert Johnson. Among the hallmarks of Johnson's governance was a plan for western expansion, which he called the "township scheme." Borrowed in part from earlier proposals, Johnson envisioned the creation of eleven new "townships" on the colony's frontiers, intending to lure settlers there with the promise of land and political representation. Johnson also hoped to expand the colony beyond its current borders, as his plans called for two new townships on the Savannah River, and two others on the Altamaha, in what is now Georgia.[64]

Additionally, Johnson revived the colony's atrophied land system. Not only had the land office been closed for twelve years, but there was also the question of what to do about the cloudy title to lands claimed under the defunct proprietorship. The answer came in the form of the Quitrent Act of 1731, which sought to remedy the colony's land and revenue problems first by voiding the old proprietary grants, requiring all claimants to have their property resurveyed and certified within eighteen months. Upon doing so, each property holder would receive a new grant from the royal government. The catch, however, was that quitrents (a fixed rent paid to a superior, formerly the Proprietors)—which had not been regularly collected in the colony—were to be raised from one shilling per hundred acres to in excess of four shillings. Another catch was that anyone who failed to register their lands in the allotted time would lose title to them. When Governor Johnson reopened the land office on November 27, 1731, all South Carolinians seeking to gain new title to their lands were forced to confront the colony's reinvigorated land bureaucracy at some point in the next eighteen months.[65] Here again we find the Musgroves in the mix of things, surmounting administrative hurdles to secure title to the St. Bartholomew's tract.

For those adept at legal maneuvering, the quitrent act probably posed little threat. Many others, however, must have found the procedures it called for a bit intimidating. Such was the case for Mary Musgrove, who remembered well the ominous day of November 2, 1731, when "an order was pas[sed] to void all possessions." This order seemed unfair to her because she and her husband "had been 14 or 15 years in undisturbed possession of the said tract and Improvements."[66] As it turned out, Mary had every right to regard the new act with suspicion, as she and her husband encountered no little difficulty in their attempts to make good on their existing land claims. So much so, in fact, that their title remained in dispute for more than twenty years.

By November 1731, John and Mary had claimed lands totaling 650 acres, indicating that they had expanded beyond the "500 acres more or less" that John had purchased from Thomas Jones. In addition to that tract, the Musgroves also seem to have acquired a half-share of a 360-acre tract in Colleton County originally granted in 1707 to the late William Steads. The Musgroves never lived there or tried to make improvements to the property, so they sold their share to John Champneys and made him clear the bureaucratic hurdles to gain royal title to it.[67]

Having divested themselves of the Steads property, the Musgroves then turned their attention to their own 650 acres. Like many planters, John's strategy was to have it divided into several smaller parts, allowing him to hold on to the most productive lands while divesting of those that were unproductive. When the land office reopened on November 27, John first obtained a warrant for 440 acres. On December 2, he had one tract of 210 acres surveyed. Then, on December 23, he had a nonadjoining tract laid out for 230 acres. That, of course, left 210 acres unclaimed and unsurveyed. When Mary recalled the episode later in life, she insisted that John wanted to rid himself of those acres, which she described as "barren," and exchange them for fertile land at "some other place."[68] While it is conceivable that John and Mary simply wanted to have the remaining tract surveyed elsewhere in Colleton County, the fact that John was not ready to claim it in November suggests that he had a more drastic plan in mind. Perhaps even then John and Mary had their sights set on land south of the Savannah River.

The following March, the Musgroves went to Charles Town to certify their surveys and complete other paperwork related to their land claims. On March 3, as required by law, Mary renounced her dower right to the Champneys tract, swearing before the chief justice Robert Right that she had sold the property "freely and voluntarily without any manner of compulsion dread or fear" from her husband John.[69] Three days later, on March 6, the Musgroves submitted the two surveys of their property to the surveyor general's office. The 210-acre tract aroused no dispute. Certification of the 230-acre tract, however, proved to be more troublesome. The new land system, combined with the emerging land boom, had made it easy for land speculators to revive old proprietary grants of dubious legality and have them validated. The biggest problem involved the colony's extensive baronial grants, which the proprietors had given out in their attempt to fashion a local aristocracy comprising "cassiques" and "landgraves." The baronies were particularly troublesome because proprietary land warrants stated their acreage, but did not specify their location. So, when certain members of South Carolina's would-be nobility tried to revive their baronial grants, they often conflicted with the land claims of ordinary South

Carolinians who had been working and improving the land rather than speculating in it.

Such were the circumstances that brought John Musgrove into a confrontation with the former Landgrave John Bayley of Ireland. Bayley, eager to leverage his baronial patent, employed an agent named Alexander French to have more than twenty thousand acres surveyed and sold to twenty-nine different South Carolinians.[70] French himself leased one of those tracts, a 407-acre spread in St. Bartholomew's Parish. After discovering that John Musgrove's 230-acre tract overlapped his, French entered a "caveat" in Bayley's name against Musgrove, which, if successful, would have prevented him from ever receiving title to it. On March 10, the dispute came before the council, which investigated the matter thoroughly. In the end, the council sided with Musgrove, on the grounds that the original transaction between Musgrove and Thomas Jones was legal and that Musgrove had "possessed the same [land] for fifteen years." French, moreover, had drawn up the lease with Bayley more than a year prior to the survey, a sure indication of their speculative designs. The council promptly resolved to grant Musgrove 230 acres as "part of the said 407 acres" leased by French.[71] Although the Musgroves never lived there again, these two tracts technically remained in their name for more than twenty years.

The key to understanding John and Mary's motives, and the timing of their move to Yamacraw Bluff, then, is the remaining 210 acres of land they intended to have surveyed at "some other place." Circumstantial evidence seems to indicate that the couple resolved to move south around that time. During the council session they attended on March 10, for instance, William Bull was ordered to lay out the town of Purrysburg on the Savannah River, which provided John and Mary with a clear indication that Johnson's township scheme would soon be implemented on the colony's southern margins. Three days later, on March 13, John sold five-hundred-pounds' worth of their property to Daniel Green, perhaps to lighten their load for the anticipated journey. Around that time, John also obtained a land warrant for the remaining 210 acres and had a document drawn up granting Green power of attorney to settle his affairs in Charles Town.[72]

While circumstances suggest that the Musgroves intended to move, it is difficult to discern whether their plans included setting up a trading post at Yamacraw Bluff. Fate would intervene, however, when a group of Upper and Lower Creeks came to Charles Town in late May 1732 to sign a peace treaty with the new governor. As it happened, the Creek delegation included Tomochichi and some of his followers, most of whom had been banished from the Creek towns of Apalachicola and Hitchiti and had probably passed by the Musgroves' home while advancing toward Charles Town. While Governor Johnson regaled the Creek leaders publicly, eventually concluding a peace treaty on June 24, private talks seem to have occurred at that time between Tomochichi, the merchant Samuel Eveleigh, and the Musgroves, who probably acted as interpreters. In the end, the three parties worked out a plan to allow Tomochichi's band of Indians to settle at Yamacraw Bluff alongside the Musgroves, who were to trade with them. Samuel Eveleigh figured into the mix as well, agreeing to provide the Musgroves with a line of credit that would allow them to buy trade goods.[73] Judging by the policies later enacted by the Georgia colony, Johnson seems to have made a verbal agreement with the Musgroves, promising them not only a monopoly of the Yamacraw trade, but also an additional grant of land on the south side of the Savannah River.[74] By June, the Musgroves and Tomochichi's band had departed Charles Town, and they settled on the Savannah River shortly thereafter.

Although the Musgroves' ultimate designs later became clear, it is difficult to say who initiated the move to Yamacraw Bluff or why John Musgrove, now a planter, would have agreed to it. Years later, Mary would assert that she and John moved there "at the request" of both Governor Johnson and the Creek nation, indicating that the initiative came from others. Yet, the Musgroves' delay in having their remaining 210 acres surveyed, combined with their activities in early March, suggests that the initiative was at least partly their own. Johnson's offer to open a trading post, then, may have only sweetened the deal.[75]

Judging by Mary's later recollections, it seems that the Musgroves never intended to sever their ties to South Carolina, and agreed to assume control of the Yamacraw trade as part of a diversified economic strategy similar to that which they had pursued for more than a decade. Hence the importance of John's as-of-yet unsurveyed land, which might have been used to claim a prime tract suitable for raising livestock or growing rice. As it happened, when the Musgroves first moved to Yamacraw Bluff, John brought with him the warrant from the South Carolina government for the remaining 210 acres of land. Mary "very well remember[ed]" that John's intention was "to have laid out the said 210 acres upon the north side of the River Savannah adjacent to his settlement in Georgia." Musgrove "had expected" one of the colony's surveyors to appear in the area, but he never arrived to survey the property. So, John employed John Chevers, a trader at the Palachacola Fort, to deliver to Daniel Green his land warrant for the 210 acres, a copy of his power of attorney, and the deeds to his Colleton County lands. Green's duty, it appears, was to have John's land grants recorded in Charles Town and perhaps to notify the authorities of the surveyor's absence. Unfortunately, Green's "neglect" led to the loss of those papers.[76]

John might have followed up with Green to make sure that his business was attended to, but in August, the South Carolina government again recruited John Musgrove and some of the Yamacraw Indians to accompany Charlesworth Glover to Fort Moore to investigate the recent murders of two traders named Shaw and Sanders. Given that Glover's party remained in the field until October, it would appear that John was too busy to attend to his own business. As a result, the Musgroves' South Carolina properties remained unrecorded, as did the 210-acre tract that had never been surveyed. Not until 1753 was Mary able to rectify the situation and have some of those lands granted to her again.

The Musgroves had only recently settled into their role as traders with the Creek Indians at Yamacraw when, on January 11, 1733, the English ship *Anne* sailed into the harbor at Charles Town. As it turned out, the ship's arrival permanently altered Mary and John's lives. On board the *Anne* was an English Member of Parliament named James Oglethorpe and roughly 120 men, women, and children. South Carolina authorities made hasty arrangements to assist them, providing food, a ranger escort, and money and other necessaries collected in Charles Town's churches. On January 12, the Council of South Carolina likewise ordered John Musgrove "to use his utmost endeavours to be serviceable to Mr. Oglethorpe and his people."[77] So he did with Mary by his side, and together they stepped out of the obscurity of St. Bartholomew's Parish and into the gaze of history as the Georgia colony's interpreters and diplomats.

4 🌿 Mrs. Musgrove of Georgia

That upon the arrival of James Oglethorpe Esqr . . . the Indians that were then settled at Yamacraw, were very uneasy, and Threatened to take up arms against them . . . had not your memorialist used the utmost of her interest and influence to persuade them from it, and to bring about a treaty betwixt Mr. Oglethorpe in behalf of his Majesty and the Indians that were then there . . . That she and her then husbands having at that time had but little experience of the world, and the fraudulent designs of bad people have greatly suffered by giving large credit to sundry inhabitants and other persons on publick service in the colony of Georgia . . . most of which are either dead, have left the colony or not in circumstances to pay her . . .

Mary Bosomworth, 1747

WHEN MARY AND JOHN moved to Yamacraw Bluff in 1732 they had good reason to be optimistic about their future. For one thing, their economic prospects looked favorable; in addition to the land they still held in South Carolina, they owned a considerable number of livestock, and had even begun planting rice. Now traders to the Yamacraw Indians, the couple could look forward to a brisk business in deerskins to supplement their earnings, and perhaps even another grant of land where their trading post stood on the Savannah River. The Musgrove family also seems to have been flourishing; sons James and Edward were growing and approaching the age at which they would begin to learn the various trades of their father. Meanwhile, through his work in Indian affairs at the behest of South Carolina officials, John had entered the realm of public service, and it might even be said that John's Indian background had opened up opportunities for advancement that non-Indians lacked.

Adding to these grounds for optimism was the establishment in 1733 of the Georgia colony, initially conceived of as a refuge for English debtors.[1] Its leader, James Oglethorpe, quickly recognized the Musgroves' value as interpreters, which thrust them into the limelight of the colony's public affairs. Its capital, erected adjacent to the Musgroves' trading post, buzzed with the activity of the first settlers, who busied themselves laying out streets and erecting houses. Savannah, Georgia, promised all the advantages of a colonial port city, including access to international markets, credit networks, and a local demand for the Musgroves' cattle.

As Mary's preceding words seem to indicate, however, Georgia did not live up to its promise. On the upside, Mary's tendency to speak of herself as the one responsible for "[bringing] about" a peace treaty with the Indians indicates that the new colony offered her unique opportunities for public service, which ultimately earned her a place in history. But, looking at the proverbial glass half empty, life as a public figure proved burdensome to Mary. Not only did her services to the colonists occupy time that might otherwise have been devoted to her family's economic endeavors, but they also impoverished her. Candidly, Mary recognized that her youthful naiveté, or lack of "experience of the world," had caused her to fall prey to the "fraudulent designs" of the colony's "bad people," who were unable or unwilling to pay for the "necessities" Mary gave to them on credit. In debt to South Carolina merchants herself, Mary continued to live in the shadow of debt for much of her life—and became increasingly embittered because of it.

While Mary is candid in some ways, her statement omits an important detail: the tragic loss of her immediate family, who were among the many "dead" Georgians referenced above. Not only did Mary lose her husband, John, in 1735, but her sons James and Edward also died soon after their father's passing. Mary rarely spoke of it in her letters and memorials, but her silence seems only to confirm how deeply these losses affected her. A prosperous wife and mother in 1733, less than four years later Mary was a childless widow, and in real danger of not being able to support herself.

It has often been assumed that Mary's second and third husbands turned her against the colony after serving it well during its infancy. Serve the colony she did, but it is perhaps better to situate Mary's later squabbles with its leaders in the context of these early personal tragedies. For Mary, the Georgia experiment represented a double blow to her economic fortunes and to the personal fulfillment she might have enjoyed as a wife and mother. Mary experienced the establishment of Georgia, then, not as a heroic endeavor, but rather as one of deep-seated disillusionment. She later needed no prodding from Mathewes and Bosomworth to fight for land and money she believed was rightly hers, and I would argue that the roots of her problems are to be found here, in Georgia's infancy, and not in the character of Mary's later husbands.

The Cowpen

In many respects the Musgrove homestead at Yamacraw Bluff was similar to their previous one and did not represent a qualitative change in Mary and John's manner of living. As was the case in St. Bartholomew's Parish, the family's economic enterprise remained diversified and involved not only the Indian trade but also livestock production and the cultivation of food crops. The Cowpen's prime location on the Savannah River was much better suited to rice cultivation, and John may have expected to improve upon the one hundred bushels of grain he had raised in 1731. The Cowpen was similar to their previous home, too, in that their closest neighbors were Indians, a group of Creek refugees known as the "Yamacraws." The Musgroves therefore would have expected to continue to participate in Creek social and ritual life, much as they probably had while living among the Pon Pon Indians.

The Musgroves' outpost at Yamacraw therefore testified to the possibilities of genuine biculturalism on the frontier. With the establishment of Savannah, Georgia, in 1733 and the flood of English settlers it attracted, however, such bicultural enclaves came increasingly to be seen as dangerous anomalies. For one thing, the proximity between Indians and English settlers occasioned disputes over land, personal property, natural resources, and even women. Moreover, the bicultural makeup of the Cowpen and the Musgroves' visibility in public affairs challenged colonial conceptions of order and English cultural supremacy. Because a certain amount of law-breaking and violence occurred at the Cowpen, some Georgians were always a little uneasy about the place and the disorder it seemed to represent.

Yamacraw Bluff was a stopping point on the south side of the Savannah River some seventeen miles from the coast and well known to Indians and traders. Mary and John probably lived there for less than a year, but they continued to use their house as a trading post until 1735. When James

Oglethorpe first visited the Musgroves in late January 1733 they negoti-ated a "treaty" by which the Musgroves and the Yamacraw Indians agreed to relocate upstream in exchange for a new tract of land, and the promise of a town lot in Savannah for the Musgroves.[2] While the provisions of this oral agreement seem to have been mutually beneficial and voluntary, it is worth noting that the Musgroves' first interaction with the Georgia colony involved their displacement, perhaps indicating the future direction of Anglo-Creek relations. Later that spring, the Musgroves established their "Cowpen" at a location approximately five miles upstream and west of Pipemaker's Creek, on well-drained lands forested in pine, oak, and hickory.[3] One mile to the east, the Yamacraw Indians built a new village and it was here that they, the Musgroves, and their innumerable guests were able to carry on beyond the immediate gaze of the authorities in Savannah.

Much about life at the Cowpen is well known and readily discernible in the documentary record, which attests to its varied functions as the Musgroves' residence, trading post, and the destination of Indian visitors to Savannah. In addition to the documentary record, recent excavations of the Musgrove home site help both to confirm and to broaden our under-standing of the residents' lives. In terms of its architectural remains, the Musgroves' home, situated more than fifty meters from the water's edge, is the only structure that can be positively identified. The remains of small postholes along the south wall seem to indicate that the house began as a hastily built wattle and daub structure that resembled a Creek Indian house. In time, John Musgrove and Jacob Mathewes improved upon that dwelling by replacing it with a "good house" that had a small cellar and was paved with flagstones and walled with cypress planks. In addition, the property included at least two "huts," which probably housed their ser-vants or slaves.[4] There must also have been a split rail pen for their cattle, which were known to stray across the Savannah River to forage in the savannahs, swamps, and Indian old fields on the South Carolina side.

As with the remains of the Musgrove house, archaeologists have also uncovered an impressive array of artifacts that reveal much about the man-ner of life at the Cowpen. Perhaps the most spectacular discovery came from the house cellar, in which eight fully intact glass bottles were found, indicating rum consumption. More than twenty meters away from the house, archaeologists found two large trash pits, which contained domes-tic refuse such as remains of earthenware plates, a butter churn, and a rare Bellarmine jar made in Germany. Complementing these artifacts of domestic life are the remains of items that were undoubtedly part of the Indian trade, including gun parts, scissors, and a pair of whittled down deer antlers that Indians used to attract deer.[5] Archaeologists have also unearthed animal remains, which likewise gives us some indication of the Musgroves' culinary preferences. The overwhelming presence of bovine remains should come as no surprise, but the Musgroves also ate chickens, pigs, and perhaps harvested wool from sheep. As they probably did at Pon Pon, too, the Musgroves also ate a lot of venison.[6]

As a residence, the Cowpen was home to an extended family that included not only John, Mary, and their two sons, James and Edward, but also several dependents. Most notable among them were the Musgroves' Indian slaves, named Wan, Nanny, and Justice, who was murdered in 1734 and replaced with another unnamed "Indian servant," most likely a man known as Nottoway. Although at the time it was illegal in Georgia to own slaves, the colony's prohibition applied only to "negroes," and the Musgroves were the first of a small minority of planters to exploit this loophole without technically breaking the law.[7] The tribal designations of the slaves are not recorded, but it is reasonable to suspect that they were Yamasees from Spanish Florida and had been purchased a few years earlier from the Pon Pon Indians.

The presence of Indian slaves necessarily raises questions—some of them discomforting—about the Musgroves' attitudes about race and the institution of human bondage. Generally speaking, the Musgroves practiced slavery much like slaveholders in the Carolinas, but with some significant variations that may betray the masters' Indian heritage. With respect to the slaves' work regimens, it is clear that the Musgroves assigned them tasks that corresponded to their age, sex, and presumed skill levels. Justice, an able-bodied adult, worked as a field hand and was probably the couple's most valuable slave.[8] Wan, on the other hand, is described in John's will as an "Indian boy" and was later groomed to become Mary's messenger. Their female slave, Nanny, was most likely a teenager.[9] As the name "Nanny" was common among female slaves who assisted in childrearing, it is plausible that she helped Mary raise her sons and was probably responsible for dairy work. At least two of the Musgroves' slaves—Nanny and Wan—appear to have been bilingual and would have been able to converse with their masters in English or Muskogee.

In some ways, the Musgroves' ideas about the institution of slavery conformed to those of white slaveholders. Most notable is that John regarded all three of his slaves as chattel property that could be bought, sold, and bequeathed, as indicated in his will. John's tendency to refer to them in the possessive case ("my man Justice") or to use the emasculating term "boy" reflects this sense of ownership. To put it another way, the Musgroves were not modern liberals who celebrated equality and the empowerment of the individual. Rather, they conceived of human relations vertically, as a system of hierarchies linking high to low. Owning property in human beings allowed Mary and John, like other planters, to conceive of themselves as "masters," whose status depended upon their ability to command the labor and lives of others.

Yet, it seems also to have been the case that the Musgrove slaves enjoyed de facto freedoms that indicated that John and Mary could sometimes be lax in exercising their mastery. The demands of frontier living may have promoted a measure of equality in the work regimens of masters and slaves. Moreover, Mary and John's Creek heritage might also have been a factor. Studies of Creek Indian slavery indicate that Creeks allowed their slaves considerable personal freedoms, such as a right to tend their own gardens, to travel, hunt, and perhaps even marry Creeks. Creek slaves also worked in a less physically demanding and less regimented environment, causing some scholars to compare Creek Indian slavery to a "modified patron-client" relationship.[10]

That the institution of slavery at the Cowpen exhibited some of these qualities can first be inferred by the lack of evidence of physical coercion, or of any acts of insubordination on the part of the Musgroves' slaves. It also appears that each slave enjoyed considerable latitude to move beyond the confines of their master's plantation and perhaps even garnered a measure of respect. John held Justice, for example, in high regard because of his agricultural skills, and the two men appear to have regularly worked side by side. Justice also once had the rare opportunity to testify against a white man in court in Savannah, where he was allowed to travel in the company of Yamacraw Indians. More so even than Justice, Mary's personal messenger Wan enjoyed considerable freedom to travel about Georgia. Nanny, meanwhile, did not travel as far and wide but fraternized regularly with the Yamacraw Indians. While these examples do not rule out the possibility that the Musgrove slaves were treated like other slaves, they nevertheless give some indication that the slave regime at the Cowpen was less coercive than its counterpart on some plantations in neighboring South Carolina.

Complicating the Cowpen's labor regime further still was the presence of white servants or employees. Among the Musgroves' white employees was Job Wiggin, a former member of the garrison at Fort Moore in South Carolina, who worked as a cattle hand. In addition to Wiggin, John purchased a servant during his trip to England in 1734. The Englishman's name, not incidentally, was Jacob Mathewes, who outlived John and later wed Mary.

The unique circumstances of Wiggin's and Mathewes' servitude at the Cowpen seems at first to confound common presumptions about race relations and the supremacy whites enjoyed over Indians and blacks. Unprecedented as the situation was, their example serves as a reminder that race relations were at the time somewhat fluid in Georgia. In fact, the situation is roughly analogous to one found in the previous century in Northampton County, Virginia, where a community of propertied free blacks owned African slaves and white indentured servants. In explaining how such a situation came into being, the historians T. H. Breen and Stephen Innes argue that property, rather than an arbitrary "racial" designation, determined one's place in society. Property, they assert, was "the foundation of liberty" that gave men legal rights, their political identities, and was "the only clear measure of another man's worth."[11] By analogy, then, we may infer that the Musgroves' status as property owners (and substantial ones, at that) was the principal measure of their worth, which empowered them to own and control the labor of others—regardless of the color of their skin. Moreover, because the bicultural Musgroves represented only a tiny minority of Georgia property owners, their actions posed little threat to the region's emerging racial hierarchy.

Any attempt to understand the cultural complexity of the Cowpen must also take into account its proximity to the Yamacraw Indian village, which was located just one mile away. The Yamacraws, with an estimated population of one hundred persons, comprised a band of Creek refugees who had been banished from the nation some time before. Their leader, Tomochichi, had been expelled from his hometown of Apalachicola for committing an unspecified (though presumably grave) offense. Many of Tomochichi's followers appear to have been clan-kin, hailing principally from the Creek towns of Apalachicola, Osuchi, and Hitchiti. How long or how intimately they knew the Musgroves prior to 1732 is difficult to gauge. But John's Apalachicola origins and their coordinated move with the Indians to Yamacraw Bluff suggest that at least a few of them may have been Pon Pon Indians.

Much is known about the Yamacraw Indians' involvement in Georgia's diplomatic and military affairs. In cultural terms, though, the Yamacraws' proximity enabled the perpetuation of Creek lifeways at or near the Cowpen, where the Creek language was spoken with regularity and where elements of Creek ritual life were occasionally on display. Added to this were certain elements of frontier culture, in which violence, hard drinking, blunt conversation, raucous behavior, and a degree of sexual permissiveness were a part of everyday life. A destination for Indians and English colonists alike, the Cowpen (and their trading post at Yamacraw Bluff) served as an interface between two cultures and might be regarded as an exotic place that at once attracted and repelled Georgia residents.

Creek rituals and entertainments, for example, fascinated some Georgia settlers, who had opportunities to observe and sometimes participate in these diversions while visiting the Musgroves. Perhaps the most intriguing case transpired on the evening of February 1, 1733, when the Musgroves hosted a "handsome supper" at their house. After the meal, the Yamacraws entertained the Musgroves' English guests by dancing around a fire they had built in front of Tomochichi's house, which stood nearby. Sitting on the sidelines as a mere spectator, however, was too much to bear for one of their visitors, a man named Dr. Cox. After becoming inebriated, Dr. Cox joined the Indians' dance "endeavoring to mimick and ape them in their antic gestures." Shocked by the elderly man's behavior, the diarist Peter Gordon urged Cox to stop, lest he make a fool of himself in front of the Indians. Still inebriated, Dr. Cox returned again to dance with the Indians, after which he was forcibly removed (this time for good) from the site of revelry.

What a sight it must have been to see an elderly, drunken Englishman dancing around the fire before the Musgroves and other Indians, who probably found his antics at worst insulting and at best amusing! Gordon, however, found nothing amusing about the incident, as the loss of inhibition was thought unbecoming in English people, particularly in an elderly man of distinction who ought to have exercised more restraint.[12] Social intercourse with the Indians, then, was to be conducted with formality and decorum befitting English gentlemen. Activity at the Musgroves' home, however, gave the colonists opportunity to behave otherwise.

As this episode indicates, the presence of alcohol made the colony's leaders—particularly James Oglethorpe—somewhat ambivalent about the Musgroves. While not strict teetotalers, the colony's reform-minded Trustees disdained strong drink such as rum for its intoxicating effects and the suffering it caused among the poor. Although the Trustees did not anticipate that alcohol would be a problem, James Oglethorpe identified the profligate consumption of rum as the cause of laziness and insubordination among the settlers. Rum also weakened the settlers' constitutions, making them susceptible to various fatal fevers. To counter rum's unwanted effects, Oglethorpe restricted its supply, which brought him into direct conflict with the Musgroves, who regularly sold the beverage.[13] Whether or not they were to blame, the traffic in rum became a mounting source of friction between Oglethorpe and the Musgroves, who were clearly leveraging their position as interpreters to resist Oglethorpe's various "prohibitions" on its sale. As Oglethorpe explained: "I do not care to disoblige them [of selling rum], as they are the only interpreters we have." Eventually, however, Oglethorpe threatened to "suppress" them and convinced the Trustees to pass a law prohibiting the beverage's sale.[14] Mary and her several husbands submitted to the law rhetorically but continued to flout it for many years.[15]

Along with hard drinking, the Musgroves' home had a reputation for interracial sexual intrigue. One incident, occurring in March 1734, must have been the source of prurient gossip in Savannah and involved the Musgroves' cattle hand, Job Wiggin, and a married Yamacraw woman called "Defatige." Wiggin, who was single, had offered Defatige his hand in marriage in the Indian manner by inviting her into his hut and giving her a blanket. Although she was already married to a Yamacraw man, Defatige accepted Wiggin's offer and proceeded to "[lie] with him in the said hut," presumably to consummate their marriage. Incensed that Defatige had been lured into bigamy, Yamacraw Indians protested to authorities in Savannah, who promptly arrested Wiggin. Meanwhile, the wronged Indian husband defended his honor by cutting off Defatige's hair and both of her ears, which he later paraded around Savannah on a stick.[16]

In spite of their differing views of sexuality and marriage, Wiggin's and Defatige's actions violated both Creek Indian and English standards of marital conduct. Also, Yamacraw and Georgia leaders understood that their behavior could threaten the stability of Indian families, not to mention the relationship between their peoples. So, Savannah authorities decided to make an example of Wiggin, devising an ad hoc method of justice that allowed for Indian participation. The setting was the makeshift courthouse in Savannah, where Yamacraws Skee and Estichee entered their complaint, as armed constables and curious Georgians looked on. Then, witnesses were called to testify against Wiggin, including the Musgroves' slave, Justice, who, like other Indians, claimed that he "saw it." Perhaps intimidated by a throng of white onlookers, the Indians at first seemed to intercede on Wiggin's behalf by insisting that no "white man should be punished for them." Wiggin, however, "seemed to laugh at" the accusation, so Georgia authorities made an example of him by shackling him in irons. Later, Skee and Estichee agreed to let Georgia authorities have Wiggin whipped, but the Yamacraws were generally uncomfortable about the shedding of Wiggin's blood and were somewhat embarrassed by the maiming of Defatige.[17]

As these events seem to suggest, unrestrained behavior was the norm at the Cowpen. Involving, as they did, unbecoming dance, alcohol, and sex, these events might be said to indicate that an eighteenth-century version of "sex, drugs, and rock 'n' roll" reigned supreme. Even if these behaviors did not violate the Musgroves' own sense of propriety, it is clear that the Cowpen, as an interface between two cultures, offered dangerous possibilities for violating the English elite's standards of behavior.

A Public Figure in the Making

It is intriguing to wonder how Mary's life might have been different had her first husband, John, lived to a ripe old age, rather than dying, as he did, in the prime of his life. Given contemporary gender expectations that elevated men above women in public life, we may imagine that John would have continued on his path as the colony's trader and point person for Indian diplomacy. The first two years after Oglethorpe's arrival were truly John's moment in the spotlight, with Mary playing only a supporting role in Georgia affairs.[18] John's long absence and eventual death, however, would provide opportunities for Mary to assume many of her husband's responsibilities. As a consequence of her ability to perform them so well, Mary more than filled the void John left and gained some of the "experience of the world" that prepared her to become a public figure in her own right, the renowned "Mrs. Musgrove."

Mary's invisibility in managing Indian affairs at the official level should not, however, be taken as evidence that she was not involved in other capacities. As was often the case, the colony's male residents and visitors probably overlooked the important role she played in the background. They may not have known, for example, that Mary had already been called on once before to interpret, as she appears to have done in June 1732, when she helped to hammer out the agreement that led to the establishment of the Yamacraw settlement.[19] Nor were they aware of Mary's behind-the-scenes politicking, which seems to have convinced Tomochichi to acquiesce to Oglethorpe's desire to locate on Yamacraw Bluff. As Mary remembered it, when Oglethorpe arrived to "choose a situation" for his town, the Yamacraw Indians became "very uneasy" and threatened to take up arms against him. By using her "interest and influence" to prevent the Yamacraws from attacking Oglethorpe, Mary was able to "bring about" peaceful relations between the Georgia colonists and "the Indians that were then living there."[20]

While Mary likely participated informally in diplomacy, her main contributions were of the domestic kind and conformed to the gendered division of labor common among both the Creek and English peoples. One brief comment by the diarist Peter Gordon is suggestive of Mary's responsibilities on the first day of the colonists' arrival:

> Not being able to compleat the Pitching of our Tents this night ... And I being but lately recover'd from my Ilness, went to ly at The Indian Town at Mr Musgrove the Interpreters House, With Doctor Cox and His Family and Lieutenant Farringtons Belonging to Captain Massy's Company. Who hade order'd a Handsome Supper to be provided for us at Mr Musgroves House.[21]

Even though he does not mention her by name, Gordon's comments suggest that Mary spent considerable time and energy that day fulfilling her duties as hostess and attending to the needs of her many visitors. Perhaps the most needy guest was the ill Peter Gordon, who came to Mary's house for some much-needed bed rest. As if a sick man wasn't enough, a throng of other visitors also crowded into the Musgrove home. Each of them, too, probably looked to Mary for help getting situated and alleviating their thirst and hunger. Most telling of all, though, is the "handsome supper" that was to take place that night in the Musgrove home. While Ogle-thorpe, Tomochichi, and the rest of the settlers busied themselves conducting diplomacy and pitching tents, we can be fairly certain that Mary spent much of that day cooking. We might imagine, too, that Mary was harried giving orders to Nanny, who would have been at her side preparing the dishes, fetching water, and perhaps attending to the needs of Mary's sons, James and Edward.

Along with hospitality, religious piety was a quality much admired in women, and it was one that Mary also admired in herself. Another important behind-the-scenes function Mary seems to have served was cultivating in the Yamacraw Indians an interest in Christianity. The conversion of the Indians was important, not only because it was a stated goal of the Georgia Trustees, but also because both Indians and colonists employed the rhetoric of conversion to convey their peaceful intentions. Known by many to be a pious woman, and herself a teen convert to Christianity, it is plausible that Mary was responsible for bringing Tomochichi to church, which he attended regularly after Oglethorpe's arrival. In fact, the first direct documentary evidence of Mary's existence occurs in the context of a religious service Tomochichi attended.[22] Circumstantial evidence suggests, too, that Mary was the one to convince Tomochichi to have his nephew Tooanohoui educated and baptized. Mary was known to teach the Indians "useful things from the Holy Writ" herself, so it would not be surprising if Mary was the first to introduce the Lord's Prayer and the Apostles' Creed to Tooanohoui, who was said to read them "tolerably" well.[23]

Nevertheless, it was not Mary's hospitality and piety that first gained the attention of Georgia colonists, but her linguistic abilities. Mary would have had ample opportunity to translate on an informal basis, and her services must have been in demand when colonists and Indians crossed paths at Yamacraw, as can be inferred by Oglethorpe's comment that John and Mary were "the only interpreters we have."[24] Moreover, colonists quickly realized that Mary had a "special talent for expressing Indian terms in English," a talent "not even possessed" by her husband, John.[25] So, Mary's reputation as a linguist seems to have been widely known and, in time, led to more work on behalf of Georgia's governing officials and ministers.

The opportunity, welcomed or not, for Mary to play a more public role came with John's prolonged absence in England in 1734, when he served as interpreter for Tomochichi and the Yamacraws. The arrangements that John made prior to his departure for England reveal much about the way he conceived of his relationship to Mary, as well as the extent and limits to which he believed her capable of managing the family's affairs. Fearful, perhaps, that he might die while crossing the Atlantic, on April 29 John drew up a brief will. Most noteworthy among its provisions is the one in which John bequeaths the "Cowpin" and his cattle to his sons James and Edward, which suggests that he expected them rather than Mary to continue the family livestock business. Each son also received one slave, as did Mary, to whom he bequeathed "all the rest." This probably included all John's personal property, remnant properties in South Carolina, and must have constituted more than the traditional "widow's third" that surviving widows received under English common law. Importantly, John named Mary as his "sole executor," which meant that the responsibility of settling John's debts and honoring his bequests would be hers.[26] While entrusting Mary with executor rights, John was nevertheless unwilling to let her manage the deerskin trade alone in his absence. Sensing the need for a male presence in that business, John entered into a partnership with their neighbor, Joseph Watson, who was to help manage the deerskin trade while he was away. Ultimately, John and Mary would come to lament their decision to partner with him.

After John's departure on May 6, Mary quickly assumed responsibilities that broadened her horizons and led to her first appearance in the colony's public record. Of most lasting significance was her involvement in Indian affairs. On June 30, Mary's kinsman Thomas Jones arrived at the Cowpen with a seemingly large delegation of Choctaw and Talapoosa chiefs, who Jones brought to Georgia to meet Oglethorpe. Politically, this meeting was an important one, as Jones and Oglethorpe had conspired to draw the Choctaws—then allied to the French—into Georgia's trade orbit. Gaining the Choctaws' friendship required that the Georgians appear hospitable, and Mary, who housed them for several weeks at the Cowpen, would have born much of the burden of making them feel at home by preparing food and regaling them with rum.

Mary's earliest surviving correspondence is a letter she wrote to James Oglethorpe (then in England), dated July 17, 1734, shortly after the Choctaws' departure from the Cowpen.[27] That letter is instructive on many levels, particularly for the way her writing evinces a cosmopolitan understanding of the colony's place in the wider world. Noteworthy among Mary's observations is that of England's rivalry with France for control over the region's Indian tribes. Mary likewise understood the disparity between British and French trade capabilities and recognized that the Georgia colony could enhance its standing among the Choctaws by exploiting England's commercial advantages. Gaining the Choctaws' allegiance had other advantages as well, including those of defense. Optimistically, Mary predicted that commercial ties to the Choctaws would enable Oglethorpe to "raise a thousand or two [men] at your Honour's Command if desired" and boasted "they design to leave the French entirely."

This letter likewise provides evidence for some of Mary's personality traits, most specifically her assertiveness in defending family interests, in this case those of her kinsman Thomas Jones. First among Jones's troubles was a town lot in Savannah that Oglethorpe had granted to him, but which he had mistakenly regranted to Robert Parker. Mary did not shy away from informing Oglethorpe of his poor handling of the matter, one that had caused a "great dispute" in Savannah and required mediation in court (by which Jones was regranted his town lot). In addition, Mary lobbied for Jones's right to the potentially lucrative Choctaw trade. "Your Honour did promise him," she reminded Oglethorpe, adding that Jones had "ventured his life" to bring in the Choctaws, who had a "very great Respect and Value" for him. Ultimately, neither the Georgia colony nor Thomas Jones could capitalize on the initiative to the Choctaws, but Mary had done her part, both in hosting them at the Cowpen and in lobbying on Jones's behalf.

Finally, Mary's words betray her worried state of mind during John's absence in England. For one thing, she was concerned about John's health, having reasonably presumed that the Atlantic crossing and urban environments he encountered might have a detrimental effect on him. Mary's intuition may even have led her to guess (correctly) that time spent in a "strange place" would exacerbate John's weakness for alcohol, in which he indulged to the detriment of his work and possibly his health while in London. Mary was, it seems, protective of John, as she pleaded for Oglethorpe to look after John on the grounds that he was "not able to take care of himself" and urged Oglethorpe to "send him home as soon as possible."

While she no doubt feared for his well-being, Mary had more immediate reasons for wanting her husband home. Left alone to manage her family's business dealings, Mary was vulnerable to the machinations of Joseph Watson, the very man John had trusted to oversee the Indian trade during his absence. Not only did Watson conduct a dishonest trade, but he also tried to slander Mary by spreading rumors of sexual dalliance and mismanagement of the trade. Whether he did so simply because she was female or because she had "little experience of the world," the so-called "Watson Incident" illustrates the varied ways in which conniving men could take advantage of unsupervised and inexperienced women. In Mary, however, Watson more than met his match.

The problems with Watson appear to have begun shortly after John's departure for England. Watson started drinking heavily and engaging in odd and dangerous behavior. At times he would go naked among the Indians and paint his body after their fashion.[28] To awe the Indians, Watson feigned spiritual powers by "threatening to bring down storms and showers of blood" and also by conducting mock baptisms.[29] Predictably, the Yamacraw Indians came to fear and distrust him and began to look to sell their deerskins elsewhere. Watson's odd and belligerent personality, though, was only part of the problem. Much more damaging to the Musgroves' finances was his dishonest conduct of the trading business. As later investigation proved, Watson bought and sold goods without Mary's knowledge and carried on trade through "another channel" rather than with the Charles Town merchant Samuel Eveleigh, who later complained of having received "no skins" since John's departure in May.[30]

Watson's belligerence first became apparent in early August when he called Mary a "witch."[31] Watson's choice of words was probably intentional, given that women—particularly those who were quarrelsome, owned property, or lived without male supervision—have historically suffered from such accusations.[32] Most importantly, Watson likely tailored his accusation to the ears of the Yamacraw Indians, who believed it possible for a human being to manipulate spiritual powers. By discrediting Mary as a "witch" before the Yamacraws, Watson probably hoped to deflect criticism of his own conduct of the Indian trade. Mary, recognizing the potential consequences of Watson's accusation, felt it necessary to respond. On August 13 Mary brought a lawsuit against Watson before the court, which rewarded her with six pounds and eight shillings in damages.[33]

After being sued, Watson escalated his attacks, and the threat became physical when Watson pulled a gun on Mary, intending to shoot her. In a manner that can only be described as courageous, Mary "overpowered" Watson, took the gun away, and broke it. Watson's rampage continued, though, when he assaulted an Indian named Estichee the next day and "defrauded him of his goods." For these infractions, Watson was again hauled into court, this time for assault and theft. The court again sided with Mary and Estichee, each of whom received monetary compensation for Watson's crimes. Although clearly dangerous, the court did not imprison Watson, who went free after posting bond for good behavior.

Watson's provocations continued even as the scrutiny of his behavior intensified. Around the time that Watson appeared in court, he began keeping company with a Yamacraw Indian named Skee, and the two stuck together as constant drinking companions over the course of several weeks beginning in August. The excessive drinking appears to have weakened their constitutions and sickened them both. While Watson eventually recovered from his illness and later managed to sober up for a while, Skee came down with a "flux" (perhaps dysentery) and went to the Cowpen in order to recover. As Skee's condition worsened, Watson boasted publicly that he had caused Skee's illness and predicted "that he would [die]." While many dismissed Watson's prediction as "drunken talk," when Skee succumbed to his affliction, many more felt inclined to take Watson seriously, and Watson persisted in boasting that he had purposefully caused Skee's death. Colony officials, who feared that such talk would irreparably damage their relationship with the Yamacraws, were not amused.[34]

Given what was transpiring in Georgia, it is no surprise that word of Mary's troubles soon reached the ears of Samuel Eveleigh, the Musgroves' creditor in Charles Town. In September, Eveleigh hired a local attorney named James Muir to demand money from Watson. Watson, who was unable or unwilling to pay, challenged the attorney to sue him in court.[35] To gather evidence against Watson, Muir and Thomas Causton, the colony's storekeeper, traveled to the Cowpen to conduct an inquiry, which, as Causton remarked, "proved to be the unraveling of all Watson's behavior." It was then that Muir learned the details of Watson's mismanagement of the deerskin trade, compelling him and Causton to examine Watson's accounts and take an inventory of the remaining trade goods. As Muir's dragnet closed around him, Watson absented himself in the woods and locked up the Musgroves' storehouse, which could not be reopened because Watson had managed to abscond with the lone key.

Watson persisted in this behavior for several days, which led to the murder of the Musgroves' slave, Justice, and ultimately to Watson's arrest. One day, Watson locked himself and Justice in the Musgroves' storehouse, when a group of Yamacraw Indians led by Estichee approached the door. Mary, who knew quite well of Estichee's murderous intent, feared having blood shed on her premises, so she begged Watson to escape by shouting to him through a window. Watson secreted himself out of the back of the house and ran away to Savannah. When Estichee finally managed to enter the storehouse, he encountered the Musgroves' slave, Justice, and beat him to death in a state of rage. To prevent further bloodshed and scandal, Georgia officials confined Watson to a house in Savannah and gently persuaded Estichee to keep his distance.

In the meantime, Georgia officials groped for a just resolution for all the parties involved, referring the debt case to arbitrators and offering Watson the chance to flee to South Carolina. Watson rejected Causton's seemingly generous proposals, choosing instead to speak ill of the arbitrators and boast of killing Skee. In retaliation, Causton drew up charges against Watson for slander and on November 21 tried the case before a grand jury. The court found Watson guilty as charged but refused to recommend punishment, instead leaving him to the mercy of the Trustees on the grounds that he was "a lunatick." Causton, though, judged Watson too dangerous to be released and placed him under house arrest in Savannah, where he would spend the next three years. While this may have pleased Mary and her supporters, others in Savannah considered it "cruel" to imprison a white man "for fear of an Indian," and his confinement continued to stoke factionalism between Watson's supporters and detractors for several years.[36] Eveleigh probably never did collect the money that was owed him.

Retrospectively, the Watson incident is perhaps best interpreted as an educational experience that enabled Mary to acquire some of the hard-won "experience of the world" that would make her a formidable person to deal with. One valuable lesson was learning to take advantage of the colony's court system, where Mary would have gained confidence in her ability to speak publicly before men as well as an understanding of the formal procedures and evidentiary demands of the legal process. Mary likewise became adept in averting cross-cultural violence, both by withholding from Skee's brother her knowledge of Watson's inflammatory speeches and also in pacifying Estichee, who had intended to kill Watson. The Georgia Trustees were so impressed with these and other acts that they rewarded Mary with twenty pounds sterling for her "great service" in "keeping the Indians in friendship."[37] This reward, in fact, marks Mary's first appearance on the Georgia Trustees' payroll. It would not be the last.

Mary also learned some important hard-won lessons about business. The most obvious lesson was to be careful in choosing one's partners, and her bad experiences with Watson may explain why she never again entered into another trade partnership, choosing instead in business to go it alone or with her several husbands. Watson's diversion of the trade through "another channel" must have likewise opened her eyes to the importance of keeping an accurate account book and taking a regular inventory of trade goods. To these business practices, we must also add something intangible—an emerging tendency in Mary, and in others, to identify her as a trader rather than as a trader's wife. The first sign that Mary had begun to think of herself this way comes during James Muir's investigation of Watson in September 1734. When interviewing the Yamacraws, Muir received a request from a man named Tallahummee that "another man" replace Watson. On second thought, however, Tallahummee seemed to prefer another option: "that [Mrs.] Musgrove may trade by herself."[38] It was a logical proposition; by then Mary had been selling beef to the colony's storekeeper for some time and had grown accustomed to making transactions on her own.[39] John's return home in January, however, made it unnecessary for Mary to find "another man" to partner with. Ultimately, though, the Georgia Trustees recognized Mary as an equal partner by confirming "Mr. John Musgrove and his wife" as the sole traders for the Yamacraw Indians.[40] The Trustees' directive, dated May 15, 1735, is the first time the colony officially recognized her in this capacity. And again, it would not be the last.

John's return from England in January 1735 likewise may have helped to expand Mary's horizon of experience, albeit indirectly. Up to that point, Creek knowledge of England consisted largely of guesswork. John Musgrove, the first Anglo-Creek ever to visit England, would doubtlessly have returned empowered with firsthand knowledge of the island nation—its size, population, military strength, commercial capacity, and imperial ambitions. Through John, Mary would have had the opportunity to gain secondhand, but nevertheless valuable, knowledge of her father's people, knowledge that must have shaped her thinking about Indian diplomacy and trade.

It is tantalizing to imagine the kind of stories John might have told Mary in moments of quiet repose at the Cowpen. The six-week ocean crossing itself must have piqued Mary's curiosity. Perhaps John chose to mention the iceberg the ship encountered somewhere in the north Atlantic, or the sense of relief he felt when they finally anchored at Portsmouth in view of the imposing South Sea Castle erected centuries earlier by Henry VIII.[41] John must have experienced a sense of exhilaration at being whisked away in a horse drawn carriage to London, which he and his Indian companions had ample opportunity to explore.[42] John would have been remiss not to mention the grandeur of London's buildings: the Royal Palace at Whitehall, where the Indians met the King and Queen, or Lambeth Palace, where the Archbishop of Canterbury hosted them for dinner.[43] Outside of London, John witnessed firsthand the manner of life lived by England's landed gentry, having spent one week at Oglethorpe's home at Godalming and dining, as he did, at The Cannons, the Middlesex estate of the Duke of Chandos.[44] While sightseeing occupied much of John's days, evenings provided him with the opportunity to experience London's many entertainments. He might, for example, have described to Mary the city's handsome theaters, like the Covent Garden, where the Indians saw a production of Christopher Marlowe's *Doctor Faustus,* or the frightful "phantasmagoria" conjured by Dr. Desaguliers's "magic lanthorn," which projected ghastly, moving images on a lit screen.[45]

John also would have been obliged to discuss with Mary the more somber aspects of the voyage, in particular the death of Hinguithi, one of the Yamacraw Indians.[46] From John's point of view, England must have seemed a diseased and dangerous place, and he probably thought himself lucky to have survived it. Ceaseless rounds of sightseeing and visits with British notables, while sometimes exciting, were also fatiguing due to the fact that John was constantly on call to interpret. Perhaps John confided (or could not conceal) the fact that he grew dependent upon alcohol as a means of coping with his unremitting schedule and his homesickness. Perhaps, too, John reached for alcohol to numb himself to occasional displays of racism, as it was reported that English onlookers sometimes stared, heckled, and made "indecent" gestures at the Indians. These experiences must have rudely awakened John to the fact that many English looked upon Indians, and by extension him, as at worst savages and at best exotic display objects.[47]

From a personal standpoint, though, John achieved some important objectives, securing a grant of 500 acres of land and one-hundred pounds sterling as a reward for interpreting.[48] At the same time, however, John found himself on the defensive during the several rounds of trade talks between Tomochichi and the Trustees. At one point Tomochichi asked the Trustees to prohibit the sale of rum, which flowed in abundance from the Musgroves' store and which the Trustees later forbade by statute. Also, John must have been furious when Tomochichi complained that his people "had been much imposed on in their trade" and asked for lower prices that cut into John's one-hundred percent profit margin (as it was then calculated).[49]

Mary and John's reunion should have been a happy one. But the couple did experience a brief period of marital discord due to prurient gossip about Mary that sowed seeds of doubt in John's mind about his wife's conduct during his absence. One rumor had it that Mary sold John's rights to the deerskin trade to the colony's storekeeper, Thomas Causton, for the sum of one thousand pounds sterling. Others reported a substantially higher figure (1,600 pounds) and insinuated that Causton had somehow gotten his money back. Hints of sexual impropriety tinged all these rumors, and word that Causton's relationship with Mary had made John "jealous" echoed throughout Savannah.[50] Although these stories were later confirmed as false, John appears to have briefly entertained their plausibility and, momentarily, became "enraged" to the point of frenzy.[51]

In addition to Mary's sexual honor, Mary and John had to defend their racial heritage when an abortive servant rebellion known as the "Red String Plot" surfaced that March. Unbeknownst to Georgia freeholders, a group of servants had organized and stockpiled arms and ammunition, intending to burn Savannah and kill Georgia's governing officials. To identify themselves, the rebels were to tie a red string around their wrist (hence the plot's name). Word of their plans leaked, however, and eventually reached the ears of the militia captain John Vanderplank, who was led to believe that John Musgrove and forty to fifty Indians were "to join the white men" in their carnage. On Sunday, March 2, Vanderplank interrupted church services by calling out the militia, apprehended three of the supposed plotters, and had the militia confiscate the rebels' stockpile of weapons. In the days that followed, Georgia officials issued search warrants against the suspected ringleaders and conducted interrogations in order to get to the bottom of the situation.[52]

While it is difficult to judge the degree to which Joseph Watson participated directly in the foiled plot, evidence gathered by Georgia leaders suggests that its ringleaders consisted of a small group of his friends. Watson also seems to have been responsible for devising the rebels' default alibi, which involved spreading the abovementioned rumors about Mary, so as to enrage John and make it easier for them to "lay it [the plot] on Musgrove and his Indians."[53] Not only was Watson engaging in a bit of revenge, but by blaming the plot on the Musgroves he also was intentionally tapping into the sometimes latent racism of the Georgia colonists, which made John and Mary inviting targets for all who believed them to be traitors.

This unspoken racial prejudice is most apparent in the actions of the servants, who repeatedly fingered John in the belief that other Georgians would accept him as their scapegoat. Perhaps a more latent form of racism is in evidence in the gullible reactions of Savannah's respectable white residents, such as Patrick Houston, who did nothing to distinguish the Musgroves from the plotting servants when he referred to them collectively as "villains." John Vanderplank, the first to sound the alarm, likewise was inclined to believe the rumor of Musgrove's involvement and sent a body of his militiamen to the Cowpen to investigate. One day after the plot's discovery, Mary and Tomochichi came to Savannah to plead their innocence, but their efforts were insufficient to fully convince Georgia officials. Still needing to "know more," Georgia officials demanded that John suffer the indignity of appearing in Savannah himself to answer the charges against him. Wary that his testimony alone might not be convincing, John brought along with him a white friend named Robert Cannon to corroborate his alibi.[54] Even Thomas Causton, who was a victim of Watson's rumors and was inclined to believe John's side of the story, remained leery of him.[55] Only after the apparent danger had passed, and Georgians had returned to their senses, did the cloud of suspicion lift.

Following the troubling events of March, Mary and John kept a low profile, remaining "wholly" at the Cowpen for the next several months.[56] Meanwhile, in London, the Georgia Trustees rewarded Mary for "keeping the Indians in friendship" and shipped to John a blue suit of clothes and a silver trimmed hat—a reward for services rendered that was to confirm the gentlemanly status he had long sought.[57] Closer to home, in Georgia, the colony's officials and Tomochichi laid the groundwork for an important visit from the Lower Creeks, whom they had invited to Savannah to receive presents from the Georgia Trustees.[58] Normally, John and Mary would have played an active role in these proceedings, but they were conspicuously absent during that important June visit. The reason for this absence is that John and his son James had contracted a fever and lay near death just as the Creek chiefs arrived. Mary, then, would have been desperately trying to nurse her loved ones back to health while her uncle Chigelly related the Cussita "Migration Legend" to the gentlemen and freeholders of Savannah.[59] Unexpectedly, Mary entered a new phase of her life, this time as a widow, and would have to draw upon her faith, and some of that hard-won "experience of the world," to see her through.

Mourning and Ministers

Mary's loss of her immediate family between 1735 and 1736 catalyzed a period of intense spirituality, which made her receptive to recently arrived ministers led by John Wesley, who came to the colony to invigorate its spiritual life and institutions. Mary at first welcomed Wesley and his companions and assisted with their evangelizing efforts to the Indians. Eventually, however, like many Georgians, Mary became displeased with Wesley for his sanctimoniousness and experienced an irreparable falling out with him. This falling out coincided with a more general displeasure with the Georgia colony, a land of poverty and sickness that had clearly failed to live up to its promise. More directly involved in the colony's business than ever before, Mary nevertheless, in her disenchantment, embarked on a path of mild rebellion, playing a small, if unintended, part in ousting Wesley. She even contemplated leaving Georgia for good. Most importantly, however, that path led her into the arms of her second husband and former servant, Jacob Mathewes, who would shape the subsequent course of her life.

John and James Musgrove probably perished in one of several outbreaks of disease that left many Georgians ill in the late spring and summer of 1735.[60] John was rumored to have "died of a fever" back at the Cowpen a few days before June 18, and it is probable that James died later that summer.[61] Some described this unfortunate occurrence as a "great loss" to the colony. No one, of course, felt it more acutely than Mary, and we can only guess at her state of mind after burying her eldest son and interring John during a military-style funeral that Georgia authorities honored him with for the minor office he held as constable.[62]

Over the course of that summer Mary struggled to pick up the pieces of her life and cope with the strain of managing the Cowpen without John. This left her with little free time for Indian affairs, and her presence was clearly missed by some who recognized she had "too much to do with her large household."[63] Gradually, however, Mary emerged from her isolation and was seen in Savannah regularly in the course of conducting her own business. In July, Mary removed to the Cowpen what remained at the trading post in Savannah, collected some money due to her, and ventured to Savannah yet again on July 29 to prove John's will and have it recorded.[64]

Eventually, however, events conspired once again to draw Mary into direct involvement with Indian affairs. After a fifteen-month absence, James Oglethorpe in February 1736 returned to Georgia with a diverse lot of new settlers and plans to erect a string of new forts on the Georgia coast in anticipation of war with Spain. Most importantly, as it would concern Mary, Oglethorpe's return marked the beginning of an invigorated evangelizing mission to the Indians. Tomochichi's visit to London gave the Trustees' long-stated goal of converting the Indians to Christianity a new sense of urgency and attracted a small, zealous circle of young ministers eager to make their mark on the world. These included August Gottlieb Spangenberg, David Nitschmann, and Andrew Dober, all ministers to a group of Moravians who, after a time in London, had come to live in Oglethorpe's colony. Joining them were three young Anglican ministers, all graduates of Oxford: Benjamin Ingham, Charles Wesley, and, most famous of them all, Charles' brother John Wesley, founder of Methodism.

John Wesley, born in 1703 and described as a "sober and studious" child, graduated from Christ Church, Oxford, in 1720, and was later ordained as an Anglican priest. He returned to Oxford about a decade after his graduation, and remained there as a Fellow until 1735. During his second stint at Oxford, John fell in with the Oxford "Holy Club," which comprised Ingham, John's brother Charles (founder of the club), and other like-minded Fellows and students. The Holy Club—or Methodists, as they were called—was a reactionary movement inspired by a perceived lack of piety among laypersons, the opulence of the English court, and the established clergy's presumed "ignorance." By their example the Holy Club intended to bring their nation back to Christ by living holy lives, defined not only by a deep and abiding faith, but also by regular—methodical—introspection and Christian practice.[65] For Wesley, Georgia's underdeveloped religious institutions, perceived religious backsliding, and Indian presence offered an even bigger challenge, as well as the prospect of attaining a higher "degree of holiness." By preaching to the Indians, Wesley hoped to "learn the true sense of the Gospel" and, in the process, to save his own soul.[66]

Shortly after Wesley's arrival, he and Mary established an amicable working relationship. The two met for the first time on February 14, when she interpreted for Wesley, Tomochichi, and Tomochichi's wife Senauky, who offered the minister jars of milk and honey as welcoming gifts.[67] Mary, whose cows likely provided the milk, probably had a hand in selecting these items, presumably because they symbolized the Biblical Israel, described in Exodus 3:8 as a land "flowing with milk and honey." Georgia, it seemed, would be a latter-day Promised Land.[68]

It wasn't long before Mary and Wesley began laying the groundwork for the conversion and education of Indian children, the likely topic of conversation when the two engaged in "necessary talk" four days later. By late February, the Moravian ministers had selected a "spot" for the erection of a school and offered their services as educators.[69] Construction of the Indian school on the top of an ancient Indian mound near the Yamacraw village proceeded throughout the summer, and the school was complete by September 1736. Meanwhile, Mary and Wesley continued to seek each other out. Wesley's diary entries for that period indicate that the two met on four separate occasions between March and May to engage in "religious talk," often over a cup of tea.[70]

In fact, it seemed that every time Wesley and Mary met, Mary's acquaintances were drawn into conversations about religion. Mary's brother, Edward, once participated in a half-hour of "religious talk" while visiting Mary at the Cowpen.[71] Mary's Coweta kinsmen, Chigelly and Malatchi, who came to visit Oglethorpe around midsummer 1736 were similarly engaged. While their diplomatic talks with Oglethorpe are more widely known, Wesley's diary indicates that the two Coweta chiefs met with Oglethorpe and Wesley for dinner on July 3 and engaged in "religious and useful talk" that continued for a full hour after the meal.[72] Wesley and Chigelly sparred a bit as they debated the respective merits of their religions. Eventually, Wesley got down to recommending Bible study for the Indians and warned that God "will not teach unless you avoid what you already know is not good." To that proposition Chigelly assented, conceding that his own people "do what is not good" and could not learn of God "while our hearts are not white."[73] Spoken in a Creek idiom that reflected Chigelly's conception of religious purity, such was the tenuous spiritual common ground on which Wesley and others hoped to prepare Indians to accept Christian teachings.

Establishing a common ground for teaching Christianity to the Indians also involved the problem of communication.[74] Although John Wesley expressed a rhetorical interest in learning Indian languages to facilitate conversion, he delegated much of that task to his assistant Benjamin Ingham, who spent a portion of his year in Georgia learning the Muskogee language from Mary. Joining Ingham were the Moravians, Andrew Dober and David Nitschmann, the latter of whom lived with Ingham that summer at the Indians' school.[75] During that time, these men and Mary collaborated in the production of what is perhaps the most tantalizing artifact related to Mary's life: a vocabulary of English, Muskogee, and German words.

That vocabulary still exists as a single, 4½ by 7 inch, sheepskin-bound volume of approximately one hundred pages. The unpaginated book was written starting from both ends and progressing toward the center in at least two different hands, and contains repetitive lists of English and German words paired with their Muskogee equivalents in parallel columns. Much of the space in these columns set aside for Muskogee words remains blank, indicating that the vocabulary was unfinished. On the first page is an "Indian alphabet," consisting of a phonetic system based on Greek letters that was used as a syllabary for the Muskogee language. The volume currently rests in the Moravian archive in Bethlehem, Pennsylvania, but remains underutilized and underappreciated because archivists have been unable to identify where it came from or when it was made.[76]

A strong circumstantial case can be made that the volume dates to the year 1736 and was the product of Mary's work with Ingham, the Moravians, and perhaps Boltzius and Gronau, the Salzburg ministers.[77] In fact, the Salzburgers were the first to develop the phonetic system based upon Greek and had already enlisted Mary to teach them when Ingham arrived.[78] Because it represents the oldest known collection of such words, the "Musgrove Vocabulary" will hopefully one day attract the attention of linguists and shed further light on the historical development of the Muskogee language. For now, it is possible to make a few preliminary observations about Mary and the language that she spoke.

First, the vocabulary features simple one- or two-word terms (body parts, cosmological terms, place names, and the like) indicating that Ingham and Nitschmann's lessons probably did not advance beyond the elementary level.[79] The list likewise gives us some indication of the antiquity and persistence of much of the Muskogee vocabulary and its pronunciation. Many, if not most, of the terms exactly conform to those of the modern Muskogee language, such as the words for "sky" (*sutv*), "king" (*mekko*), "sun" (*hvse*), or "stone" (*cvto*).[80] The same can be said for words expressing kinship, which closely, and in many cases exactly, follow those collected by the anthropologist John R. Swanton around the turn of the twentieth century.[81] Altogether the vocabulary, limited as it is, confirms that Mary was deeply immersed in her native language and culture. That she could use Muskogee terms to describe every part of her body (down to her fingernail and entrails) and those to whom she was related offers proof that she was not limited to the simple phrases used in business transactions, as were other interpreters.[82]

The Musgrove Vocabulary indicates as well that the work of a linguist involved not only translating between two languages, but also between two cultures. For example, Mary seems to have been trying to convey a sense of the Creeks' matrilineal clan system when she was asked to translate the words for "uncle" and "aunt." As was done elsewhere in the text, the Creek words are arranged side-by-side with their English equivalents, but with the phrase "by the mother" scratched in between the columns, as if Mary had to qualify the meaning of those words and explain that they applied only to maternal kin. Creek conceptions of religion and cosmology also required explanation. Entered in parentheses next to the Creek word for "air" is the word "breath," which suggests that Mary informed her interviewer that Indians regarded air and breath as like manifestations of the deity, who was also known as the "Master of Breath." Mary and her interviewers also appear to have broached the subject of social and political organization. Creek entries for "Carolina" and "Savannah" (in this context, Georgia) are left blank, as if Mary had to explain that the Indians conceived of political entities as "towns" and lacked the vocabulary to describe political units like "colonies." Beneath each of these entries, however, are the words "Charlestown" and "Savannahtown," for which the Creek Indians did have words; Charles Town was known as "talofa thlakko" (big town), whereas the Creeks used the phonetic equivalent of "Savannah" to describe it.[83]

Such is the tangible evidence of Mary's work that summer, during which she had infrequent contact with John Wesley. That fall, however, Mary and Wesley began again to spend more time in each other's company and their "religious talks" seem to have intensified. Wesley's diary, in fact, suggests that he acquainted Mary with some sophisticated works of theology and other literature. On September 27, Mary arrived at Wesley's door at eight o'clock in the morning, interrupting him as he was reading the "Mystics," undoubtedly the works of several German Pietists that influenced much of Wesley's thinking.[84] Mary stayed for a half hour of "religious talk," and the two must have at least broached the subject of these writers, who emphasized the importance of inward religion and the attainment of Christian "perfection."[85] Perhaps the Mystics' teachings were still on her mind a month later, when the two walked together in the Trustees' garden and meditated.[86] On one occasion, Wesley read to Mary the work of Thomas Bray, who founded the same missionary society responsible for her baptism in South Carolina a quarter century earlier.[87] Mary even had the opportunity to return the favor by tutoring Wesley when they read together from the "Account of Florida," a tract quite possibly written by Daniel Coxe describing the flora, fauna, and people of eastern North America.[88] Mary of course was familiar with the terrain and Indian tribes Coxe described and would have been able to provide critical commentary on his work.

Given the closeness of their relationship it is not surprising that Mary turned to Wesley when her remaining son, Edward, died that fall.[89] The end for him probably came around November 22, when Wesley made a hurried but unsuccessful attempt to reach the Cowpen. At four o'clock the following afternoon Mary and Benjamin Ingham arrived in Savannah with Edward's body, and Wesley conducted the burial service held that evening. Mary, weakened due to the stress of losing her son, had fallen ill herself with what Wesley described as "violent rheumatism." Evidently concerned about Mary's health, Wesley ventured to the Cowpen two days later to check up on her, finding her ill at home with Ingham and several others. There, he tried to alleviate Mary's suffering by praying, reading religious tracts, and engaging in a full hour of "religious talk" with her.[90]

Two weeks later, Wesley returned to the Cowpen relieved to find Mary "better," and by the end of December she appears to have recovered from her affliction.[91] While Mary remained sound in body, the same could not be said about her state of mind. As her health returned, Mary had clearly formed an ill opinion of the colony's land policies and fretted about losing the estate she and John had worked so hard to build. At the time of the colony's founding, the Georgia Trustees had placed certain restrictions on land ownership in order to promote (as they argued) its equitable distribution to male heads of household, who were needed for the colony's defense. These restrictions limited the size of land grants to a maximum of 500 acres and implemented a "tail male" system of inheritance, by which land could be transferred only to the surviving sons of a deceased owner. In the event that a landowner died without male issue, his grant would revert back to the Trustees, who could then reissue the land to another male head of household. While the Trustees never enforced the "tail male" policy rigidly, widows and surviving daughters faced the very real prospect of having no permanent claim to any portion of their family's estate.[92]

Troubled by that possibility, Mary summoned Benjamin Ingham to her defense and, shortly before his departure from the colony in late February, convinced him to plead her case before the Georgia Trustees. When Ingham finally appeared before the Earl of Egmont in late July, he asked if Mary "might have leave to appoint a successor to her lot," which she deemed necessary because "her children by Musgrove [were] dead." Mary tried to leverage her service as interpreter by having Ingham inform the Trustees that she intended to "leave the colony and settle with her new husband in Carolina." This, Ingham remarked, would be a "great loss to Georgia," reminding the Trustees that Mary was "our best interpreter" and had "great influence" among the Indians. Egmont, wary of "disobliging her on account of [her influence with] the Indians," agreed to take the matter to the Trustees for future consideration.[93]

Importantly, Ingham's remarks also clearly indicate that Mary had decided to remarry some time before Ingham's departure. Normally, Wesley would have presided at her wedding, but the self-righteous Wesley had a habit of arbitrarily excluding people from church rituals and rites of passage, particularly Dissenters. Wesley could be equally hard on Anglicans, making inordinate demands on them to fast or engage in physical "mortifications" before allowing them to partake of communion. Predictably, many Georgians quickly became averse to their sanctimonious minister, and some cast about to find more flexible ones.[94] Ultimately, this search led them to the Salzburgers, Boltzius and Gronau, and Henry Chiffele, the Swiss minister at Purrysburg, South Carolina, all of whom were willing to overlook incidental matters of dogma, a willingness that led some Georgians—Mary and Jacob included—to seek their services.

To understand how she managed to evade Wesley, it is important to realize that Mary Musgrove's social networks included not only Indians and government officials, but extended to the colony's female settlers. Their number included several married women, such as one "Mrs. Bush," a "Mrs. Deikin," and also "Mrs. Salter," the wife of one of the Salzburg settlers living upstream. Others were considerably younger than Mary, such as Margaret Bovey, one "Miss Fawsett," and Sophie Hopkey, who appear to have looked to Mary as a kind of mentor. These women regularly visited Mary at the Cowpen, perhaps to take a walk with her in the woods, or to share a cup of tea. Following the death of her son, they helped nurse Mary back to health, provided emotional support, and probably helped out with the cooking, cleaning, and other chores that Mary could not do in her sickened state. When Mary came to town, she kept company with these same women, who shared tea, walked the streets of Savannah, and engaged in "religious talk," usually in the company of John Wesley.[95] Excluded from participation in secular and church politics because of their sex, Mary's cohort nevertheless found the opportunity to engage in what the historian Mary Beth Norton calls the "small politics" of the neighborhood, in which women gossiped and took other measures to influence the public perception and behavior of others.[96] Actions spoke louder than gossipy words when in March 1737 Mary and two of her young friends sought out other ministers to perform nuptial services. By voting with their feet, they sent a strong message of protest that provoked Wesley's wrath and eventually led to his unceremonious departure from the colony.

Significantly, following her son Edward's death, Mary forged a close friendship with Sophie Hopkey, the eighteen-year-old niece of the colony's storekeeper Thomas Causton. Sophie Hopkey was among several young women in Savannah who were initially attracted to John Wesley's religious message, and the two spent considerable time together. So much so, in fact, that Hopkey and Wesley became romantically involved and Wesley hinted of a marriage proposal, only to hesitate after having second thoughts about the compatibility of clerical and family life. Meanwhile, as Wesley demurred, Sophie became romantically involved with William Williamson, her uncle's clerk in the storehouse, and accepted his proposal of marriage. Around the same time, another friend, Margaret Bovey, became engaged, and rather than subject themselves to Wesley's humiliations, the three women secretly began looking elsewhere for a minister to preside at their weddings.

Curiously, Mary, Sophie, and Wesley appear to have gotten along well in the fall of 1736. One notices, however, that Wesley's relationship with the two women had become strained by January, probably because Mary was influencing Sophie's choice of marital partners and had expressed her intent to wed her servant, Jacob Mathewes.[97] Mathewes, a noncommunicating Anglican, struck Wesley as spiritually unfit and thus unworthy of receiving the benefits of the Church. Mary must have pleaded with Wesley to change his opinion and consent to marrying them, only to be rebuffed by him as many others were. Meanwhile, Sophie had secretly become engaged to Williamson, who on February 14 ventured to Ebenezer to request the services of the Salzburger ministers. A sympathetic John Boltzius at first agreed to Williamson's request, but then delayed, fearing that "not much could be gained and some ill will might be incurred by such an exercise of our ministerial functions."[98]

In spite of the hesitation of the Salzburger ministers, Mary, Sophie, and Margaret Bovey were encouraged after hearing that they were sympathetic to their plight and decided to act. The plan was for the three women and their fiancées to meet at Ebenezer on Sunday, March 12, to attend church services and demand that the nuptial ceremonies be performed on the spot. Mary, Jacob Mathewes, and "a few [other] Englishmen" arrived on the assigned day and requested that Boltzius join them in marriage. Boltzius refused, but promised to take up the matter with Thomas Causton and inquire whether or not the Trustees "might consent to [Boltzius's] performance of marriages." Irritated, Mary nevertheless decided to stay in Ebenezer, where she appears to have calmed down a bit, even taking the time to attend an afternoon prayer and music service. The following day, Mary waited nervously for the arrival of Hopkey and Bovey, who she expected to "come down here in their boat" carrying "some words from Mr. Causton addressed to me." Unfortunately, Sophie and Margaret never arrived. Boltzius, however, promised to accompany Mary to Savannah the next morning to seek permission to marry her and Jacob.[99]

On March 14, Mary, Jacob, Boltzius, and several other Salzburgers traveled downstream on a boat headed for Savannah. On their way, they stopped at the Swiss town of Purrysburg, on the South Carolina side of the river. While there, Mary learned that Henry Chiffele, the town's "French preacher," had married "three other couples from Savannah," including Margaret Bovey and Sophie Hopkey. Deciding that "this privilege was due also to her," Mary stayed behind at Purrysburg, where Henry Chiffele married Mary and Jacob on March 15. Thus did Mary Musgrove become Mary Mathewes.[100]

Upon learning that the three couples had gotten married behind his back, Wesley became defensive of his spiritual jurisdiction. In early April, Wesley ventured to South Carolina to, as he phrased it, "put a stop to the proceedings of one in Carolina [Chiffele] who had married several of my parishioners with out either banns or license." Returning to Georgia on April 30, Wesley stopped again at Mary's house, probably to explain his position.[101] Such was the tense state of their relationship when, on July 12, Mary visited Wesley at his home in Savannah to engage in an hour of "religious talk." Mary probably used that opportunity to request that Wesley baptize Thomas Jones's infant son, a "near relation" of Mary's. Wesley agreed, and ventured to the Cowpen four days later to christen him. Wesley's diary for that day describes a brief encounter: "Cowpen; christened." What Wesley failed to record was his refusal to allow Jacob Mathewes to stand as godfather, sidestepping Anglican rules that mandated two godfathers for male infants.[102] Clearly, Wesley's refusal strained his relationship with Mary even further, and he would not return to visit the Cowpen for a full month. On August 18, Wesley met with the couple and engaged in a "necessary talk," describing them afterward as "affected" as if to indicate that some kind of heated discussion had taken place.

Two weeks later, Mary and Jacob added their complaint to a list of charges against Wesley, who stood before a grand jury accused of ten counts of ecclesiastical misconduct. One charge was for denying communion to Sophie Hopkey, formerly the object of his romantic attentions. The tenth and final count involved Wesley's refusal to allow Jacob Mathewes to serve as godfather for the Jones baptism.[103] Indicted in August, Wesley demanded a jury trial, which the court kept postponing. His reputation sullied, Wesley on December 2 "shook off the dust" from his feet, sailed back to England, and left Georgia for good.[104] Nor did Wesley and Mary seem to repair their relationship, which had once been close. Wesley never mentioned Mary again in the copious writings he left behind and, to add insult to past injuries, allowed her nemesis Joseph Watson, recently released from his confinement, to receive Holy Communion.[105] For her part, Mary never again spoke Wesley's name.

✦

One evening, shortly after Wesley's departure for England, a curious ceremony took place on an open spot of ground formerly occupied by the Yamacraw Indians. At the center was a table on which a cloth had been spread. Sitting at one end, feasting on a young pig that had just been taken off the barbecue, was Mary Mathewes, her husband, Jacob, two young girls, and Tomochichi. Several visitors came from Savannah, including William Stephens, the colony's recently appointed secretary. Stephens joined them at the table and enjoyed several glasses of wine, which he soon realized were intended as a toast to Tomochichi for "making a grant of that spot of land to Mrs. Mathewes and her husband." Tomochichi returned the favor with a short oration asserting "his claim and property in that land" and likewise that of the recipients. Perhaps anticipating that this action might be cause for dispute, Tomochichi pleaded that he "hoped the Trustees would not be offended" and demanded that all livestock not belonging to Mary and Jacob be removed from the property. Stephens, perhaps underestimating the significance of this act, glibly promised to "take notice" of Tomochichi's requests.[106] Little did anyone realize it at the time, but that single property conveyance would catalyze a decades-long dispute that gradually turned Mary away from her mild path of rebellion and toward a series of assertive actions against the colony. In this we see not just the origins of a certain land controversy but also the making of Mary Mathewes, the "malcontent."

5 ✍ *Mary Mathewes,*
Malcontent

[Mary] not only employed her own interest to continue the Creek Indians steady in their Friendship . . . but constantly supported at her own expence, great numbers of her friends, and other war Indians . . . by which means her trade daily decreased and almost interely went to ruin. The Indians who were her hunters most frequently employed on some expedition for the publick service, and thereby rendered unable to pay the debts they had before contracted . . . some being dead and others killed in his Majesty's service particularly her own brother and other near relations at the Siege of Augustine in the year 1740.

Mary Bosomworth, 1747

I can answer that Mrs. Mathews has always been very desirous of advancing His Majesty's authority amongst the Indians . . .

James Oglethorpe, 1742

It is the evident effect of such disorders fomented by this [Jacob] Mathews, who has very much disturbed the peace of Savannah, and at whose house cabals have been carried on . . . the Trustees desire your Authority and Influence to interpose with him and his wife [Mary] to restrain him from such dangerous behavior in the future.

Georgia Trustees, 1741

. . . immediately the Rum was seized and staved. Whereat Mrs. Mathews was so provoked, that she could not forbear uttering many hard words and threats, what Revenge we might expect from the Indians, for whom she said 'twas designed. In such manner are we to be terrified, if any Obstruction is given to the Domineering Will of that Family.

William Stephens, 1742

TO PUT IT IN PLAIN TERMS, Mary's short but eventful marriage to Jacob Mathewes ended much as it began: in controversy. Mary and Jacob's decision to take their wedding vows outside the colony was one of the many insubordinate acts that provoked Rev. John Wesley into fleeing the colony. Fast-forward to the year 1742. Jacob Mathewes is ailing and just weeks from the grave, having been imprisoned for stubbornly refusing to serve on a grand jury because he believed the judge was a criminal. Even in death Jacob Mathewes sparked controversy, as the conduct of his funeral elicited a dispute between his friends and the colony's president, William Stephens, over whether to bury him with full military honors, an honor Stephens ultimately denied Mathewes.

These passages from Jacob's life share a common thread in that each was a manifestation of an organized opposition to the colony's government. Dubbed "Malcontents" by their opponents, these disgruntled Georgians opposed the "tail male" land tenure system, sought the institution of a representative assembly, and, most importantly, demanded that the Trustees rescind the law prohibiting African slavery. While not their most prominent spokesperson, Jacob Mathewes had a hand in all the Malcontents' activities, and his obnoxious challenges to authority earned him the distinction of being the colony's "Champion of Misrule."[1] Given Mary's intimacy with the man, we have to wonder whether she identified with the causes he espoused.

As indicated by the above epigraphs, Mary probably did not think of herself as a "champion of misrule," but rather as a selfless servant of the colony. Judging by the numerous sacrifices she made for the colony—of money, of loved ones—Mary was justified in thinking as she did, as was James Oglethorpe, who defended her record in Indian affairs and considered her a friend.

Yet, for all her sacrifice, Mary's relationship to Georgia was marked by a chronic ambivalence about its economic and governing policies. Manifest in the colony's first years, this ambivalence became even more pronounced during Mary's marriage to Jacob Mathewes, as can be seen in 1742 when Mary and Jacob got caught red-handed trying to evade the colony's law prohibiting the sale and consumption of rum. When confronted by the authorities, Mary responded much as Jacob might have, with an impassioned outburst and thinly veiled threat to unleash the Indians on the colony.

It may be tempting at this juncture to raise the question of whether Mary was a friend or foe of the colony. But much like Mary's cultural orientation, her actions defy simple binary categorization.[2] Due to her formidable ability to conflate her interests with those of Georgia, Mary saw nothing contradictory about asserting loyalty to colony and king while expressing displeasure with governing officials and Trustee policies. What set Mary apart, though, was her ability to conflate her personal interests with those of the Creek nation. Because of Mary's unique diplomatic role, her fiscal solvency involved more than the interests of her own household, as her ability to provide gifts was necessary for conducting Indian affairs. By trading rum to the Indians, for example, she not only lined her own pockets, but helped secure the Creeks in their friendship, so perhaps Mary was justified in asserting her "domineering will" to defend a practice that was technically illegal.

The extent to which the Malcontents influenced Mary has been a hitherto neglected aspect of her life and is one that merits further investigation. Not only was she married to a notorious rabble-rouser, but she also hosted many Malcontent gatherings in her home and regularly interacted with their leaders. Consequently, Mary was on hand to hear them voice grievances, plot strategy, and draft several important manifestos that circulated on both sides of the Atlantic Ocean. Given her privileged access to Malcontent politicking, it stands to reason that she learned a few lessons along the way.

Most importantly, the land controversy that later would consume Mary was born of the Malcontent struggle and at this early stage cannot be easily distinguished from it. Originating as one of many attempts to circumvent local authority, only much later, after the Malcontents achieved many of their goals, did Mary's claims take on a life of their own and evolve into the infamous Bosomworth controversy. As it took Mary nearly two decades to resolve her case, it is plausible that she never ceased being, at some level, a Malcontent.

Starting Over with Jacob Mathewes

Jacob Mathewes was an enigmatic figure in colonial Georgia, where he lived in anonymity for two years before bursting onto the scene as Mary's husband.[3] Not much is known about his early life, but it is clear that he was born in England and had three sisters there. As Jacob came to Georgia as an indentured servant, we can guess that his family was not prosperous, but neither were they destitute, as evidenced by the rights to family property in England he left to his sisters in a 1741 will.[4] How he came to the colony is difficult to determine, but the evidence suggests that Jacob contracted himself to John Musgrove while John was in London interpreting for the Indians.[5] John, it seems, intended to employ Jacob in endeavors other than agriculture, perhaps as a cattle hand or in the Indian trade.[6]

Indentured to Musgrove, Jacob must have arrived in Georgia with his new master in January 1735. Interestingly, Jacob's name would not surface for another two years, indicating that those who visited the Cowpen took no particular notice of him. Overlooked by Mary's visitors, Jacob nevertheless would have been on hand to witness all the recent ups and downs of Mary's life. Importantly, Jacob would have been present to mourn with Mary after the passing of her husband and two children. Perhaps he also stepped up his responsibilities during Mary's prolonged sickness, and, in this emotionally charged context, the two decided to marry no later than February 1737. As with most eighteenth-century marriages, economic considerations likely factored in their decision as much as did romantic love. For Jacob, marriage brought his servitude to an abrupt end. For Mary, marriage ensured that her estate would not, in the event of her death, revert to the Trustees under the rules then governing the transference of property.

As previously noted, the Mathewes' marriage began in controversy due to the couple's decision to marry outside of the colony. John Wesley's eventual flight from Georgia eased that controversy, but the couple inherited another problem when Mary's nemesis, Joseph Watson, was released from house arrest that November. Within days, Watson was up to his old tricks, spreading word that he intended to go to England to "[call] all people to account for what was past." Sensing that Watson meant to sue him for debts incurred when Watson was partnered with John Musgrove, Jacob promptly had Watson hauled before the authorities, and the two wound up in court for an "intricate and tedious" trial that was twice postponed.[7] Finally, in February 1738, a jury delivered a verdict largely favorable to Mathewes, who was ordered to pay Watson only a nominal sum of ten pounds.[8]

While in retrospect the Watson-Mathewes case was financially inconsequential, it is important to recall that matters between the two men were still unresolved when, on December 13, 1737, Tomochichi first made the controversial gift of land to Mary. Facing the prospect of having to compensate Watson for his (seemingly large) losses, Mary and Jacob probably looked upon the acquisition of Indian land as a way to enhance their financial security, which was precarious due not only to Watson's claims, but also to the thousand-pound debt Mary still owed to merchants in South Carolina. In this context, it appears that the land dispute that eventually generated hundreds of pages of paperwork and raised theoretical questions relating to Indian sovereignty was rooted in Mary and Jacob's immediate financial concerns.

A critical moment in the assertion of Mary's land claim came in October 1738 during an important visit of Lower Creek headmen to Savannah.[9] More than fifty lower Creeks arrived in late September and were promptly directed to stay at the Cowpen with Mary.[10] Judging by the content of the Indians' speeches, it is clear that the Creek leaders had come primarily to talk with James Oglethorpe (who had recently returned from England) about matters of trade and the looming war with Spain.[11] Yet, it is equally evident that Mary used the opportunity of the Creek visit to acquire title to the land Tomochichi had given to her ten months earlier, and a great deal more. In an effort to secure this enlarged land grant, Tomochichi and Mary invited the colony's secretary, William Stephens, the commander of Fort Frederica, William Horton, Mary's neighbor Robert Williams, and several other "Gentlemen" to witness a "solemn" twig and turf ceremony, which involved the ceremonial exchange of turf between buyer and seller.[12] Tactically, it was a shrewd move. Dating to a time in English history when most people were illiterate, the twig and turf ceremony's ritual symbolism could be understood by unlettered peoples like the Creeks, some of whom were also on hand and knew very well Tomochichi and Mary's intentions.

The surviving record makes it clear that the Creek witnesses readily assented to the conveyance of land.[13] Conversely, the transaction discomforted Georgia officials, so much so that it paralyzed them from taking action to deny or confirm the transfer of property. "I could not help thinking at that time," recalled William Stephens some years later, "that it boded no good" because he feared the aggrandizement of Jacob Mathewes.[14] As with Stephens, the colony recorder Thomas Christie was unsure of how to act when first pressured by Tomochichi to record the transaction, due to a certain "hesitation" that the Trustees would not agree to it. When pressed further by the Indians, Christie was reported to have made an equivocal promise to "comply therewith" in the future.[15] James Oglethorpe, too, seemed reluctant to recognize the gift of land. When informed by the Indians on October 13 that the transfer to Mary had occurred, he responded skeptically, asking whether the Indians would "desire it [the land] again" when they saw white people in possession of it. Although assured by the Indians that "no body will trouble them," Oglethorpe nevertheless sat on his hands and did nothing to secure Mary's right to the property before leaving the colony for good in 1743.[16] That Christie's minutes went unrecorded for fifteen years (during which time Mary held them in her possession) may indicate that the colony's leaders did not want to be implicated for anything that might have earned the Trust's disapproval.

In addition to gaining land title, Mary and Jacob tried to shore up their finances by relocating their Indian trading operation to a more favorable location on the Altamaha River. The couple was already rumored to have begun living "at the forks," and Jacob had recently left the management of the Cowpen in the hands of their neighbor, Robert Williams, and a man named Critchley.[17] Perhaps coached by Mary to voice a predetermined set of demands, on October 14, the Indians informed Oglethorpe that they "wanted Mrs. Mathewes to settle on the Altamaha River" near the fort at Darien built two years earlier.[18] Oglethorpe did not respond immediately to their request, but nor did he protest, evidently aware of the potential strategic benefits of allowing Mary to trade on the Altamaha.

Probably before the spring planting season of 1739, Mary and Jacob built a new trading post on the Altamaha River called Mount Venture, which was later converted to a small fort during the war against Spanish Florida. The settlement's location has yet to be confirmed archaeologically.[19] A map composed more than twenty years after it had been abandoned, for example, places Mount Venture on the Altamaha sixty-six miles downstream from the convergence of the Ocmulgee and Oconee Rivers.[20] Recent archaeological excavations, though, hint that Mount Venture was located a few miles further downstream, at Sansavilla Bluff, in modern Wayne County, Georgia. Trading paths ran along both sides of the river, and a ford situated several miles upstream connected Mount Venture to another path leading into Savannah, a two-day journey by land. Maps depicting various "Indian houses" along that course of the river indicate the presence of small-scale Creek settlements, most notably that of "Captain" Aleck, a Cussita headman.[21]

Although the evidence is thin, a few modest conclusions can nevertheless be drawn about life at Mount Venture. First, the presence of nearby Indian houses indicates that the area was a multicultural enclave that replicated the residential patterns at Pon Pon and Yamacraw Bluff. Mount

Venture itself was culturally diverse also; Mary and Jacob's Indian slave Nottoway lived there, as did their friend William Francis and his family, and several English and German militiamen-rangers.[22] As indicated by the Sansavilla Bluff excavations, Mount Venture probably consisted of the main trading post and a handful of other small buildings. Eighteenth-century artifacts litter the area, too, most of which reflect the residents' occupations in trade and warfare. These include gunflints and trade beads, portions of which were found melted and fused, perhaps in the fire set by Yamasee Indians that destroyed the post in 1742. Shards of ceramics, pewter, iron, and lead all indicate that the site had been in use since the 1730s and that settlers—Indian and European—continued to frequent the area decades after Mary abandoned it.[23]

While Mary and Jacob might have regarded it as a home-away-from-home, the couple lived at Mount Venture only intermittently between December 1738 and November 1742. Useful as the post might have been for the colony, the extended stays at Mount Venture nevertheless had a deleterious effect on the economic enterprises Mary and Jacob had back at the Cowpen. Mary seemed to think so, later claiming that her "own private affairs and improvements on her lands, at or near Savannah, daily went to ruin, being in her absence on publick service entirely left to the care and management of servants."[24] Interestingly, Jacob Mathewes identified himself in a 1741 will as an "Indian trader," perhaps indicating the degree to which trade overshadowed the family's other economic activities.

Indeed, it seems that Mary and Jacob were stretched too thin. Their overseers Williams and Critchley had difficulty managing the Mathewes herds properly; each was accused of butchering cattle that belonged to the Trustees rather than Mathewes, and each ran afoul of the law during Mary and Jacob's absences.[25] The couple's agricultural endeavors likewise suffered for a time. Whereas in 1738 Mary and Jacob had thirty "well planted" acres, they apparently planted nothing during the 1739–40 growing seasons, which Jacob's detractors attributed, perhaps unfairly, to his idleness.[26] Jacob and Mary did, however, begin to devote most of their attention to the Cowpen in the year before Jacob's death. In January 1742 it was reported that Jacob had been "making preparation for putting a variety of seed into the ground," indicating his intent to plant that season. At the same time, Jacob was in the process of moving the couple's belongings from their house in Savannah to a new "large house" in the final stages of construction at the Cowpen, where Jacob died just a few months later.[27] Whether these expenditures exceeded their income is difficult to judge, but what cannot be denied is that the Mount Venture experiment enhanced their visibility in Indian affairs as the colony lurched toward war with Spain.

Jenkins' Ear and the Indians

Even though Mary never donned a military uniform or fought in the shadows of the castillo at St. Augustine, the so-called War of Jenkins' Ear was one of the seminal events in her life. As James Oglethorpe's best interpreter and most trusted diplomat to the Creek Indians, she was essential to the recruitment of Indian warriors, and, having the trust of important Creek leaders, was one of the best informants on the southern frontier. Mary gave of herself, too, by allowing the men in her life to serve for extended periods of time in the colony's militia, leaving her alone to manage her family's trade and other enterprises. These men gave not only their time but also their bodies to the colony's cause. Her husband weakened under the strain of field campaigning, and her brother and one of her cattle hands died in the ill-fated siege of St. Augustine in 1740. So, as the colony placed itself on a war footing, Mary experienced the War of Jenkins' Ear in a direct and visceral way.

The War of Jenkins' Ear remains one of colonial America's most enigmatic wars due to its unusual nickname and inconclusive results. The conflict's origins can be traced to the unresolved territorial disputes between Spain and Britain and to more recent disagreements over Britain's right to trade in the Spanish Caribbean. Principally a naval war, regiments from South Carolina and Georgia, with their Indian allies, nevertheless engaged Spanish forces on land several times, most notably during two sieges of the fortress at St. Augustine. The result as the year 1743 drew to a close was a virtual stalemate. Peace, however, did not come officially until the 1748 Treaty of Aix-la-Chapelle, which ended the series of conflicts in Europe known as the War of the Austrian Succession. While it successfully ended the war in Europe, the treaty failed to address adequately the territorial disputes in the New World, and these disputes would remain fundamentally unresolved until the Treaty of Paris in 1763.

Local circumstances also help to explain the brewing conflict between Britain and Spain and provide insights into the rationale Indians used when picking sides. From the perspective of Charles Town and Savannah,

Spain represented an imminent threat due to recent infusions of Spanish soldiers at St. Augustine, Spanish naval reconnaissance of the coast, and Spain's general refusal to acknowledge Britain's territorial claims in the Southeast. British colonial officials were also painfully aware of Spain's repeated attempts to draw the Creek and other Indian tribes into an alliance that could have led to an invasion from the western backcountry. Conversely, Spanish officials in St. Augustine considered the establishment of Georgia an intrusion into territory that was properly Spain's, and lamented the hypnotic effect that English trade goods had upon the Indians. Also at issue were the forts recently erected on Georgia's barrier islands, some of which were situated dangerously close to the town of St. Augustine. Like the European actors, the region's Indians had an interest in the conflict, as participation in the war would enable them to demand favorable trade concessions and gifts from the European powers. Hence, the importance of picking what promised to be the winning side. Importantly, the Yamacraw Indians had a long-standing feud with the Yamasees of Florida, and violent encounters between the two long predated the declaration of war in Europe in 1739.[28]

As all sides braced for conflict, Oglethorpe worked diligently to secure the support of Indians, who factored significantly into the general's war plans.[29] To solidify Indian support for the British, Oglethorpe seized upon an invitation the Creeks had floated to him the previous fall to visit their villages. Setting out in late July, Oglethorpe's party reached the Chattahoochee River on August 9, and spent more than two weeks in the towns of Coweta and Cussita.[30]

The end result of these meetings was the famed 1739 Anglo-Creek treaty, the second of two important agreements made since the establishment of Georgia. In the treaty, the Indians declared the Creek nation's adherence to "their Antient love to the King of Great Britain" and reconfirmed the treaty of 1733.[31] Probably at Mount Venture at the time, Mary appears to have played no direct role in the treaty proceedings. Nevertheless, the 1739 Treaty had important implications for the land claims she had made the previous October. In circumscribing colonial settlements, for example, the Creeks reserved for themselves "Indian lands" on the Savannah River, which encompassed the very tract Tomochichi intended to give her. In addition, the Creeks claimed the islands of St. Catherine's, Ossebaw, and Sapelo, on which they camped and hunted while en route to Georgia's coastal towns and fortresses. If those assertions weren't ominous enough, the treaty's text includes the following statement: "That the said Commissioner [Oglethorpe] doth declare that the English shall not enlarge or take any other Land Except those granted as above by the Creek Nation to the Trustees and doth promise and Covenant that he will punish any Persons that shall intrude upon the Lands which the Creek Nation hath reserved as above." While aware of Mary's situation, Oglethorpe nevertheless seems to have persuaded the Creeks to nullify Tomochichi's conveyance of land to Mary. Perhaps the Creeks did so unwittingly. But the Creek chiefs' resolve to maintain control over the "Indian lands" set them on a collision course with Mary and the Georgia Trustees that would explode in the not-so-distant future.

Of more immediate concern, however, was the undeclared war that finally became official on October 23, 1739, when Britain expelled Spain's ambassador and declared war on his country.[32] Although news of the war's declaration in Europe would not reach the colonies for several weeks, Georgia and Spanish officials had already taken matters into their own hands when, in mid-November, Spanish troops killed and beheaded two English sentinels stationed on Amelia Island.[33] News of the killings reached Oglethorpe at Fort Frederica, prompting him to call upon Tooanohui and Hillispilli, who led a small Yamacraw war party to St. Augustine to exact revenge. Stalled at Amelia Island when the Spanish launched a second attack against the English fort there, the Yamacraws promptly returned to Fort Frederica, where Oglethorpe began making more definitive war plans.[34]

In Oglethorpe's formulation of these war plans, Mary Mathewes figures prominently as a consultant, most often as it related to the recruitment of Indian warriors. When planning to retaliate for the Amelia Island killings, for example, Oglethorpe summoned Mary from Savannah to meet him at Fort Frederica, where she likely helped to convince roughly thirty Creeks and Yamacraws to join in the fight with her husband, Thomas Jones, and the trader William Grey.[35] In addition to having her recruit Indians, Oglethorpe likely looked to Mary for advice on how to gain assistance from South Carolina. As a former resident, Mary knew well many of that colony's old frontiersmen and perhaps dropped the names of acquaintances knowledgeable of the terrain and experienced in war. In a letter to South Carolina's Lieutenant Governor William Bull, himself an old hand in frontier warfare, Oglethorpe recommended that Bull raise a volunteer company, pleading that William Macpherson or "[Tommy] Jones of Pon Pon" could show them the path to St. Augustine.[36] When the South Carolina company eventually formed six months later, it included not only Macpherson and Jones, but also several other St. Bartholomew's residents who were well known to Mary.

Mary's husband, Jacob, saw some of the first action in Oglethorpe's war against Spain, when he led a party that included more than thirty Indians in coordinated strikes against forts Picolata and Pupo. While these victories on the St. John's River were not insignificant, everyone knew that the real prize was St. Augustine, the capture of which would have virtually guaranteed British control over much of the Southeast. Forcing the surrender of the town's imposing castillo, however, required more troops and firepower than Oglethorpe currently had at his disposal. To remedy these shortcomings, he recruited men and war material from South Carolina, gained support from the British navy, and enlisted the support of allied Indians. With this enhanced war-making capacity, Oglethorpe planned to invade Florida once again and force the submission of St. Augustine in a grand siege planned for the summer of 1740.[37]

It was about this time that Mary also joined the war effort as an interpreter, agreeing to a fifty-pound annual salary.[38] Oglethorpe offered, and Mary probably accepted, these terms when the initial forays into Florida were being planned in November and December 1739. The details of this arrangement are important because Mary would later assert that much of her work went uncompensated, claiming that she had agreed to twice that salary beginning in 1733. Oglethorpe may have made a verbal commitment for higher compensation, or to make it retroactive, but extant documentary evidence suggests that Mary later submitted "vouchers" and was paid 200 pounds for four years' work between 1739 and 1743, the year Oglethorpe left the colony. As she did in most of her claims against the Georgia Trustees, Mary probably embellished, rather than falsified, evidence in order to increase the amount of her award.

Mary's whereabouts during the invasion are unknown, but it is probable she spent most of her time at Mount Venture, perhaps making occasional stops downstream at Frederica. Her decision to reside there at precisely that time had strategic benefits, as Mount Venture's location put her in closer proximity to the Creek nation and directly in the path of mobile Creek warriors and hunters who ranged between their homes and

Fort Frederica. This allowed her to serve as the eyes and ears for James Oglethorpe, as well as for Creek Indians seeking news about the colony's war plans.

Among Mary's likely visitors that spring were her kinsman from Coweta, Malatchi, and three other Creek Indians who in late April followed her to Frederica to speak with Oglethorpe. Before Oglethorpe, Malatchi complained that his uncle Chigelly was openly persuading his people not to "interpose among the white men's quarrels," thus advocating the policy of neutrality for which the Creeks were already famous. Malatchi not only announced his disagreement with Chigelly's assertion of neutrality, but also raised the question of political authority in Coweta. Appointed his "guardian" years earlier, Chigelly governed as a kind of regent in behalf of Malatchi, who was picked by his "father" Brims to assume leadership once he had reached the age of maturity. Now approaching his thirtieth year, Malatchi began to chafe under Chigelly's tutelage and felt that the time was right to begin asserting himself as the leader. So, to counter Chigelly's neutralist policies, Malatchi ventured east to speak with Oglethorpe at Frederica. Assuming he liked what Oglethorpe had to say, Malatchi planned to return to Coweta and "try who had the best Interest in his country, he or Chigelly."[39]

After leaving Oglethorpe at Frederica, Mary and Malatchi headed north to Savannah, where they met with Secretary Stephens on May 3. Malatchi explained the situation again, referring to Chigelly's intransigence and boasting of his willingness to "cut off his head" if he kept up his attempts to keep the Creeks out of the war.[40] The next day, Malatchi went to the Cowpen with Mary, where they remained for an undisclosed amount of time.[41] From that point on, she and Malatchi were close confidants, and their relationship later had important consequences for Mary's land claims and the Anglo-Creek relationship as it evolved in Georgia.[42]

Meanwhile, the invasion of Florida—a coordinated land and sea maneuver—was well underway.[43] Oglethorpe launched the operation in early May, arriving on May 8 at the St. John's River, where he established the main camp and rendezvous point for his forces. Over the next month, the British captured Fort Diego (a small private fortress), conducted reconnaissance missions, and positioned themselves around the city. On June 9 Oglethorpe assembled a "flying party" of 137 men comprising Highland Rangers, volunteers from South Carolina and Georgia, thirty Yuchi Indians, and perhaps no more than ten Yamacraws and Creeks. Two days later, the flying party took possession of Fort Mose, an abandoned installation formerly manned by escaped slaves from the Carolinas. Unopposed, they set up camp at the fort, and were instructed to prevent Spanish foraging parties from rounding up cattle and horses. Meanwhile, Governor Manuel de Montiano of Florida realized that a victory of some kind was needed to boost Spanish morale, so on June 14 he ordered Captain Antonio Salgado and three hundred men to launch a predawn counterattack against Fort Mose, where the first real battle of the war took place.

Of the many skirmishes in Florida, the battle of Fort Mose affected Mary the most on a personal level. Some of the men stationed there were old acquaintances of hers from South Carolina. As for the Creek participants, several were Mary's clan-kin, including their leader, Thomas [Tommy] Jones of Pon Pon. Closer still was her brother, Edward Griffin, who had an Indian wife and three children back in the Creek nation. That these men happened to converge at Fort Mose at the same time illustrates the extent to which Mary worked through both Indian and English networks to recruit fighters.

In the course of several hours of fighting, Mary's kinsmen paid dearly with their blood. In all, at least sixty-eight men lost their lives and thirty-four others were taken prisoner, two of whom the Spanish later killed, chopping off their heads and genitals. Several of Mary's "near relations" from the Creek nation died there, as did her brother, Edward Griffin. Kinsman Thomas Jones, William Steads, and a few others managed to fight their way through the Spaniards and escape. Only ten Spaniards died in the melee, and by any measure, the battle of Fort Mose was the most embarrassing defeat for the British of the entire war, causing a loss of morale and foreshadowing the futile siege of St. Augustine that ended unceremoniously a month later.[44]

Mary seems never to have gotten over the battle of Fort Mose and referred to her losses on several occasions in memorials and petitions she later submitted in defense of her land claims. Mary might have been consoled, somewhat, by hearing stories of her brother's bravery. James Oglethorpe, for one, singled out Griffin as being "worthy of the Greeks or Romans" as he fought off the Spaniards from the moat surrounding the fort. After receiving gunshots in both legs Edward fought from his knees, using the bank of the moat for additional bodily support. Refusing quarter offered by the advancing Spaniards, Griffin continued to fight, "loading and firing several shots" before finally dying.[45] These laudatory comments, however, probably did not do enough to deflect whatever blame Mary might have assigned to Oglethorpe for her brother's death. One of her other kinsmen, Thomas Jones, later held Oglethorpe responsible for placing the garrison at Fort Mose in an untenable position, something he must have also communicated to Mary.[46]

Reports of the Fort Mose tragedy began drifting into Savannah in late June, and it was probably then that Mary first heard of her brother's fate.[47] Later, news of the failed siege at St. Augustine sparked a panic in the colony from which Mary could not have been immune. By early July, it was rumored that Spanish Indians were planning to attack, causing the residents of the Orphan House (located east of Savannah) to flee to the city for safety. Those living in the vicinity of Frederica and Darien abandoned their homes on the Altamaha River, while in Savannah many fled for what was believed to be the safer confines of South Carolina. So extensive, in fact, was the flight that many depicted Savannah as a ghost town in a "droopy and languid" condition ill-suited to its purpose as the front line of defense against Spanish Florida.[48]

Mary and Jacob likewise fled from their home that summer, choosing Coweta as their destination.[49] Why they chose Coweta is difficult to say, but Mary was probably grieving with her Coweta kin over the recent loss of her brother, who was married to an Indian woman named "Scotcheneha" and probably considered Coweta his permanent home. In addition to his widow, Edward left three young children; two boys, ages nine and one, and a five-year-old girl.[50] Circumstantial evidence suggests that Mary proposed bringing the children to the colony to have them baptized and educated. Improbably, Scotcheneha agreed to the proposal, and the three Griffin children accompanied Mary and Jacob on their return to Mount Venture in September. Soon thereafter, Jacob took ill and the couple returned to Savannah.

Mary and Jacob's return to Savannah gave them a brief respite from the war and enabled them to attend to more personal matters. Now experiencing episodes of paralysis, Jacob recognized that he was "weak in body" and feared being not long for this world. So, on January 15, 1741, Jacob drew up a brief will that named Mary as the executor and main beneficiary of his estate, which included remnant properties in South Carolina.[51] Sometime in February or March, Mary took her nephews and niece to Savannah, where they were baptized by the missionary William Norris. Reflecting proudly on the accomplishment of having Indian children baptized, Norris described Mary as a "good woman" and was glad that she had taken them into her home "to better direct their conduct and instruction."

Following the failed siege of St. Augustine, Georgia assumed a defensive posture against Spain, as the colony was unable, and unwilling, to mount an offensive on the scale of the misadventure of 1740.[52] Nevertheless, Mary continued recruiting warriors for small-scale assaults, even as she was busy at the Cowpen laboring to save a sick husband.[53] Through it all, it would appear that a kind of routine set in whereby Mary, busy attending to her own business, would be summoned to Fort Frederica whenever Creek Indians arrived and forced to drop what she was doing to head south on a boat sent to retrieve her. At Frederica, she not only translated for the general, but also capitalized on her blood ties to the Creeks to encourage a few kinsmen to venture their lives against a common Spanish foe. When her work was momentarily done, Mary would return home and repeat the cycle at each summons. During interludes in Savannah and at the Cowpen, however, we find that matters other than Indian diplomacy and warfare engaged her time and energy.

Malcontents

Important as Indian affairs were, the storm being raised in Savannah over the future direction of the colony was equally significant in Mary's life. Economic sluggishness, combined with recent setbacks in the war against Florida, only intensified this growing unrest. Gradually, dissonant calls for reform harmonized into a more unified insistence upon rescinding the prohibition on slavery, as well as limitations to the size of individual landholdings and the "tail male" land inheritance policy. These reformers also demanded the institution of an elected assembly, which, unlike every other British colony in North America, Georgia lacked. The Trustees' rejection of these proposed reforms and the elevation of the colony secretary William Stephens to the position of president only steeled the resolve of the colony's critics, earning them distinction as "Malcontents."[54] Intent on achieving their goals by fair means or foul, by pen or by fist, Malcontent protests did not immediately achieve their desired effects. However, the Trustees gradually relented to some of their demands, permitting female land inheritance in 1739 and establishing a representative assembly in 1750.

By 1751, slavery had been legalized, and when a royal government was installed in 1754, it could be said that the Malcontents had achieved most of their aims.[55]

Mary and Jacob's association with the Malcontents was not necessarily predetermined, as some of them harbored anti-Indian attitudes that could not have sat well with Mary.[56] Malcontent writings, in fact, at times exhibit a seething contempt for Tomochichi's people. Most inflammatory was Patrick Tailfer's satirical 1741 narrative, which mocked the 1733 treaty with the Yamacraws as a "solemn" agreement with "a parcel of fugitive Indians."[57] Mary, of course, had done much to bring about that agreement. Mary and Jacob nevertheless ended up casting their lot with the Malcontents, presumably due to the colony's lack of economic progress, and their general agreement with Malcontent prescriptions for reform. The couple also had disputes with a few of the Trustees' placemen, making their grievances personal, as well as political, in nature.

Jacob first surfaces in Malcontent politicking late in 1738, when he signed his name to a December 9 petition demanding fee simple land tenure and the use of Negro slaves.[58] Jacob then engaged in various acts of law breaking, as if intentionally trying to subvert local authority. On one occasion, Jacob tried to sell some land he did not own. In April, the storekeeper Thomas Jones accused Robert Williams of killing and marketing Trustee cattle at the behest of Jacob Mathewes, who had to submit to a humiliating interview before James Oglethorpe.[59] The general ultimately exonerated Jacob of the crime, but Mathewes never forgave Jones, and his dislike for him only intensified as time passed.

Military action kept Jacob out of the limelight for a while, but upon returning to Savannah in January 1740, Jacob resumed his association with the Malcontents and, more than ever before, turned to drink and violence. On February 14, an inebriated Jacob pitched a fit with a Trustee servant employing an ox that Jacob claimed was his. Jacob verbally abused the servant and knocked him to the ground, prompting the storekeeper Thomas Jones to intercede on the servant's behalf. Mathewes then directed his wrath at Jones, whose accusations of misappropriating Trustee cattle still burned fresh. After exchanging verbal barbs, Mathewes punched Jones in the face and kicked him in the belly, cursing and swearing while several onlookers attempted in vain to restrain him. Several of Jacob's friends promptly whisked him away to the Cowpen, where they hoped he would return to his senses. Not incidentally, later investigations proved Mathewes "much in the wrong" for mistaking the ox for one owned by James Millidge, who branded his livestock with the same initials.[60]

Following the altercation with Jones, Jacob hosted a gathering of friends at the Cowpen, where they carried on for several days. Mary was not mentioned by name as being present, but the work required to feed and house more than ten visitors, including their wives, suggests that she was on hand toiling at domestic tasks. Their guests included several men and women identified as Malcontents, such as their neighbor Patrick Tailfer, soon to emerge as a leading Malcontent penman, and Thomas Upton, a frequent petitioner. Also in attendance was the Reverend William Norris, who later threw his weight behind Malcontent causes, and Mrs. Alexander Heron, wife of the captain stationed at Frederica and a friend of Mary's. Georgia officials were not quite sure what went on there, but William Stephens suspected the "Company" (as he called them) of dealing in politics. The problem, as Stephens saw it, was that Jacob's quick promotion in status from servant to the husband of a well-connected woman had the "usual effect" of inflating his ego, causing him to grow "vain," "dress gaily," and become in all manner "insolent." From that moment on, Stephens had his eye on Jacob, as his recent antics made it "necessary to observe, of the future behaviour of Mr. Mathews."[61]

As it happened, Stephens had little occasion to observe Jacob's "future behavior" over the next few months, during which time the war with Spain seemed to eclipse the colony's internal political squabbling. Jacob drew attention to himself again in September 1740, when he was accused of instigating a "riotous" assembly in Coweta, prompted by his attempt to arrest some Creek traders. Stephens and Jones must have been aghast, therefore, to learn that Oglethorpe had appointed Mathewes to command a troop of rangers stationed at Mount Venture, where he remained for much of that fall. Mathewes did not return to Savannah until November 1740, when Malcontent politics resumed with a new intensity.

If any single action can be deemed responsible for galvanizing the Malcontents, then the publication of William Stephens'"State of the Province of Georgia" surely qualifies. "State of the Province" was Stephens' response to what he believed were troubling developments in Georgia following the disastrous 1740 invasion of Florida. Not only was the colony hemorrhaging residents to its more prosperous neighbor, but it also continued to suffer from the Malcontents' conspiracy against its government. To set matters straight, "State of the Province" focused on the colony's virtues and cast its governing officials in a favorable light. The result was propaganda depicting Georgia as a bountiful land of mulberry trees and grape vines, where hard-working people reaped what they sowed. Accordingly, Stephens refused to recognize the widespread poverty in the colony, due to its poor soils and ill-conceived agricultural experiments. Nor did Stephens acknowledge the many grievances filed by persons he deemed "Malcontents" or give serious consideration to any of their proposed reforms.[62]

The Malcontents responded by composing a "Remonstrance" that detailed the colony's economic woes and called upon the Trustees yet again to consider their proposed reforms, which they detailed in six "Articles." Completed on November 22, the document was signed by sixty-four men, many of whom soon became notorious for their conspiring activity. These included the Malcontent ringleaders Fallowfield, Grant, and Duchee, along with the tavern keeper Peter Morell, the recorder John Pye, and William Ewen. These consultations took place at the Mathewes home, and Jacob Mathewes was among the signatories of the "Remonstrance," as well as of a similar petition sent to the king just a few weeks later.[63]

As Jacob ventured further down the slippery slope of political opposition, one wonders whether Mary approved of his actions.[64] While his indulgence in alcohol and violent outbursts may have caused her some embarrassment at times, it is nevertheless the case that Mary stood by her man. In other words, the turbulent political events of that year politicized Mary, much as they did the wives of other Malcontent leaders.[65] Mary's political sentiments can be inferred from her willingness to open her home in Savannah for days on end to the numerous Malcontents who flocked there to draft what became the "Remonstrance" of November 22, 1740. Had she disagreed with its six articles, it is difficult to imagine Mary inconveniencing herself to host them. In that light, we can read each Malcontent gathering that took place at Mary's home as an expression of her political will, exercised within the domestic sphere, which was considered proper for women.

Mary also expressed her politics indirectly through smaller acts consistent with English gender norms. Take, for example, the baptism of her niece and nephews, which took place in February or March 1741. Her choice of minister is revealing, as the Reverend William Norris's association with leading Malcontents raised the eyebrows of the Trustees' placemen, who were also aware of rumors indicating that Norris was a womanizer. Even more telling is the list of individuals who stood as godparents, which reads as an all-star cast of leading Malcontents. In addition to Mary, the sponsors included John Fallowfield, John Pye, Robert Williams, William Ewen, Andrew Duchee, and, last but not least, the notorious Sir Richard Everard, the Malcontents' lobbyist and legal consultant. Not only did Mary accept them as godparents, but even lent one nephew Everard's name, baptizing the eldest boy as "Richard Everard Griffin."[66]

Perhaps Mary's political orientation can also be gleaned from two episodes involving women whose out-of-wedlock pregnancies unwittingly put them at odds with the government. The first involved Mary and Jacob's friend William Francis and a young German servant girl. Importantly, the servant worked for the storekeeper Thomas Jones, who discovered that she had become pregnant and took it upon himself to make the matter public. After learning that William Francis was the father, Jones demanded monetary "sureties" from him to ensure that the baby would not be a charge on the public. Jacob Mathewes and Andrew Duchee agreed to put up the money, but Jacob reneged when Jones forbade the servant girl from residing at the Cowpen, where Francis was living. This enraged Mathewes to the point of attempting (unsuccessfully) to enter Jones's house late one night to "beat" him, and Jacob continued to rampage drunkenly with a gang of "loose, idle people" throughout the Easter weekend.[67] As a political controversy, the William Francis episode seems to end there, probably because the two were eventually allowed to marry and live at Mount Venture.

The second such episode involved the Reverend William Norris, who was accused of impregnating his servant, a German girl named Elizabeth Penner. The two lived together at Frederica, where her pregnancy (and Norris' dalliance) was a source of ridicule.[68] Secretly, the couple made plans to flee to South Carolina, stopping first in Savannah that February to find transportation north. While Norris collected his belongings in Savannah, Elizabeth Penner took up residence with Mary and Jacob at the Cowpen.[69] Thomas Jones, who had suspected Norris' guilt several months earlier, had Elizabeth brought back to Savannah for questioning. The young girl first exonerated Norris, then signed an affidavit attesting to his paternity, only to change her story again by claiming that another man from Frederica (whose name she conveniently could not remember) was the real father of the child.[70] Pressing on, Jones conducted interviews with several inhabitants of Frederica, each of whom attested that Norris had impregnated Penner.[71] As the reverend had already petitioned the Trustees to return to England, Jones happily encouraged Norris to leave the colony, wishing to bury the issue "into oblivion." What happened to the expectant Elizabeth Penner unfortunately is not known.

Perhaps it was simply the common bond of womanhood that compelled Mary to offer her home to two women encumbered by out-of-wedlock pregnancies. But when viewed in a broader context, these pregnancies figure not merely as private matters, but as public controversies involving the upkeep of "bastard" children and the conduct of the minister at Frederica, who was hardly a private citizen. Mary, then, knew full well that her offer to harbor these expectant women came into direct conflict with Georgia officials, who had other plans for them. Importantly, as the Mathewes' arch-nemesis Thomas Jones acted as Grand Inquisitor for each pregnancy, Mary's actions directly and purposefully countered Jones's attempts to get to the bottom of the situation. So, again, Mary's actions within the private sphere of her home had broader ramifications that can be construed as being political.

Soon after the controversy surrounding the two pregnancies settled down, there was a shift in Malcontent tactics, which became more personal—and malicious—over the course of the next eighteen months. During the summer of 1741, Malcontents enlisted a South Carolina printer to publish Patrick Tailfer's scathing account of the Georgia colony, initiating an intense print war that lasted for another two years.[72] Malcontent leadership also seems to have undergone a shift, as the local authors of the recent petitions turned to two prominent men with connections in London—Sir Richard Everard, and the president's own son, Thomas Stephens—to plead their case. On a local level, Malcontent tactics also underwent a significant transformation, as Savannah's ringleaders decided to use the local courts to hang (possibly trumped up) charges against Thomas Jones and William Stephens—in effect taking the fight directly to them via the arm of government itself.

One example suffices to illustrate the Malcontents' use of the courts against Stephens and Jones. The troubles began around mid-June 1741, when the clerk John Pye submitted an affidavit against Thomas Jones for "mal-administration" of public money.[73] The Malcontents pressed harder when a grand jury was empanelled on July 7 and secretly began taking witness affidavits, which prompted a dispute over its power of discovery. The court dissolved on July 9, and when the grand jury was sent away the Malcontents gathered at Mary Mathewes' home in Savannah to plot their next moves. Mary therefore was present to witness firsthand their attempts to manipulate the English legal system. In particular, because they wanted to clarify the extent of the grand jury's authority, Sir Richard Everard obtained two popular law treatises, Giles Jacob's *Law Dictionary* and Henry Care's *English Liberties*.[74] The comprehensive *English Liberties* was probably the more useful work, as it employed language that could easily be construed as supporting the sweeping powers claimed by the current grand jury. In Section III, for example, Care explains that the grand jury was obliged "to discover the villainy," and that it was their job "not only to inquire, but diligently to enquire."[75]

Moving forward at Everard's behest, the Malcontents continued to assemble a case for themselves at the Mathewes' home. The same day, they drew up a silly indictment against Thomas Jones for failing to arrest one Thomas Upton for swearing. They also drew up a bill of indictment against William Stephens for the more serious crime of refusing to appear in court.[76] While many of the affidavits they collected targeted Jones and Stephens, others appear to have been drawn up for the more general purpose of rebutting Stephens' "State of the Province of Georgia." A deposition by Kennedy O'Brien, for example, countered Stephens' claim that the area around Augusta was flourishing, arguing that Stephens had inflated the number of white men settled there and the amount of corn they raised.[77]

The expelled grand jury used the Mathewes home as a base of operation for several weeks, taking more depositions that implicated the regime in Savannah and raising all manner of hell in town.[78] Most important were a series of meetings held on July 24 and 25, when Malcontents drew up yet another "representation" to the king, signed by sixty-one Georgians.[79] In addition, John Pye, who initiated charges against Jones, was deposed twice on July 24 at the Mathewes home to help buttress his case.[80] Jacob meanwhile took the opportunity to go on a weeks-long rampage that lasted through the first half of August. Witnesses accused him of causing "great disorders" in the streets, as Mathewes and his friends repeatedly got drunk and satirically mocked Georgia authorities. Ominously, Jacob was also using Mary's Indian friends to ill effect, getting drunk with them and roaring through the streets demanding provisions. Some faulted Mary for selling the rum to the Indians in the first place.[81]

Given the stirrings emanating from her own home, it is not surprising to find that Mary also got swept up in the spirit of protest, often by insisting upon fair treatment for Indians.[82] One memorable encounter took place in late July, when Mary told a local Yamacraw Indian named Tenorchy that he was to receive five horses from a Georgia official. The official in question (who did not bother to identify himself in writing) resisted, saying that he had received no such order to give horses to the Indian. Mary did not believe his story, and she and Tenorchy left "not well pleased."[83] A few weeks later, Mary confronted William Stephens and asked him to give the Indians more provisions. Stephens refused her on two occasions, which did little to endear him to Mary.[84]

As one of the chief targets of Malcontent wrath, William Stephens was, perhaps fittingly, the first to see the connection between Jacob's riotous behavior and Mary's unconfirmed land claims. Reflecting upon the transaction that transpired between Tomochichi and Mary three years earlier, Stephens concluded that it "foreboded no good," and Jacob's recent outbursts seem to have justified that sentiment. From Stephens' perspective, Jacob's marriage to Mary not only inflated his ego, but also his willingness to use "what influence he thinks he has" over the Indians for his own gain. By encouraging them to drink to excess and go roaring through the streets of Savannah, Jacob hoped to demonstrate his "power" over the Indians, expecting that the Trustees would "have a singular regard to that, and be careful to oblige him in all he should expect." Now that Jacob was attempting to capitalize on his marriage to Mary it seemed to Stephens that all his worst fears had come to pass.[85]

In October 1741, another court session was held, and in it William Stephens announced recent reforms of the Georgia government and his elevation to the position of "President."[86] This ominous news catalyzed a new wave of Malcontent protest, during which the disaffected assumed the appearance of a formal political party by naming a salaried "agent" and appointing a committee of correspondence.[87] Of particular significance is how discontented Georgians became more assertive in their use of formal legal documents. To demonstrate the mismanagement of the colony and to press individual claims for money and property, Georgians petitioned for the arrest of Jones and Stephens, and for back wages, land, relief for poor widows, and even compensation for good deeds, such as one man sought after saving a mother and child from drowning. The number of written petitions sent to the Trustees that fall and winter is striking and indicative of the desperate mood that had set in among cash-strapped Georgians.[88] Among the many petitioners were Mary and Jacob Mathewes, who named Sir Richard Everard and Robert Williams as their legal representatives and had them draft a letter of attorney empowering them to press their case. Mary and Jacob made two demands on the Georgia Trust; the first was for a 450-acre grant comprising the land that Tomochichi had given to Mary in 1737, and the second was for an unspecified sum of money for Mary's services as interpreter. In addition to the letter of attorney, Mary and Jacob sent a copy of a "talk" with the Creek Indians (the Christie minutes of October 13–14, 1738) in which the Indians appear to have consented to the land conveyance. James Oglethorpe was mentioned as being present at that talk, a fact that Mary and Jacob hoped to use as leverage with the Trustees.[89]

Mary and Jacob's claims were on one level nothing out of the ordinary. Nor was the couple alone in having the Trustees deny their claims. What distinguished the Mathewes' demands was the nature of the land transaction between Tomochichi and Mary. At a fundamental level, the method by which Mary acquired the land from Tomochichi violated the English principle by which all land titles derived from the king. This meant that no colonist could receive English title to land that was given to them directly by Indians. Rather, land titles derived from the colonial governments that, by virtue of their royal charters, had been empowered to grant lands in the king's name. To put it another way, the means by which Mary acquired the disputed tract of land was illegal and, at least abstractly, shook the foundations of royal rule.

After receiving Mary and Jacob's letter of attorney that February, the Trustees gathered three times to consider it. Had they not handled their claims so poorly and perhaps so undiplomatically, the issue might never have been blown so out of proportion. First, the Trustees unceremoniously denied Mary the monies she had requested for interpreting, claiming that they knew "of no service done for them, but what she has been paid for." The Trustees were equivocal, however, when it came to the Mathewes land claim, most likely because it appeared that James Oglethorpe had given his consent to the transaction and knew more about its details. So, instead of refusing Mary's claim outright, the Trustees referred the matter to Oglethorpe's judgment. In a letter penned by the Georgia treasurer Harman Verelst on February 16, the Trustees recommended having the Indians first grant the land to Oglethorpe on behalf of the Trustees in order to establish the proper chain of transmission from the king. Then,

Verelst urged, Oglethorpe could convey the same land on the Trustees' behalf to Mary, thus allowing her to acquire undisputed English title simply by adding this middle step to the process.[90]

Meanwhile, as the Mathewes petition was making its way to the Trustees, Jacob's battles with Georgia's leaders continued. In January 1742, Jacob learned that William Stephens had sent scathing reports of his riotous behavior back to authorities in London and had brought to their attention the sad state of his plantation.[91] Somewhat surprisingly Mary and Jacob seem to have developed a grudge against James Oglethorpe after intercepting some correspondence of his that appears to have confirmed what others said about Jacob's troublesome behavior.[92]

So, with Mary and Jacob angry even at Oglethorpe, it seems only fitting that Jacob would find one last opportunity to confront Thomas Jones in court. Seeking to press the charges against Jones that he had initiated in January as jury foreman, Jacob arranged for a summons to be sent to Jones, requesting his appearance in court that May.[93] When the grand jury finally met on May 18, Jones was inexplicably installed as second bailiff in place of John Fallowfield (a Malcontent). Thinking it absurd that a man indicted for numerous felonies should be named bailiff, Jacob Mathewes and two other members of the grand jury resigned in protest, prompting their arrest by the third bailiff, none other than the implacable Joseph Watson. Confined to the "log house" for a short time, Mathewes and the others were released after paying fines. Because of its constant bickering, the grand jury was dismissed on May 20, and Jacob Mathewes' supporters left in a huff and reconvened at the Mathewes home in Savannah for a night of revelry.[94]

It was not all fun and games that evening, however. In the midst of the celebration, members of the grand jury sympathetic to Mathewes composed yet another "Representation" asserting their right to present "all such matters that come before them" and defending the sweeping investigative powers that several recent grand juries had assumed.[95] On May 21 the grand jury met one last time, only to spar verbally with the unsympathetic bailiff, Robert Parker, who likened the grand jury to a "pack of scoundrels" before dismissing it for good.

Perhaps it was all too much for Jacob Mathewes' fragile constitution. Already weakened by a debilitating chronic illness, Jacob's health took a turn for the worse following his confinement in jail. About that time Jacob received another blow in the form of a letter from James Oglethorpe, in which the general excerpted some of the accusations Stephens and Jones had made against him.[96] Jacob's friend John Fallowfield mused retrospectively that Jones's and Stephens' scathing words were responsible for "shorten[ing] his days."[97] Perhaps learning that a Yamacraw Indian had broken into their Savannah townhome and stolen two of Jacob's finest suits hastened the end. On June 5 Jacob returned to the Cowpen in a "fit of sickness" and succumbed to the inevitable a day later.[98] Still in the prime of her life, Mary was left alone to endure war, manage three Georgia properties, and stay afloat financially while awaiting settlement of her claims against the Trust.

Widow Again

After a protracted illness, Jacob Mathewes finally succumbed to the chronic "fits" he knew might shorten his days. The day after his death, Mary had Jacob's body loaded onto a boat and sent downstream to Savannah for burial. If the writings of Stephens and Jones make it appear that Jacob Mathewes was a disagreeable person with an insatiable appetite for controversy, his funeral would seem to indicate otherwise. Throngs of townspeople turned out for the event, compelling even William Stephens to recognize that "most part of the town" was there. As Jacob's body was lowered into the ground, eight cannons fired at minute intervals in honor of his distinction as ranger captain. At least a few of his friends thought that ceremony insufficient and demanded that the militia assemble to fire their "small arms," a request William Stephens could not find it in himself to accommodate.[99] Weeks later, John Fallowfield eulogized Mathewes as a "man of honor and resolution," lauding his "agreeable" relationship with the Indians. So, while he may not have impressed William Stephens and Thomas Jones, many of Jacob's contemporaries—perhaps a majority— held a different opinion of him as a man of "trust and worth."[100]

William Stephens seemed almost exuberant over the demise of his arch-nemesis, observing that an "uncommon tranquility" had descended upon Savannah since Mathewes' death.[101] Mary's life, however, was anything but tranquil, as Indian affairs summoned her attention even as Jacob's body lay fresh in the grave. Just two weeks after Mary buried her husband, James Oglethorpe, tipped off to the long-anticipated Spanish invasion of Georgia, invited Mary to come to Frederica to assist him with the Indians, presumably to interpret and persuade warriors to fight.[102] Given Jacob's recent death, it is no surprise that Mary delayed accepting the offer and chose instead to stay at the Cowpen to attend to her crops and cattle and to direct her servants. It was probably a wise decision, as a Spanish fleet of thirty-six ships and nearly two thousand soldiers advanced on St. Simons Island that July for what proved to be one of the pivotal battles of the War of Jenkins' Ear.

The Spanish invasion of Georgia was long in the making, and preparations to overwhelm the English settlement with a superior show of force had been underway in Cuba for some time. By late June, a Spanish invasion fleet of more than fifty ships carrying upward of two thousand soldiers began its advance on St. Simons Island, arriving on July 5. After securing the southern part of the island, the Spanish sent parties of regulars and Yamasee Indians north along the path leading to Fort Frederica, to which most of Oglethorpe's troops had retreated. Hot, tired, and isolated from their defenses, Spanish soldiers were quickly overrun in a series of battles that took place on July 7. Fearful that a British naval convoy might soon appear, the Spanish hastened to Florida in mid-July and made no more attempts to invade Georgia.[103]

Mary was not on hand to witness these memorable events. She did witness, however, the chaos that set in among the colonists when word of the Spanish invasion reached Savannah in early July. William Stephens described a scene of "much confusion," as men sent their wives and children upstream to Abercorn and Ebenezer, while others crossed into South Carolina.[104] While out of harm's way, this massive influx of people created health problems, and it became difficult to feed the refugees and maintain proper sanitary conditions. Some Georgians succumbed to diseases that incubated among the refugees, among them the Reverend Christopher Orton, who died soon after sickening at Ebenezer.

Once victory on St. Simons Island had been secured, James Oglethorpe resumed his correspondence with Mary and boasted of his success. In defeating the Spaniards, he reasoned that they had obtained some "satisfaction for the blood at Mose," a direct reference to the deaths of Edward Griffin and other of Mary's Creek relatives who had lost their lives fighting the Spaniards two years earlier. Here, Oglethorpe's choice of words is telling, as "satisfaction" was typically used to convey the Indians' concept of blood revenge. By describing the victory against the Spaniards in this way, Oglethorpe hoped to engage Mary's Creek emotional subconsciousness, perhaps in an effort to stimulate her efforts to recruit more warriors.

Evidently this tactic worked, as Mary continued to send Indians to Frederica that summer.[105]

Although she was repeatedly invited to join Oglethorpe at Frederica, Mary chose to remain at the Cowpen. She had enough to do at home tending to her crops, which she somehow managed to do "by her self," raising the sixty-two bushels of corn, seven bushels of peas, and one hundred five pounds of potatoes that earned her in excess of four pounds.[106] It was perhaps the first harvest on the Mathewes plantation in four years, indicating that Mary had gotten down to the business of cultivating and harvesting produce soon after Jacob's demise earlier that summer.

Mary's decision to remain at the Cowpen proved not only productive, but also fateful, for in November, a party of Spanish and Yamasee Indians attacked her trading post at Mount Venture, killing most of the garrison and taking several others prisoner. Among the dead was Mrs. William Francis, the same woman to whom Mary and Jacob had offered sanctuary in their home more than a year earlier. Sadly, the Indians also killed Francis's infant daughter, whose conception had once been controversial.[107] Reflecting upon that misfortune several years later, Mary lamented that she never had the chance to return to Mount Venture, as her affairs "on the account of [Jacob's] death being in great confusion" required her to stay put. This was, she added, detrimental to her trade business, as the Indians that lived and hunted in the vicinity of Mount Venture got "uneasy" and retreated, leaving the garrison exposed to the Spanish surprise attack. The destruction of her settlement also had economic consequences, as she "greatly suffered" from the lack of trade.[108]

The attack on Mount Venture proved to be a Pyrrhic victory for the Spanish, however, as their affront to Mary Mathewes seems to have stiffened the resolve of Creek warriors who volunteered to defend her. The destruction of the trading post also caused Mary to relent and accept Oglethorpe's invitation to visit him. When Mary arrived at Frederica in April, she quickly fell into some of her old routines as Oglethorpe's interpreter and gatherer of intelligence. Mary also had an agenda of her own, primarily of obtaining information about the recent destruction of Mount Venture. On April 13 she interviewed a Creek Indian named "Smilly," who related how the Spanish were trying to turn the Creek Indians against Oglethorpe by offering them money for English prisoners and scalps. Nine days later Mary interviewed two Chehaw warriors named Talgier and Wyawney, who remembered hearing of the destruction of Mary's trading post in the Creek nation. At Coweta, they reported that Chigelly had mourned for Mary, calling upon warriors to assist Oglethorpe in his recent attack on St. Augustine. In mourning herself, Mary was probably pleased to learn of her uncle's fulfillment of kinship obligations that no doubt had been strained by the demands of imperial rivalry and warfare.[109]

Shortly after arriving at St. Simons Island, Mary settled in at her abode in Frederica, a fourteen-by-twenty-foot tabby house with a small garden. Listed on one city plan as "lot 61," Mary's home was actually owned by a widow named Grant and had housed Spanish prisoners. Although a widow, Mary was certainly not alone in her island home. In fact, a census taken on June 1 indicates that Mary, the "half Indian interpretess to the Indians," gave shelter to five servants.[110] Their identities are not revealed, but it is possible that three of them were Indians, including her old hands Nan, Wan, and Nottoway, who had escaped from the Yamasees and Spaniards after being captured at Mount Venture. Mary also owned the rights to one German servant, and that spring was offered the use of two Spanish "crown prisoners" who agreed to serve a term of indenture in exchange for their eventual freedom.[111]

While Mary must already have known many of Frederica's residents, her prolonged residence there enabled her to deepen her existing acquaintances and friendships. Just two blocks north of widow Grant's home lived Captain William Horton, who later assisted Mary by penning favorable accounts of her service to his superiors in London. Two doors down from Horton lived the family of Frederick Hobzendorf, a surgeon, who in a few short years would loan money to Mary and her husband to cover a debt.[112] Most important was James Oglethorpe, with whom Mary had ample opportunity to consult on matters that were as much personal as they were related to the public interest. In addition to Indian affairs, the two seem to have discussed Mary's precarious financial circumstances and her pending claims for land and money. Oglethorpe, in fact, had invited her to Frederica for the express purpose of allowing Mary the opportunity to "acquaint me if I can be of any service to you in Mr. Mathew's affairs."[113]

Evidently, Mary pled her case with some success, as Oglethorpe paid her 200 pounds (she later claimed to have received only 180 pounds) as compensation for four years of interpreting, and gave her a diamond ring from his own finger. At the same time, the general may have issued a verbal promise to pay her more and to exercise whatever influence he had with the Trustees to make good on Mary's land claim.[114] In retrospect, it seems clear that Oglethorpe, by placating Mary with verbal commitments, heightened her expectations of financial support from the Trust. In time, when it became clear that Oglethorpe could not make good on those promises, Mary would blame the general for abandoning her.

When James Oglethorpe left the colony for good in July 1743, Mary returned to Savannah, as his absence meant that there was less need for her services. Mary arrived in Savannah to the welcome of yet another large household that included eight servants and one "inmate," her servant, William Ewen.[115] That summer, she seems to have settled into a quiet routine, as is perhaps best indicated by her surprising appearance at church in the company of a little girl and a "plentifull entertainment" she hosted in August for a group of recently arrived settlers.[116]

As was often the case, however, the calm that Mary experienced at home was soon interrupted by a summons to duty. William Horton, who had recently assumed Oglethorpe's duties as commander of the Frederica garrison, found that he, too, could not manage Indian affairs without her. By December, Horton had asked Mary to send Indian warriors to scout and make quick raids into Florida. Intending to stage another invasion in March 1744, Horton requested even more warriors and begged Mary to visit Frederica to speak with the Indians, on the grounds that "they will be more open with you."[117] Pressed into duty, Mary seems to have been instrumental in organizing the war party that descended upon Florida when, in March 1744, her long acquaintance Tooanohoui died in a skirmish against the Yamasee Indians.[118] Mourning the young man's death, Mary went again to Frederica to converse with the Indians stationed there that spring. By the time she returned to Savannah on May 17, William Stephens had concluded that her ventures southward were routine, commenting that Mary was accustomed "to helping the commander there [at Frederica] as usual" and offering no indication of the recent controversy involving her late husband.[119]

It would appear that Mary's second state of widowhood afforded her a quiet life devoid of the tumult she experienced during her marriage to Jacob Mathewes. This leads one to wonder: what became of Mary Mathewes the Malcontent? Suffice it to say that Mary never forgot about her claims or the promises Oglethorpe had made to her. That these matters burned fresh in her memory is evident in her decision to begin archiving important self-serving documents. She not only carefully preserved Thomas Christie's minutes from the fateful 1738 Creek conferences but also began saving dispatches sent to her by Oglethorpe and William Horton, which offered proof of her services to the colony. This should not come as a surprise. Creating a paper trail favorable to oneself was, after all, one of the important lessons she learned while observing the Malcontents, who amassed an impressive number of affidavits espousing their cause and sparred repeatedly with the Trustees' placemen over the maintenance of the colony's official records. We may reasonably presume, then, that Mary held these papers and her grievances close to the chest when on June 23, 1744, she boarded a boat bound for Fort Frederica, where she intended to engage in another of her "usual" consultations with its commander. Fortuitously, one of the passengers on board that day was the Reverend Thomas Bosomworth, whose destiny was about to become inextricably linked with Mary's and whose nimble mind was perfectly suited for the unfinished business that lay ahead.[120]

Eight bottles similar to these were found in the remains of a cellar at the Grange site (Mary Musgrove's homestead) on property now owned by the Georgia Port Authority, some five miles northwest of Savannah. In the eighteenth century such bottles were used for storing rum, which flowed freely at the Musgroves' home and was an important trade item for Indians and colonists alike. (Photo courtesy of Southeastern Archaeological Associates and the Georgia Port Authority.)

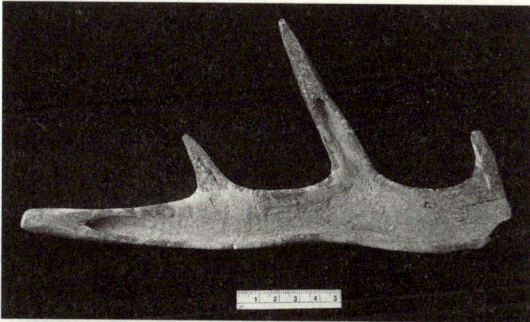

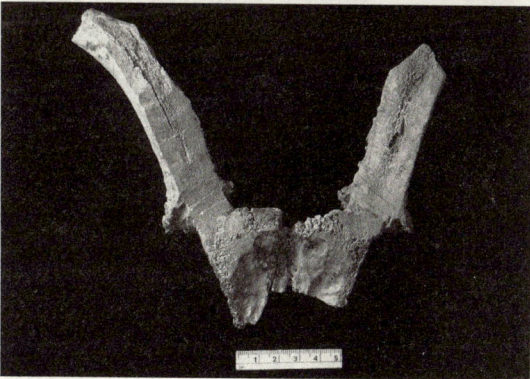

Smoothed deer antlers found at the Grange site. Documentary evidence suggests that Southeastern Indians attached antlers such as these to deerskin mantles, which hunters wore over their heads to lure whitetail deer. The antlers recovered at the Grange site are the first of their kind to be found in the archaeological record. (Photo courtesy of Southeastern Archaeological Associates and the Georgia Port Authority.)

Butter churn. This artifact from the Grange site indicates that the Musgroves probably made butter for home consumption. As women typically did most of the dairying work, we may presume that Mary or one of her female servants handled this item before committing it to the trash heap. (Photo by the author, courtesy of Southeastern Archaeological Associates and the Georgia Port Authority.)

This Bellarmine or "Bartmann" (Bearded man) jar is similar in style to those manufactured in Germany between the sixteenth and eighteenth centuries. Its recovery during excavations of the Grange site indicate that the Musgroves had contact with the Moravians living at Ebenezer, upstream on the Savannah River, or with the many Salzburgers who immigrated to Georgia in the eighteenth century. (Photo courtesy of Southeastern Archaeological Associates and the Georgia Port Authority.)

This assemblage of ceramics found at the Grange site is representative of the kind of tableware eighteenth-century colonists used in their homes. The remains of a large platter (*bottom right*) suggest that the Musgroves ate roasted meats in addition to stews, which were commonly served in bowls. (Photo by the author, courtesy of Southeastern Archaeological Associates and the Georgia Port Authority.)

Gun parts, like this discarded flintlock hammer, constitute evidence of the Musgroves' trade with the Indians. Upon their introduction in the Southeast in the late seventeenth century, flintlocks quickly became one of the most eagerly sought after trade items among Indian men. (Photo courtesy of Southeastern Archaeological Consultants and the Georgia Port Authority.)

"Indian alphabet." This is a monochrome reproduction of the first page of the Muskogee-English-German dictionary currently held at the Moravian Archives in Bethlehem, Pennsylvania. Circumstantial evidence strongly suggests that it is the work of Mary Musgrove, Benjamin Ingham, and David Nitschmann, the last of whom studied the Muskogee language under Mary's tutelage in 1736. The "alphabet" employs Greek letters as a means of creating a phonetic system for rendering the spoken Muskogee language into written form. (Courtesy of the Moravian Archives, Bethlehem, Pennsylvania.)

This page from the Creek dictionary is representative of the vocabulary lists contained therein. Note the entries for "uncle" and "aunt." Written to the right of these words, "by the Mother" indicates that the Muskogee terms referenced in the right-hand column applied only to maternal kin. Such evidence suggests that, in the process of translating, Mary had to explain how the Muskogee language reflected the Creeks' matrilineal kinship system. (Courtesy of the Moravian Archives, Bethlehem, Pennsylvania.)

Another image derived from the Creek dictionary. Observe the entry for "air." To the right of the Muskogee equivalent is the word "breath," written parenthetically in English. This inclusion perhaps indicates that the Creeks regarded air and breath as manifestations of their deity, to whom they referred as "the Master of Breath." (Courtesy of the Moravian Archives, Bethlehem, Pennsylvania.)

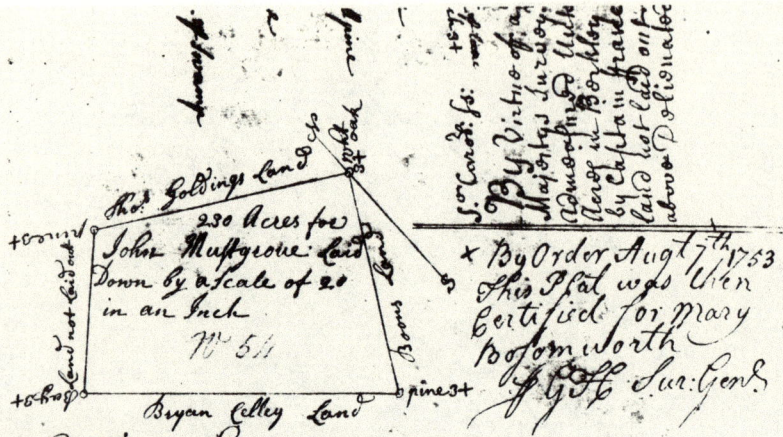

This is a land plat for John and Mary Musgrove's 230-acre tract in Colleton County. John purchased the land in 1717 but had it resurveyed in 1731 in compliance with the Quit Rent Act, which enabled landholders to obtain new grants issued by South Carolina's newly installed royal government. Note that this particular tract was not contiguous with the other 420 acres the Musgroves claimed, which likely indicates that John intended to hold on to fertile land while divesting himself of unproductive land. Also note the annotation on the right-hand side, which indicates that South Carolina authorities examined the old records when Mary (then Bosomworth) petitioned for the restoration of her Colleton County properties in 1753. (Courtesy of the South Carolina Department of Archives and History.)

6 🖋 *Mary Bosomworth*

She at present Labours under every sence of Injury; and
Circumstance of Distress; Destitute of even the Common
Necessaries of Life, being Insulted, Abused, contemned and
Dispised by those ungratefull People who are indebted to
her for the Blessings they Injoy. The Only Returns she has
met with for her past Services, Generosity, and Maternal
Affection (she has at all times shewn for the whole colony)
has been injust Loads of Infamy and Reproach; Branded and
Stigmatized with the Odious Name of Traytor ...

Mary Bosomworth, 1747

OF THE MANY colorful characters to appear on colonial Georgia's stage,
perhaps none was more loathed than the Reverend Thomas Bosomworth.
His critics—and there were many—thought him greedy to an extent unbecoming in any person, much less a man of the cloth. Some mocked his
pretensions of becoming an author; others were put off by his delusions of
grandeur and ridiculed what real talent the country boy possessed. Back in
England, church officials scratched their heads at Thomas's insubordinate
behavior, while those connected to him financially came to mistrust him
because of his chronic indebtedness. Much as he failed to impress many
of his contemporaries, Bosomworth has not fared well in the hands of
historians, who have tended to blame him for corrupting Mary. Given the
unflattering portrait of Thomas handed down to us by history, we must
pause for a moment and consider how Mary possibly could have been attracted to him when the two sailed together for Frederica that fateful June
day in 1744.

It is possible that Mary was attracted to Thomas not in spite of these
aforementioned characteristics, but because of them. Ambitious to the
core, Thomas Bosomworth received more education than most persons

of humble birth, gaining skills along the way that made him a match intellectually for his social superiors. Instilled with a scholar's soul, Thomas also possessed an attorney's eye, which enabled him to parse meaning from the slightest phrase and to match word for word any argument set against him. He was, in fact, a nimble legal thinker who combined existing ideas of Native property rights, British law, and natural law to press Mary's land claims. Best of all, Thomas was persistent and tireless in anything that served his own ends. In other words, there was much in Thomas to admire, particularly if one had pending legal issues.

Therefore, rather than Thomas exploiting Mary's Indian ancestry as a means of fulfilling his lofty ambitions, it is plausible that the reverse is true: Mary took advantage of Bosomworth's status as a clergyman and his education to fulfill ambitions that she had not been able to realize when wed to her rabble-rousing ex-servant, Jacob Mathewes. The pursuit of these ambitions, however, came at a tremendous personal cost to the couple, who were ostracized for their persistence and branded "traytors." The controversies surrounding the Bosomworths may be partly attributed to their clashes with particular governing officials but should not be ascribed simplistically to their personalities alone. Rather, we must look to broader historic trends that prompted settlers and governing officials alike to recalibrate their aspirations for the Georgia colony.

Among the important developments in Georgia was the repulsion of the Spanish invasion at St. Simons Island in 1742, which restored confidence in the colony's viability on the southern frontier. With this confidence came European settlers, who arrived in the colony in increasing numbers in the late 1740s, initiating sustained growth in both the white and black populations that continued well beyond the achievement of Independence in 1783. Also drawing settlers to Georgia was the fact that by mid-century, the colony had become a better place to do business. In 1750 the Trustees altered their land policies, allowing settlers to obtain "absolute" fee-simple title to unlimited acreage. A year later they rescinded the well-intended law prohibiting African slavery. This touched off a frenzy of speculation and settlement by South Carolina planters, who eyed the colony as a zone for expanding the plantation system they had developed a few decades earlier. Also important, in 1751 the colony held its first elections for the newly constituted Assembly, giving its citizens the representative voice that the "Malcontents" had demanded a decade earlier. By these reforms, then, the image of Georgia as a refuge for hard-working debtors gave way to that of a prosperous plantation colony like the one on its northern border and, as Julie Ann Sweet rightly observes, Georgia "came to resemble the older settlements more than it may have intended."[1]

The recalibration of Georgia's economic and political design also entailed a significant recalibration of Indian affairs. At the time of the colony's founding, the Anglo-Indian relationship assumed the trappings of a partnership because the balance of power between the two was relatively equal. By mid-century, however, this partnership had begun to unravel. Tomochichi's death in 1739 was perhaps the first blow, as the Yamacraw Indians' alliance with the colony was very much a manifestation of his personal relationship with James Oglethorpe. By the late 1740s, Oglethorpe was long gone and many of the Yamacraw Indians had dispersed, as had nearby groups of Yuchis and Chickasaws. As a result, the colony's Indian affairs became less personal, less mutual, and more susceptible to the clashing aims of imperial officials in London and Creek chiefs on the Chattahoochee River. As Indian and English visions for the colony diverged, relations between the two groups became strained, and white settlers in particular became more sensitive to matters of race. Consequently, persons of mixed ancestry like Mary found themselves in the uncomfortable and perhaps untenable position of having to choose a cultural orientation. In this manner, Mary became an anomaly in the colony she had helped found, and her vision of it as an institution that could mutually advance Indian and English interests gave way to pessimism and, at times, a single-minded pursuit of self-interest. This is not to cast aspersions on her, for Mary had to recalibrate in her own mind the colony's purpose, and her actions should be regarded as a realistic response to the fact that Georgia's frontier past was giving way to a plantation future.

"His Mercury Not Yet Fixt": Thomas Bosomworth

Of Mary's three husbands, Thomas Bosomworth is the best known, and his importance in Mary's life certainly makes him worth getting acquainted with. Born to humble parents in rural England, Thomas's life story can aptly be summarized as a quest to transcend his low social standing and provincialism. Thomas's aspirations for social advancement were so transparent, in fact, that William Stephens could not help but observe that when the young man arrived in the colony in 1741, his "mercury" had not yet been "fixed." In that respect, Bosomworth's history speaks to broader trends in colonial social mobility as much as it does to the controversy bearing his surname.

Thomas Bosomworth was born in 1719 in the tiny English village of Potto, making him nearly two decades younger than his future wife.[2] His father, described as an "honest countryman," was undoubtedly a farmer. While little can be known about the family, Thomas described it as "large," and the family's "small estate" must have made it difficult for his father to provide for his brood. While male children often took up their father's calling, the elder Bosomworth appears to have intended his children for more prestigious occupations. To this end he made considerable sacrifices to pay for their schooling, which was, according to Thomas, "their only likely means of making their fortune in the world."[3] In addition to Thomas, two of his siblings have come before the light of history: Abraham, who joined Thomas in Georgia in 1743, and Adam, who followed him there six years later.

Thomas's hometown of Potto was by any definition a provincial place, located in the North Riding of Yorkshire, where a branch of the River Leven cuts through a diverse landscape of hilly moorland, woods, and low-lying agricultural fields. Potto, situated within the parish of Whorlton, was a tiny village, which as late as the 1840s comprised a mere 148 individuals. Most of the area's residents made their living from the land, and the Bosomworths probably tended sheep and cattle and raised a variety of grains, including wheat, barley, and oats. Much as the region's economic activity was rooted in tradition, so was its landscape, upon which stood ruined buildings echoing Yorkshire's medieval past, such as Whorlton's Chapel of the Holy Cross, which housed a monument to a Knight Templar who had fallen during the Crusades.[4]

In the North Riding of Yorkshire, a flourishing regional subculture made it different from places elsewhere in England. Most conspicuously, people of the North Riding spoke (and continue to speak) a dialect derived from Old English and Old Norse known as Tyke, which speakers of standard English found difficult or impossible to understand.[5] Linguistically antiquated, rural Yorkshire's belief system was similarly situated in tradition that, in some cases, predated the arrival of Christianity. Belief in fairies was widespread; legend had it that a race called the "little people" inhabited the moors and vales and occasionally played merry elven pranks on humans.[6] Ghosts also figured prominently in the Yorkshire worldview.[7]

While the people of Yorkshire were (and are) at one level proud of their local culture, it nevertheless seems to be the case that they were self-conscious about their provinciality, their dialect, and their seemingly backward ways. Londoners and other cosmopolitan types who mocked rural traditions helped to reinforce this self-perception.[8] Born into Yorkshire's provincial culture and perhaps self-conscious of his backwardness, then, the young Thomas Bosomworth spent much of his early life attempting to remake himself into a cosmopolitan man of learning. Where he was schooled remains impossible to prove, but evidence suggests that he received instruction or mentoring from three men of the Church—George Slainthorpe, William Deasom, and Thomas Thwaites, all from nearby villages—who later sponsored Thomas's ordination as a priest.[9] At school and at church Thomas appears to have fallen under the spell of these and other learned men, all of whom had an Oxbridge education, spoke standard English, and advocated Orthodox Anglican teachings. Following their example, Thomas embraced the King's English and religious orthodoxy in order to transcend his Yorkshire upbringing and become, like them, a man of distinction as an Anglican priest.

Because Church rules required a baccalaureate degree for ordination into the priesthood, it can be assumed that Bosomworth attended university, hence the Trustees' description of him as "well educated."[10] At university, Thomas received the "usual" course of instruction for those preparing to take Holy Orders, which would have included considerable training in theology and Biblical languages. Latin, it seems, was the second language over which he developed the best command. In the course of his education, Thomas also learned to write using a complex script akin to calligraphy, which was beautiful to look at but time-consuming to produce and thus impractical.[11] So, in some respects, the ornaments of Thomas's education were not well-suited to the practical tasks that lay before him in Georgia.

That Thomas ever went to Georgia can be attributed to his friend, Christopher Orton, who came to London to receive Holy Orders. Orton recommended Bosomworth to the Georgia Trustees, and Thomas followed him to London in June 1741, after which he received an appointment as William Stephens' clerk (basically a job copying the secretary's copious correspondence). Upon Orton's appointment as minister, the two men set sail on the ship *Loyal Judith* with a group of Salzburgers and Highland Scots. After spending six weeks crossing the Atlantic, Bosomworth and Orton arrived in Savannah, Georgia, on December 3 to begin their careers.[12]

Billed by the Trustees as a "young gentleman" of "good character and behaviour," Bosomworth at first impressed his employers with his intelligence, self-motivation, and sobriety. At the same time, however, he revealed qualities that in hindsight help to explain why he had such trouble getting along with local officials. For one thing, Bosomworth was something of a tattler and was quick to document the misdoings of others to advance his reputation. Even on board the *Loyal Judith*, for example, Bosomworth at his own initiative began keeping a daily journal in order to document the captain's tyrannical behavior and later submitted it to the Trustees to have him reprimanded.[13]

Another of Thomas's personal characteristics was his exalted sense of entitlement. Having beaten the odds set against him by his provincial upbringing to receive a university education, Bosomworth believed himself above the "dry copy work" he had been assigned to perform under Stephens and quickly searched for a different occupation more suited (as he believed) to his talent and learning. Complicating matters further still was Bosomworth's indecisiveness about his calling. Trained in the manner of a clergyman, Bosomworth was at first reluctant to enter the priesthood and toyed with the idea of a career in business or government. His employer, William Stephens, struggled in vain to find more meaningful work to engage the young man's precocious mind. So, very quickly after arriving in Georgia, Stephens was having "doubts" and the question became what to do with Thomas Bosomworth.[14]

Although he was unsure what direction his career might take, Thomas Bosomworth spent ample time trying to demonstrate his genius to his superiors. Around March, Thomas began working at odd hours of the day to compose two lengthy reports, one an exposé of the colony's orphan house and the other a treatise on the state of religion in Georgia. Of the two manifestos, only the report on the orphan house survives, but it and other early writings give us good insight into the Anglican orthodoxy of its perplexing author.[15] Bosomworth's report on the orphan house was a scathing indictment of the institution, which he viewed as "seminary" for indoctrinating children in the precepts of the revivalist Methodism espoused by George Whitefield, the orphan house's founder and fundraiser. Bosomworth called the orphan house "dangerous" and labeled itinerant preachers such as Whitefield "desperadoes" intent upon destroying church, state, and all earthly authority. As Thomas's idea of the church embraced this life as well as the next, Bosomworth depicted the revivalist ministers as misguided in their seeming denial of earthly needs and pleasures. Their sermons, he argued, encouraged people to "cast off all obligations" and neglect all "concerns in life" so as to "give themselves entirely to prayer & meditation." That message, Bosomworth added, only served to "amuse & captivate the indolent part of mankind" and gave license to slaves and servants to refuse work.

If significant for what it reveals about his orthodoxy, the style and tone of Bosomworth's orphan house report shed even more light on the author's personality. Verbose, repetitive, and steeped in arcane, learned phrasings, it would appear that Bosomworth wrote as he did as a means of compensating for his social insecurity and of demonstrating the "genius" that had been underappreciated by the Trustees. To start with, the report is ridiculously long, a product of Bosomworth's tendency to repeat himself, to wax philosophically on points tangential to his argument, and to use florid language. At certain points, the pages drip with false modesty, as Bosomworth deferentially points out his "weak abilities," only to brashly indict the renowned Whitefield and drop the occasional biblical or Latin quote. Bosomworth also employed arcane diction to further demonstrate his advanced learning, such as when he drew upon the Book of John to describe the Methodists as "thrasonical Diotropheses."

In the report's conclusion, Thomas finally gets to the main point when he laments how "obscurity" serves as a barrier for career advancement, even for a young man of "genius." This is, of course, a thinly veiled reference to himself, and Thomas's repetition of the word "obscurity" is characteristic of several other of his early writings.[16] His motivation for finding new employment was not simply monetary, but also one of overcoming his provincial upbringing and earning respect for his intellectual gifts. Toward that end, Bosomworth finished the report by begging for a job that would elevate him. While Thomas probably was genuinely concerned about the institution's Methodist leanings, the orphan house report appears to have been little more than a vehicle for advancing his career.

Bosomworth's fortunes took a favorable turn that spring. During one of Orton's sojourns to Frederica, Bosomworth had the opportunity to conduct church services in Savannah for several consecutive weeks in May and June.[17] When the Spanish invaded St. Simons Island that July, Bosomworth joined a volunteer company raised to defend the island, thinking it an opportune moment to "[show] himself in arms."[18] Although he arrived at Frederica after the Spanish had evacuated, it would appear that

Bosomworth used the occasion to introduce himself to James Oglethorpe and solicit his recommendation for a higher position in the colony. After returning to Savannah in August, Bosomworth found his friend Orton gravely ill and the young minister soon succumbed to his affliction. After his friend's death Bosomworth delivered his funeral oration and began conducting church services again.[19]

Orton's death most likely prompted Bosomworth finally to answer the call to the priesthood. That fall, he returned to Frederica and solicited a recommendation from General Oglethorpe, presumably to fill a vacant post as chaplain in the regiment stationed there. Rather suddenly in November, Bosomworth boarded a ship bound for England by way of New York. The aspiring minister finally arrived in England around Christmas and took lodging in the Redriff district of London.[20]

Upon hearing of Orton's death, the Trustees dithered in their search for a replacement.[21] Into this vacuum stepped Bosomworth, who penned a long letter to Trustee James Vernon on March 22, 1743, soliciting his recommendation. Bosomworth later met with Vernon to discuss his prospects, and in late April the Trustees resolved to have him ordained and "go missionary to Savannah." Thomas then spent much of the spring preparing for ordination, which would have required him to submit to "examinations" of his character and theological leanings and to solicit recommendations from churchmen in Yorkshire who knew him. On May 29, at the Chapel Royal at St. James, Thomas was ordained a deacon of the church, and on June 24, at Fulham Palace, he was finally admitted to the priesthood. On July 4 Bosomworth received his official appointment to Georgia from Benjamin Martyn, the Trustees' secretary.[22]

The document appointing Bosomworth minister of Georgia makes clear that the SPG and the Trustees expected Thomas to focus his efforts in Savannah, where he agreed to reside and deliver books and furniture to the parsonage.[23] Much as he rebuffed his appointment as clerk, Bosomworth tried to set his own terms in the exercise of his ecclesiastical office. First, he delayed his departure from England by several months and did not arrive in Georgia until December 21. Rather than report for duty in Savannah, however, Bosomworth went to Frederica, where he remained until late February. Colonial officials in Savannah, who for months had been waiting patiently for him, seemed perplexed at Bosomworth's delays. Across the Atlantic, leading officials among the SPG and the Georgia Trustees must have been similarly dismayed, as Bosomworth did not begin corresponding with them for two months, and then only to inform them that he had been spending his time at Frederica and Darien, the Highland Scots' town several miles up the Altamaha River. Clearly, the Georgia Trustees were not well pleased by his conduct and ordered Bosomworth again to Savannah, where they "expect[ed] he should go and reside."[24]

After finally arriving in Savannah on February 21, 1744, Thomas for a time diligently fulfilled his duties as priest. Each Sunday morning, Bosomworth performed divine service and spent much of his afternoons catechizing children. Many of Savannah's residents seem to have embraced both him and his message, as he drew record crowds to the Church's Easter services. Meanwhile, Bosomworth was on hand to oversee construction of the city's new church and presided when its cornerstone was laid on March 28. Generally, he made a "good impression" on his flock, but nevertheless decided the first week of April to return to Frederica, where a widowed Mary Mathewes was busy consulting with commander William Horton.[25]

As Bosomworth's earliest surviving writings speak almost entirely to his professional concerns, nowhere does he give any indication that he desired to marry. Nor did Bosomworth mention any encounters with the woman who was to become his wife until after the fact, which suggests that Thomas and Mary's courtship was brief and their marriage hastily entered into. It is plausible that the two had in fact met as early as June 1742, when Mary came to Savannah to bury Jacob Mathewes. Bosomworth's lengthy stays at Frederica and in England, however, make it highly unlikely that the two had much significant contact until April and May 1744, when their stays at Frederica overlapped. Mary returned to Savannah on May 17, with Thomas arriving there ten days later. In mid-June, Mary was again asked to recruit Creek Indians for the colony's defense, and on June 23 she and thirty warriors boarded a boat for Frederica. Bosomworth hastily decided to join them, and on July 9, the two married at Frederica in a private ceremony conducted by Frederica's German Lutheran minister, Johann Driesler.[26]

When word of the Bosomworths' marriage reached Savannah a couple weeks later, it created all manner of stir among the citizenry. William Stephens called the news "very surprising," noting that many residents found the idea of them as a couple "so incredible" that they "looked upon it as a piece of merriment" and gossiped about them relentlessly.[27] This was not the first time, of course, that Mary's intimate life had been the subject of gossip in Savannah. Recall that nine years earlier Mary was rumored to have had an affair with Thomas Causton while John Musgrove was away in London. Just months before her marriage to Bosomworth, in fact, word had briefly circulated that Mary intended to wed John Mackintosh, the leader of the Highlander colony at Darien.[28] What probably made the union of Mary and Thomas "so surprising" and worthy of prurient gossip, was that the bride was two decades older than the groom. Others who held a low opinion of Indians, however, may have been dismayed to learn that a university-educated man of the cloth had decide to marry a dark-skinned woman who was half "savage."

Given the age and cultural differences between he and his bride, Thomas's expectations for his marriage probably differed from those of most first-time bridegrooms. By then, Mary was beyond her prime childbearing years, so Thomas must have realized that no children—and no heirs— would come from their union. Moreover, Thomas was fully aware that Mary's Creek heritage factored significantly in her life and that his marriage to her would bring him into close company with Indians. Thomas welcomed this prospect and later justified marrying her on the grounds that it would "better enable me to carry on the great work of promoting Christian knowledge among the natives of America." Echoing John Rolfe's famous letter explaining his marriage to Pocahontas more than a century earlier, Thomas clearly was sensitive to how others viewed their unconventional marriage, hence his need to point out the greater good it served in promoting Indian conversion to Christianity. Likewise, Thomas felt it necessary to explain that Mary was not like other Indians, emphasizing that she was "brought up in Carolina" and possessed an "unexceptionable character," meaning that she conducted herself in the manner of a Christian wife.[29] Significantly, Mary was also a woman of property, and Thomas must have known that by marrying her he would enjoy a larger estate than he had ever known in England. Little, perhaps, did he realize how much work lay ahead if he and Mary were to enjoy it.

Claims Renewed and Revised

When Mary and Thomas returned to Savannah as man and wife in August 1744, they celebrated their nuptials with a grand party. As there was no edifice big enough to hold the large number of expected guests, William

Stephens offered the use of his home, moving aside his furniture and personal effects to make way for three long dining tables and open space for dancing. On the night of August 20, sixty or more revelers enjoyed "good wine" and all manner of boiled, roasted, and baked meats. As it was hot at that time of year, the guests imbibed of a weak punch to quench their thirst, which intensified as they danced to a fiddle well into the night. Everyone, it seems, had a good time, and even Stephens was happy to report that that "no disorder" had occurred in his home.[30] Blissful as the occasion was, Mary and Thomas probably never again experienced this kind of revelry in one another's company, as Mary's pending (and ever-expanding) claims for money, land, and respect quickly came to dominate all other aspects of their partnership.

Once again, the antagonisms of the irrepressible Joseph Watson provide the backdrop for Mary's decision to revive her case. After spending several years in South Carolina, in 1743 Watson returned to England and submitted before the Trustees several claims that were potentially damaging to Mary. First, he petitioned the Trustees for several hundred acres of land, one hundred of which fell within the "Indian lands" at Yamacraw and partially overlapped with those claimed by Mary. At the same time, Watson petitioned the Trustees for a three-year license to trade with the Yamacraw Indians, which would have effectively ended the monopoly Mary and her husbands had enjoyed since 1733. Surprisingly, while the Trustees denied Watson's petition for Indian land, they responded somewhat favorably to his other requests, granting him five hundred acres adjacent to the Cowpen and recommending that Watson be granted a trading license "if no objection arose thereupon."[31]

When Watson finally returned to Georgia around March 1744, he petitioned for a trading license, only to find William Stephens reluctant to honor his request because of his "caution concerning Mrs. Bosomworth's interest." Thwarted, Watson fell back into some of his old and odd habits, such as dressing as a monk purporting to convert the Indians to Christianity. He then began trafficking rum and applied for a trading license for St. Catherine's Island, where some of the Yamacraw Indians now lived. Wary of Watson's scheming, Stephens again refused him.[32]

Denied access to a legal trade with the Indians, a stubborn Watson proceeded to carry on an illicit trade with them that summer, which led to numerous instances of disorderly behavior. Watson stole from the Bosomworths and later spread rumors among the Indians that Mary was cheating them, offering to sell trade goods at cheaper prices. He insulted Mary by calling her a "heathen" and lampooned Thomas as an "insignificant fellow" who was "unfit for exercising his function as a divine." Predictably, Watson's behavior drew protest from the Bosomworths, who took him to court. After some delays, the court found Watson guilty of trading without a license and several other misdemeanors, for which he was fined. Mary and Thomas, however, could not have been pleased with the verdict, as Watson left a free man after paying the fines and having two others pay "sureties" for his good behavior.[33]

While it would be a stretch to say that the Bosomworths renewed Mary's claims solely because of the threat Watson posed, Watson's actions nevertheless must have heightened their anxiety and caused Mary and Thomas to act quickly. Plans clearly had been hatched shortly after their nuptials at Frederica. Evidently the couple intended to make a personal appeal to James Oglethorpe, and they broadcast their intention to go to England just days after arriving in Savannah as man and wife. Thomas wrote to Oglethorpe soon after the wedding, expressing their intent to meet him in England and giving him at least a vague account of Mary's financial difficulties.

Significantly, the couple began expanding the scope of Mary's claims at around the same time. On September 12, Thomas went to Stephens in his wife's behalf, asking "how it came to pass" that Mary was not paid crop bounties in 1739. Stephens was perplexed, thinking the question "somewhat extraordinary after so many years." Unable to answer Thomas satisfactorily, Stephens promised to make an enquiry, musing to himself that the request was "a little strange."[34] Although Thomas did not press Stephens for an answer at that time, the encounter is nevertheless significant because it marks a turning point in that Mary included additional claims that she and her late second husband had not made in earlier petitions.

Meanwhile, in London, James Oglethorpe waited patiently for the Bosomworths. By mid-February 1745 it had become clear that the couple were delayed, so Oglethorpe penned a brief letter to Thomas, informing him that he had "hoped before now to have had the pleasure of seeing [him] and Mrs. Bosomworth here." "If I can be of any service," he wrote, "you may freely let me know in what I can be useful."[35] Finally, Thomas decided to take Oglethorpe up on his offer to present Mary's case to him personally. In early June, Thomas secreted himself to Charles Town and secured passage on a ship bound for England, curiously making no arrangements to have someone else conduct church services in his absence. Thomas was in dire financial circumstances of his own making, and his indebtedness may explain the secretive and hurried manner by which he departed Georgia. Bosomworth arrived in London shortly after July 17, leaving Mary back home to manage the Cowpen and to keep his creditors at bay.[36]

After arriving in London, Thomas wrote to his superiors at the SPG, pleading their forgiveness for leaving his ministerial post and telling them that he would give further account of the "absolute necessity I was under." Hinting at his indebtedness, Bosomworth went on to explain that "vile & base means" had been used to "murther" his and Mary's reputations and to "distress us in every shape." Seemingly aware that he had fallen out of favor in London and anticipating (correctly) that he would have to forfeit his ministerial position, Bosomworth proceeded to Yorkshire to transact some "private business." While there, he drew another quarter salary that was due to him before he left Georgia, citing his "necessities for cash."[37] Being a Yorkshire native, Bosomworth had ample opportunity to meet with some "friends in the country," but his real motive was to confront James Oglethorpe, who was then in York preparing to lead the king's men against Scottish rebels who had flocked to the standard of "Bonnie Prince Charlie."

Although Mary was not in England, her interests were central to Thomas's meeting with the general that October. Before departing Georgia, Thomas had Mary draw up a "memorial" highlighting her past services to the colony and presenting in detail her varied claims against the Trustees. Oglethorpe would have learned that Mary was now demanding the entire Yamacraw tract, having expanded her claims beyond the 450 acres for which she and Jacob had petitioned four years earlier. In addition, Mary demanded twelve years' annual salary as the colony's interpreter in the sum of 1,200 pounds, thereby doubling what she had agreed to in 1739 and making it retroactive. Added to these demands was another for crop bounties that had been withheld from her in 1739 and 1742, totaling more than two hundred pounds.[38]

It is not known specifically how Oglethorpe reacted, but Thomas asserted years later that the general had promised to help Mary after the Scottish rebellion had been put down. Meanwhile, Oglethorpe extended credit to the Bosomworths by allowing them to draw bills upon him not exceeding one thousand pounds, presumably anticipating that the Trustees would eventually reward Mary. Oglethorpe never denied making such promises, and his correspondence suggests that he gave Mary's memorial a favorable hearing. On November 12, Oglethorpe wrote to William Horton at Frederica, urging him to support Mary for the "friendship she has at all times shewed to me, as well as the interest of the colony." Months later, Oglethorpe repeated his offer to recommend Mary's past services to the government and explained to Thomas his desire to "be of service to you in any proper way."[39]

After receiving another letter from Bosomworth on May 19, the Georgia Trustees finally decided to take a close look at some of the bills he had recently drawn upon the Trust's account, as well as the memorial sent in Mary's behalf the previous December. Unfortunately for Mary, her avowed friend James Oglethorpe had been court-martialed for alleged dereliction of duty while leading the king's forces and was unavailable to put in a good word for Mary. Also unfortunate was that Mary's enemy, the former storekeeper Thomas Jones, happened to be on hand when the Trustees met and opined that Mary was not owed what she claimed because her former husband (Mathewes) had died owing 114 pounds to the public store. Jones's skepticism seems to have rubbed off on the other Trustees, who denied that Mary was owed anything more for interpreting and observed that her claims for crop bounties were not made properly during Jacob's lifetime. In the end, the Trustees referred Mary's land claim to the judgment of the Trustees' Common Council and ordered the colony's President and Assistants to investigate the validity of the crop bounties, authorizing them to pay Mary only if she could prove that they were "really due" to her.[40] At that point Mary and Thomas knew that no compensation would soon be forthcoming, and with that realization, the couple found it necessary to devise new strategies for advancing their case.

Mary and Malatchi

Thomas's brief return to England was just the opening salvo in a longer struggle for the justice the Bosomworths believed was their due. As the Trustees and their placemen in Savannah responded coolly to Mary's claims, she and Thomas gravitated toward others who were willing to lend support. These included not only Mary's Creek kin, but also the commanders of Frederica, William Horton and Alexander Heron, who, more than any other officials in Georgia, gave Mary's claims a fair hearing. Branded "traytors" in Savannah, Mary and Thomas also repositioned themselves geographically, first by erecting a trading post at the Forks of the Altamaha River and later by building an estate on St. Catherine's Island. In particular, the trading post on the Altamaha brought Mary into closer proximity to the Creek nation, allowing her frequent intercourse with the many hunters and "war Indians" who passed their way.

Among Mary's regular visitors was her younger cousin Malatchi, the *Opiya Mico* of Coweta and presumed heir to the Lower Creek "emperorship" held by the late Brims. Bearing grievances of his own against the southern colonies, Malatchi conspired willingly with Mary to support her land claims in Georgia, hoping to reverse or stall the recent dispersal of white settlers onto lands the Creeks claimed. Drawn together because Mary's personal interests seemed to converge with those of the Creek nation, the two devised a creative set of documents intended to solidify Mary's claims. Aided by the legal acumen of Thomas Bosomworth, their artfully composed paper trail not only emphasized Mary's service to the colony, but also presumed to elevate Mary to a position of leadership in the Creek nation. In effect, their strategy was, first, to define the Creek grant of land to Mary as an Indian-to-Indian transaction, and, then, through a process akin to alchemy, to transform Native land rights into English title. As might be imagined, colonial and imperial officials bristled at the Bosomworths' audacious tactics.

The plan to relocate the Bosomworth estate appears to have been instigated by Mary during Thomas's sojourn in England in 1745. Around November Mary wrote to William Horton at Frederica, explaining her intention to open a trading post at the forks of the Altamaha River. Horton responded favorably to the proposition, commenting "the Forks is the best place you could have thought for a trading house." Clearly, the two conceived of the trading house as serving both a private and a public function. "I cannot but see that it will be very beneficial to you & agreeable to the Indians," Horton wrote, adding that a trading post at that location would also "contribute to the public service."[41] Horton, whose straitened finances made it difficult for him to buy gifts for the Indians at Frederica, reasoned that Mary could entertain them more economically.[42] Thus encouraged by Horton, Mary and Thomas went to the Forks around March to set up their operation, and the trading post served as their principal residence for the next three years.

Around the time they opened up their trading post at the Forks, Mary and Thomas also staked a claim to St. Catherine's Island, which was then inhabited by eight to ten families of Creek or Yamacraw Indians.[43] Thomas first purchased a herd of cattle in South Carolina and shipped them to the island. Then he went to William Stephens to ask if he had any objections. Surprisingly, Stephens raised none, perhaps because he did not know that the Bosomworths intended to keep the cattle there permanently. Anticipating (wrongly for the moment) that the Trustees would soon rescind the prohibition on slavery, Thomas purchased a few slaves in South Carolina and brought them back to St. Catherine's Island. When apprised of these developments, the Trustees predictably responded with indignation, chastising Stephens for his leniency and ordering him to remind the Bosomworths of the Trustees' prohibition of slavery and the maximum size of land grants (500 acres).[44] As the years passed, Mary and Thomas came to regard the island as their permanent home.

While the Bosomworths were busy getting situated, the colony's relationship with the Indians took a precipitous turn for the worse, which greatly altered the dynamic of the Bosomworth case. Up to that point, Mary's claims had been largely between herself, the local Yamacraw Indians, and the Trustees. But Mary's expansive claim to the entire Yamacraw tract and her later claim to a similarly large tract on St. Catherine's Island, involved lands that the Creek nation understood to be theirs, making them an interested party. Importantly, by the mid-1740s white settlers had begun spilling into lands elsewhere claimed by the Creeks, an alarming trend that the Creeks met by protesting to colonial governments, by the occasional show of force, and by courting alliances with France and Spain. The convergence of these developments quickly elevated the Bosomworth Affair into a multifaceted phenomenon involving Indian affairs, warfare, and imperial competition.

To understand how this came about, it is best to focus upon a series of localized disputes involving the town of Savannah and the remnant Indians still living on the nearby Yamacraw tract. As many of the Indians had dispersed by the mid-1740s, Savannah's residents cast greedy eyes upon choice lands at Yamacraw. Some fancied settling there outright, but most infringed upon Native rights by cutting of timber on Indian lands. For a time the Indians remained somewhat tolerant, murmuring in protest privately to Mary. Soon after Mary relocated to the Forks, however, the scope of the timber cutting appears to have increased, causing the Indians to howl in protest. In March 1746 they became "clamorous" and threatened to "take satisfaction themselves," unless Mary would write a letter to colonial officials registering their complaint. Mary tried to explain the Indians' perspective on the matter in writing, but William Stephens responded by saying that he would investigate the cutting of the timber if a "Christian person" testified under oath in court.[45] As the court was to convene in only two short days, Mary could not reach Savannah in time to offer testimony herself, leaving the Indians defenseless in the face of English justice. A few Yamacraw Indians went to the magistrates to protest anyway but were denied on the grounds that no Christian testimony had been taken. To add insult to injury, the Yamacraws were informed that Tomochichi had given those lands to the king while in England, news of which came much to their surprise.[46]

The magistrates' rough handling of the Indians proved important, as the Yamacraws—indeed the entire Creek nation—viewed it as unjust and as a violation of Indian rights. Their decision only to admit "Christian evidence" in particular was indicative of the shift in the colony's attitude toward Indians. Just twelve years earlier, in 1734, the Savannah court had admitted the non-Christian Indian testimony of Mary's Indian slave Justice, who attested to the adultery committed by Mary's servant, Job Wiggin. That year Thomas Causton had consulted with the Indians when he investigated Joseph Watson's erratic behavior and misdeeds relating to the Indian trade, a consultation that ultimately led to his confinement. So, in refusing to register Indian grievances, the magistrates actually were breaking with precedent and treating the Indians as less valued partners in the colonial venture.

Stephens' refusal to acknowledge Indian grievances in court also came at a bad time. Rumors of an imminent Creek attack on the English settlements were in the air, and at a recent meeting at Augusta the Yamacraws provided Chigelly of Coweta with a detailed account of the timber cutting on their land.[47] Back in Coweta that summer, Chigelly informed his nephew Malatchi of what had transpired at Augusta. Alarmed at the possibility that they had inadvertently given their lands to the English, the two men retrieved a piece of paper that James Oglethorpe had given to them years earlier. Chigelly took the paper to the trader George Galphin, who read it and confirmed that the "the contents of that paper was that [the Creeks] had given away all [their] lands." Malatchi later confided that this revelation "vexed us very much," prompting him to deliver a hostile speech in the Coweta square denouncing Oglethorpe. Malatchi's hostile words soon became common currency on the frontier and alerted colonial officials to the possibility of an Indian war.[48]

After delivering this speech, Malatchi became persona non grata in the colonial capitals. To improve his reputation among English officials, he ventured to South Carolina in late October to meet with Governor Glen. There Malatchi found himself accosted by the governor, who annoyingly tried to persuade Malatchi to attack the French at Fort Toulouse and to accept the erection of an English fort on Creek territory. Malatchi resented Glen's attempt to manipulate him, and he remained staunchly opposed to the governor's proposals, which other Creek leaders appear to have approved.[49] On his way back to Coweta, Malatchi stopped at the Forks to pay Mary a visit. The two undoubtedly discussed their recent suspicion that the British were using trickery to steal Creek land, and Mary responded with a scathing talk that Malatchi later delivered in Coweta.

Although Mary's words come to us third hand from a trader, it is clear that she identified with the Indians' interests and was alarmed at the rate at which Georgia was evolving in ways that were not beneficial for the Indians. She began her tirade by calling James Oglethorpe a "rogue" and blamed him for taking land away from the Indians so that the king could "send over all his poor people" to settle. Major William Horton, a professed friend to Mary, did not escape blame, as she castigated him for failing to deliver enough presents to the Indians. Mary likewise knew that white colonists employed the written word against Indians to steal their lands and made reference in particular to the deerskin traders who "were always writing down against the Indians." Wary that so many white people were settling on Indian hunting grounds, Mary urged Malatchi to protest before it was "too late." "As she was an Indian herself," she added, she "wanted to have justice done [to] them," a comment noteworthy not only because it is the first time Mary identified herself in writing as "an Indian" but also because Mary's own land claims hinged on the Creeks' ability to defend theirs.[50]

Mary's speech may have convinced Malatchi that they were of like minds. Nevertheless, it is clear that he and other Lower Creeks harbored suspicions about her role in the land negotiations. By then, the Lower Creeks were aware that Mary claimed at least a portion of the Yamacraw tract, and they also probably knew of Mary's plans to settle St. Catherine's Island.[51] These maneuvers, combined with Mary's linguistic dexterity, led the Indians to believe (probably erroneously) that they "never talked about any land, but when [Mary] was the interpreter." Fearing that Mary had double crossed them, Malatchi sent his uncle Chigelly to the Forks in early December to ask her a few questions, which he did in a mildly accusatory tone: Did you give any of the lands away? Do you know anything about the papers that Galphin told us signified that we had given our lands away? Did you interpret when those papers were drawn up? If you were not the interpreter, who was?[52]

Mary must have been taken aback by her uncle's line of questioning, which she deflected by saying that she could not answer him unless she could see the papers (Chigelly had left them behind in Coweta).[53] Chigelly departed from the Forks, and soon afterward Mary and Thomas reinitiated their claims for crop bounties, probably because the bills Thomas had drawn upon them had been unpaid for nearly a year. So, to avoid being sued again for debt, Mary returned to Savannah in early January to meet with President Stephens to inquire about the status of her claims. Stephens informed Mary that they would consider her case if she could produce "what vouchers or other evidences she had to prove the quantity of corn, &tc raised" in 1739. Seemingly unprepared, Mary had brought nothing in writing to prove she was owed anything, so she promised to return bearing Jacob Mathewes' account books.[54]

Mary promptly returned to the Forks. Thomas was home at that time and the couple sifted through the documents Mary had archived over the last several years, documents Thomas would use as the basis for his "state of the case" chronicling Mary's service record and claims. Thomas sent along the paperwork to William Horton, who promptly forwarded it to James Oglethorpe.[55] Mary was unable, though, to find Jacob Mathewes' account book, if any such thing existed. In lieu of the missing documents, Mary had her old neighbor, Robert Williams, swear to an affidavit attesting that Jacob had never received crop bounties despite having "a larger crop than any planter raised by the labor of white hands" in 1739. When Thomas sent the Williams affidavit to President Stephens in late March, however, the President and Assistants found it "too loose and generall," and they postponed taking further action.[56]

Spurned yet again by Georgia officials, Mary and Thomas amplified their efforts, resolving to go behind the backs of Oglethorpe and the Georgia Trustees and petition higher authorities. The result was a lengthy "memorial" that Mary composed on August 10 and directed Lieutenant

Colonel Alexander Heron to forward to none other than Thomas Pelham-Holles, the Duke of Newcastle and Secretary of State to King George II.[57] Arguably the most important document relating to Mary, the 1747 memorial is infused with biographical detail that many historians—this one included—have mined in their attempt to sketch out the first half of her life.

We can gain a more comprehensive appreciation of the 1747 memorial, however, by situating it in context. Among other important developments, rumors of an impending Creek attack had persisted since the previous spring. Also alarming was the accruing evidence that the French were courting the allegiance of the Lower Creeks, particularly of Malatchi, who had recently visited the French fort and related to its commander the details of his sensitive discussions with James Glen.[58]

To counteract French influence among the Lower Creeks, William Horton naturally turned to Mary. Around May, Horton repeatedly solicited Mary's help, asking her first to orchestrate the capture of French agents rumored to be living among the Lower Creeks and later to distribute two-hundred pounds' worth of presents to the Indians. When a party of Creeks led by Stemachuha came to Mary's home in July, she provided them with gifts "necessary to secure their friendship" and secured a commission for her brother-in-law, Abraham Bosomworth, to go as an agent to the Lower Creeks.[59] Mary outfitted Abraham and his Creek guides and promptly sent them to Coweta, where they arrived on July 31. There, Abraham found that the rumors of French intrigue and a "rupture" with the Indians were true, and he pacified the Lower Creeks by promising them more presents. In addition, Abraham convinced Malatchi and his followers to visit Frederica to meet the newly installed commander, Colonel Alexander Heron, which seems to make his agency a successful one that, in his own words, "retarded the ill consequences that were then apprehended."[60]

The problem, however, was that the procedure Mary and Major Horton agreed to did not go exactly as planned. Horton's intent was to provide Mary with an annual allowance of 200 pounds, which she could in turn use to buy presents for the Indians and reduce the costs of entertaining them at Frederica. As it turned out, Horton was broke, and he had been forced to incur personal debts to keep Georgia's defenses afloat. Consequently, Mary had little choice but to provide the Indians with gifts from her private stock of trade goods and personally to fund Abraham's agency to the Lower Creeks that July. Anticipating that she would be compensated in the near future, Mary must have been distraught upon learning instead that the colony had decided to reduce its expenditures for frontier defense by dismissing the Highland company and the rangers and by eliminating the scout boats. Because of these cost-cutting measures, Horton's proposal for an annual fund fell by the wayside, forcing him to confess to Mary that he had no means of compensating her.[61] When Alexander Heron replaced Horton as Frederica's commander in June, he confided to Mary that he could not honor Horton's promises, though he agreed that their plan would be cost-effective. In the end, Mary was left to foot the bill not only for the expenses she had incurred that summer but also for the future gifts her brother-in-law had promised in Coweta.[62]

These events had a specific effect on the content of the 1747 memorial. In particular, Heron's inability to follow through with Horton's promises and Oglethorpe's silence caused Mary to direct her words at the highest levels of the British administration, which she believed would more likely offer her financial support. These levels included not only Parliament, but also "his Grace the Duke of Newcastle one of His Majestys Principal Secretarys of State." Interestingly, Mary also begged assistance from the governor and the Council of South Carolina, arguing that the colony had benefited from her services. Georgia, she noted, had served as a barrier that enabled the king's subjects in South Carolina to improve their estates unmolested by putting a stop to "the frequent ravages of Enimy Indians, etc."

The recent troubles between the colony and the Creek Indians also influenced Mary's line of argument. Playing to Britain's worst fears, she repeatedly invokes the specter of a Franco-Creek alliance, warning of the incursions of "French emissaries" who doled out presents to buy the Indians' loyalty. Shrewdly, Mary presents herself as the solution to Britain's problems in Indian affairs and recommends that the government send "a proper person . . . in whom they repose faith" to engage in diplomacy with the Creeks. The "proper person" to whom Mary refers is, of course, herself, and she boasts that she has "interest enough to command a thousand fighting men" and therefore the ability to thwart French and Spanish overtures to the Creeks. This she would do, but only if "suitable encouragements" were given to her, namely, Horton's proposed annual stipend of 200 pounds. Mary confidently predicted that if she received financial backing, then she would be able to protect "every foot of his Majestys Possessions" in Georgia. If she did not, Mary warned, then she would be driven "to the necessity of flying to her Indian friends for bread," adding that this would "greatly confirm the jealousies and uneasiness which his majesties enimies have so industriously fomented and spirited up" among the Creeks.

If at one level Mary's assertions appear bold, one can nevertheless detect a degree of pathos in her words. Mary's immense debt and unpaid income, estimated in excess of 5,700 pounds, was clearly one depressing factor. Hence she focused much of her narrative on misfortunes, employing words such as "ruin," "destitute," and "suffering" to describe her financial condition. Perhaps even worse than Mary's financial suffering was her social stigmatization. As Mary explained, Georgians branded her "traytor," and her Indian ancestry was also probably a factor, as the land claims rested upon the fundamental argument that "her ancestors were the Natural born heirs sole owners and proprietors of every foot of land which is now his Majestys colony of Georgia." Mary, in fact, seems painfully aware of the prejudice directed at her Indian relatives, whose bravery and independence she defended against the common assumption that they were "Savages, or Barbarions." It is a telling commentary, written out of frustration and referring to the Georgians' slights, jokes, and sneers that Mary had probably endured silently for years, leaving her bitter and hurt. Perhaps Mary was able to reconcile her bicultural heritage in her own mind, but the inability or unwillingness of others to accept her Indian relatives as equals must have made it an anxiety-filled enterprise requiring constant introspection and negotiation.

After penning the memorial, Mary forwarded it to Alexander Heron, who sent it along to Andrew Stone, the Duke of Newcastle's Undersecretary of State. Heron, recently installed as the commander at Frederica, had known the Bosomworths for several years, was favorably inclined toward them, and was supportive of Mary's financial claims. For example, in a cover letter Heron penned to Stone on September 8, he described Mary as a "most useful person" who had been of "infinite service" to the colony.[63] Tellingly, Heron continued to sing Mary's praises in subsequent letters to Stone and others, which led some Georgia officials to regard Heron as the Bosomworths' co-conspirator, a charge not entirely lacking in merit.[64]

Heron was also a quick study in Indian affairs and favorably inclined toward the many Creek Indians who had fought with him against Spain in the War of Jenkins' Ear. Eager to meet with the Indians in his new capacity as Frederica's commander, Heron invited Malatchi and Chigelly to visit him at the fort that fall. After several delays, Malatchi and at least sixteen

Lower Creeks passed by Mary's trading post at the Forks in November, and she joined them on the final leg of their journey to Frederica. Malatchi and Heron finally met face-to-face on December 7, when they exchanged conciliatory speeches. Seemingly impressed by Malatchi's oratory, Heron agreed to Malatchi's proposal to send Abraham Bosomworth to England, where he was to articulate Creek grievances and request an annual allotment of presents.[65]

If on one level a peace overture, Malatchi's speech was also significant for its promotion of Mary's interests by corroborating the claims she made in her August 1747 memorial. Malatchi likewise supported Mary's assertion—which Georgia authorities later contested—that she was descended from Coweta's leading family. On nine separate occasions during the oration, Malatchi referred to Mary as "my sister" or "our sister," artfully adding that she was "of my own blood." This did not mean, however, that Malatchi and Mary were siblings. Rather, it is likely that Malatchi was using the Muskogee compound word *cewvnwv*, which literally means "my sister" but was commonly used to refer to a range of women, roughly equivalent in age to the speaker, who belonged to the same clan.[66] If Mary is to be believed, she and Malatchi were, by English reckonings, cousins on her mother's side and related to Brims, the "old Emperor" of Coweta. As the term could also be applied to adoptive relatives, Malatchi was not wrong in using it euphemistically on behalf of other members of his entourage, who claimed different clan affiliations.

Given that Mary was interpreting, the words she attributed to Malatchi may actually have been her own. At least one witness to the December 1747 proceedings believed that Mary was putting words into Malatchi's mouth and accused them of collaborating to press Mary's land claims.[67] In fact, the Bosomworths and Malatchi had been conspiring since August to devise a paper trail suitable for that and other purposes. When Abraham went to Coweta that month, for example, he had several deerskin traders sign an affidavit attesting to Mary's services to the colony. More importantly, Malatchi and Chigelly signed a deed granting Mary, Thomas, and Abraham an equal share of the Yamacraw tract and of St. Catherine's Island.[68] In return, Abraham offered to go to England to voice Creek grievances to the highest British authorities and to request an annual allowance for presents amounting to three thousand pounds. At the same time, Abraham was to represent his brother and sister-in-law by requesting for them a portion of the presents he expected to be allotted to the Creeks and to present the secretary of state with further documentation in support of their land claims.

A flurry of new and improved paperwork followed Heron's encounter with Malatchi. To give a semblance of legitimacy to Malatchi's authority to convey land, the Bosomworths drafted a "Declaration" in which the Creeks declared Malatchi their "natural prince." On December 14 sixteen men, all from Lower Creek towns, signed their names to the document, which empowered Malatchi to "stand by, ratify, and confirm every act and deed of his as much as if we ourselves were personally present" and "transact all affairs relating to our nation." Three days later, Alexander Heron and several other officers from Frederica put their names to an affidavit acknowledging Mary's influence with the Creeks and the Bosomworths' loyalty to the Crown, a maneuver intended to diffuse forthcoming accusations of treason. Having empowered Malatchi on paper to act on the Creeks' behalf, on January 4, 1748, Thomas and Mary had him affix his mark to a deed in which he granted them title to the three coastal islands—Sapelo, Ossebaw, and St. Catherine's—to which the Creeks had a historic claim. In exchange, Malatchi received a handsome array of presents, ranging from gunpowder to pistols, as well as thirty head of the breeding cattle the couple kept on St. Catherine's Island.[69]

While the Bosomworths kept these transactions private and did not have them entered into the public record for several more years, Georgia officials nevertheless learned more or less what the couple was up to. Undeterred, Bosomworth responded to one critic by saying that obtaining grants directly from the Indians would force the king's hand to honor them. His reasoning was simple: the Creek Indians were a sovereign entity and not subjects of the king. As "allies" rather than subjects, then, the Creeks had the full power to sell land as they saw fit. Some believed the illegal conveyance of land was tantamount to treason, but Thomas professed loyalty to the Crown and continued to insist that, because the Creeks had granted him the land, the king would be "obliged" to honor the deeds.[70]

The course on which Mary and Thomas embarked in the summer of 1747, namely to compile a more robust paper trail, thus set the Bosomworth controversy on a new track. Up to that time, Mary's petitions had presented her past uncompensated service to the colony as the primary justification for honoring her claims. While Mary continued to invoke her service record, the later documents not only made Malatchi and other

Creeks complicit in her affairs but also asserted the territorial sovereignty of the Creek nation. This assertion effectively elevated the dispute to a new and abstract level involving British conceptions of law and empire, as well as the evolving concept of Creek nationhood. Abstractions put to paper, however, had real-world consequences for the parties involved, and their eventual confrontation in the streets of Savannah would be anything but abstract.

7 🖋 *Coosaponakeesa*

Wee the General Assembled Estates ... of the upper and lower
Creek Nations ... declare and grant to our beloved Woman
Cousaponakeesa (alias Mary Bosomworth) as our rightful and
natural Princess of the said Upper and lower Creek Nations, our
full power and Authority ...

Creek Headmen, 1750

The white people always respected her, until She Married
Bosomworth, but she has since been fond a Lyer; that if She was
a relation of yours (speaking to Malatchi) she would be looked on
[as] such; but we well know that She is not of your Family, being
a Daughter of a Woman of the Tuckabatchee Town (of no note or
family) by a White Man.

William Stephens, 1749

As I am informed ... that there is an immediate necessity of sending
an agent to the Creek Nation. . . . My zeal for His Majesty's service
lays me under obligation to make an offer of my best services in
negotiating those matters with the Creek Nation, provided the
government will employ me in such a manner as is consistent with
my character. . . . I believe your Excellency is not insensible of the
present unhappy situation of my Husband's affairs.

Mary Bosomworth, 1752

BY 1748 THE PAPER WAR BETWEEN the Bosomworths and Georgia
authorities was well under way. The confrontation would turn physical, or
nearly so, when in 1749 Mary and Thomas descended upon Savannah to
wrest from the government some Indian presents that she believed were

her due upon royal authority. To exert pressure upon the officers in charge of their distribution, the Bosomworths brought Malatchi and certain of their Creek friends, who sparred verbally with the Georgia magistrates by day and nearly came to blows during several memorable nighttime encounters. Skeptical Georgia officials, who denied owing Mary anything, employed divide-and-conquer tactics to temporarily isolate the Bosomworths from the Creeks and withhold from Mary the presents she had expected to receive. Over the course of their stay, Mary was jailed twice for disturbing the peace, and Thomas wound up in jail for debt. By any measure, the so-called Savannah incident was a disaster for the Bosomworths, and did their case far more harm than good.

With the odds seemingly stacked against them, the Bosomworths happened upon an opportunity to restore their reputation (as well as their finances) when South Carolina's governor put out a call for an Indian agent to obtain satisfaction for the Creek murder of some Cherokee men. Happening to be in Charles Town at just the right moment, Mary and Thomas volunteered for the position and improbably succeeded in orchestrating the execution of one man and laying the groundwork for a peace agreement between the Cherokees and Creeks. Successful by any standard, the Creek agency earned the Bosomworths the respect and support of the South Carolina governor James Glen, which effectively revived their case and renewed their hope for future restitution of their claims.

To plead her case in a way that was consistent with Thomas' (and the Creeks') theory that the conveyance of land was a matter between Indians, Mary continued to embellish her Coweta heritage in order to claim the improbable title "natural princess" of the Creeks. This marked the beginning of a period of in Mary's life when she identified more openly as an Indian. To complete the makeover, Mary assumed the name "Coosaponakeesa" (meaning "Coosa language holder/bearer"), which was in keeping with the Creek practice of assuming different names over the span of one's life and justifiable because of her decades of service as an interpreter. Those who would deny Mary's claims, in particular President William Stephens of Georgia, thought that these embellishments were tantamount to fabrications and that the Creeks had never acquiesced to Mary's presumed authority as their princess. What cannot be denied, though, is that the Creeks honored Mary with the title of "great beloved woman," and in that role she exercised real authority that would prove instrumental in the conduct of the Creek agency.

The "Savannah incident" refers to a series of tense confrontations between the Bosomworths, the Creek Indians, and Georgia officials that took place in the colony's capital over July and August 1749. Events in Savannah did not materialize out of thin air, but had been gradually building for about a year. Around November 1748, Thomas received letters from England indicating that the Trustees had received affidavits "tending to prove me guilty of treason" for illegally purchasing Indian land.[1] News of these charges was apparently widespread, as the Bosomworths' friends at Frederica had been apprised of the situation, and even the Cowetas entertained rumors that Mary and Thomas were "shortly to be sent to England in irons."[2]

In the midst of this brewing maelstrom, Mary and Thomas went about their business as best they could. Mary seems to have resumed trading, while Thomas earned a bit of extra cash filling in as the chaplain to the regiment at Frederica.[3] Meanwhile, Abraham Bosomworth was busy carrying out his assignment in England. After shipping off sometime in January or February, Abraham arrived in London that spring and submitted several proposals devised by his brother, Mary, and Alexander Heron. In a stroke of good fortune, Secretary of State John Russell, Duke of Bedford, consented to many of the Bosomworths' demands. First, Bedford convinced the king to agree to an annual stipend of 3,000 pounds for presents to the Indians of Georgia and South Carolina, to be distributed by two agents representing each colony. To ensure that Mary and Thomas's interests would be represented at the bargaining table, Bedford recommended Abraham Bosomworth as South Carolina's distribution agent.

In all likelihood Mary and Thomas learned of the arrival of Abraham and the king's presents sometime that spring. They also had good reason to expect that Mary would receive a share of them, leaving it to the discretion of the distribution agents to decide how much. The surviving correspondence of the Duke of Bedford, the governor and the Council of South Carolina, and even the Georgia Trustees suggests such an arrangement.[4] The only person standing in their way, then, was Georgia's distribution agent, President William Stephens, with whom Mary had a long and checkered history.

What happened next is somewhat difficult to determine. The most likely scenario, though, unfolded as follows. During the summer of 1749 Mary and Thomas were again seriously considering going to England.

Upon hearing that Abraham had arrived in Charles Town with the royal presents, however, the couple postponed their voyage, expecting to receive a portion of the presents as a windfall. Knowing, however, that it would be difficult to convince William Stephens to invest them with the gifts, Mary and Thomas decided to bring Malatchi to Savannah to exert pressure on the president. Thomas then ventured to Coweta in July and lured Malatchi and two Cussita headmen to Savannah by telling them that Abraham had returned from England with a "talk" from the king—presumably a response to Malatchi's December 1747 speech to Heron. Thomas also seems to have tried to dispel the rumor that he and Mary were to be sent to England "in irons" and wanted Malatchi to see with his own eyes that his "sister" intended to go there on her own free will.[5]

While he never confessed to as much, Thomas probably made it known that the royal presents for the Indians had arrived, which may explain why other parties of Creek Indians (totaling upward of seventy-five) set off for Savannah eight days after Bosomworth departed with Malatchi.[6] On the evening of Friday, July 21, Thomas and Malatchi met up with Mary in Savannah, thus setting the stage for the most famous Indian confrontation in the history of colonial Georgia.[7]

Following Thomas's arrival in Savannah, a three-week game of cat and mouse ensued, as the Bosomworths and the magistrates each tried to gain the upper hand at the proceedings.[8] First, the Georgia magistrates removed Mary from the position of interpreter and replaced her with the trader John Kennard, undoubtedly to lessen Mary's influence. The Bosomworths and Malatchi appear to have employed scare tactics in retaliation, when on August 9 Thomas Bosomworth loaned one of his boats to Malatchi and a group of followers, who paddled against a high tide to reach Savannah in the middle of the night. Firing their guns as they approached town, some interpreted the gunshots as a "menacing and insulting" gesture. The magistrates countered the next morning by sending a few workmen to cut a path from the site of the Musgroves' old trading post to the western terminus of Savannah, thereby intentionally transecting the disputed Yamacraw tract the Bosomworths claimed. In protest, the couple had Malatchi's followers seize the cutting tools and deposit them back across the town line.[9]

The magistrates' first public conference with the Creek Indians began on Friday, August 11. At 10 o'clock that morning the Indians disembarked at the old Musgrove trading post, where the militia cavalry met them. Following an old custom, the Indians and cavalry responded in kind by laying down their weapons as they approached the town line. There, the entourage was met by the main body of the militia, which led the procession through town, followed by Thomas Bosomworth dressed in his "canonical habit," with Mary, Adam, Malatchi, and the rest of the Indians trailing behind. When the Creek delegation reached William Stephens' house, they took their places "in order" of rank and passed around pipes and glasses that had been distributed for toasting. Once the pomp had ended, Malatchi rose to speak, explaining that he had come to town to hear Abraham Bosomworth's "talk" from the king and to see whether Mary was to be arrested and sent to England in irons. After the magistrates dispelled that rumor, Malatchi insisted that Mary be reinstated as interpreter.

The Georgia magistrates denied Malatchi's request, and Mary responded with her first notable outburst, declaring herself the "Empress and Queen" of the Creek nation and denying her allegiance to the king of England. When the acrimonious talks ended, the magistrates invited the Creeks to dinner, at which point Mary and Malatchi abruptly left with some of their followers. Six of the Creeks stayed behind, evidently to show that their "esteem and authority" equaled Malatchi's. Importantly, it would not be the last time that Creeks would point out the limits of Malatchi's authority.

By five o'clock that evening, the magistrates and Indians had finished their dinner and gone their separate ways. Stephens expected to enjoy a quiet evening, but Adam Bosomworth, his servant Joseph Piercy, and Malatchi's followers got hold of a drum and began beating it as they paraded through the streets of Savannah. The locals interpreted this parade as some kind of war signal, fueling an errant rumor that the Indians had cut off William Stephens' head and spurring the militia into action. When a few of the magistrates finally caught up with the parade, they promptly arrested Piercy and Adam Bosomworth. Protesting their innocence, Malatchi offered to talk things over at William Stephens' home. Once there, Mary burst onto the scene in a "mad and frantic" state. Before a group of onlookers, Mary spoke her mind. "You talk of your white town, your general and his treaties," Mary began, proceeding to curse Oglethorpe's name and remind her audience that the land now occupied by Georgia had originally belonged to the Creeks. Mary added a theatrical twist by stamping her foot as she declared that "the very ground was hers," a thinly veiled reminder that she and John Musgrove had lived there before the arrival of the first Georgia settlers. By that point, the magistrates had heard enough, and they seized Mary and put her in detention in a nearby "private house."

After cooling down for a while, the magistrates agreed to release Mary and Adam Bosomworth, on the condition that they bring the Creeks into town the next morning at eight o'clock for another round of talks. When morning arrived Malatchi and the Bosomworths tried to postpone the meetings on the grounds that, despite their promises to stay sober, the Indians were hungover from the last night's drinking binge. Facing the threat of jail time, Mary and Thomas managed to convince the Indians to meet with the magistrates at three o'clock. When they arrived, Stephens shrewdly used the opportunity to drive a wedge between Malatchi and the Bosomworths. First, he told Malatchi that the Bosomworths were only using him to advance their own "selfish aims" and asked the Indians bluntly if they were "willing to receive two blankets and let Bosomworth have the third, and so in proportion of all that the great king had sent them"? The Indians responded "no," having been unaware that the Bosomworths' share of the presents was to come directly out of theirs. Stephens then took the opportunity to ask Malatchi about Mary's position as the "empress and princess" of the Creeks. Again, he put it to him bluntly, "Are you the chief or is she?" To that question Malatchi responded angrily that he could never be ranked "with an old woman." With his mission accomplished, Stephens sent the chiefs on their way, informing Malatchi that his people would receive their presents from the king in a few days.[10]

It is curious that Malatchi was so quick to deny the Bosomworths their presents and Mary the authority she claimed as a Creek "princess." Rather than nursing a hangover that morning, Malatchi probably spent his time holed up with the Bosomworths as they drafted a document recognizing "Coosaponakeesa" as the Creeks' "rightfull and naturall princess," empowering her to negotiate in their behalf. Composed under duress and in haste, it was perhaps the least effective instrument Thomas had devised, not least because the sobriety and allegiances of its signers (most were close friends of Malatchi) were questionable, as was Mary's status as a Creek "princess." Still, Thomas partly succeeded in covering the tracks of Mary's outburst the previous day.[11]

The August 12 "recognition" is especially important because it marks the first recorded instance of Mary identifying herself as "Coosaponakeesa," long thought to be her childhood Creek name. A careful examination of the word's literal meaning and of the context in which it first appeared, however, tells a different story. "Coosaponakeesa" is a compound of three Muskogee words that translates as "Coosa language holder/bearer," a highly unusual name for a baby or young girl who could not yet speak. A better explanation is that Mary adopted this name (or had it bestowed upon her by Creeks) as an adult, and that it was a recent construction acknowledging her prominence as a translator. Her timing is also of consequence; Mary had only recently been removed as the interpreter for the Savannah proceedings, and identifying herself as the "Coosa language holder" was perhaps a means of protesting her dismissal. Constructed in the heat of the moment or not, the name stuck, and Mary continued to employ it in subsequent petitions.

Finally, on Thursday, August 17, more than seventy Indians, including women and children, descended upon Savannah to receive the presents that had been promised them several days earlier. Thomas Bosomworth also happened to be in attendance and, after drinks were served, Malatchi delivered a long talk in which he reiterated Mary's land claims and defended her pretensions to authority as "empress." Malatchi then pulled out the "recognition" of Mary as "Princess" that he had helped to compose on August 12, and it was read aloud. Needless to say, the English members of the audience were "universally displeased" with its contents. Observing that the audience regarded the document as a "bad talk," Malatchi requested to see it again, proclaiming that he "did not know what was in it."

With even Malatchi questioning the motives of his "sister," Stephens used every trick in the book to denigrate Mary and her husband. He began by lying about Mary's social standing at the time the colony was founded, insisting that she was in "mean and low circumstances" but had been elevated by Oglethorpe because of her ability to speak Muskogee. Mary, he added, had no land to give to the settlers, and he further insisted that Oglethorpe had obtained consent to settle from "all the Head and Old men of the nation." Stephens even denied her relationship to Malatchi, ridiculing Mary as the progeny of a white man and a Tuckabatchee woman "of no note or family." Sensing that the time was right, Stephens asked if the Indians were "willing to let [Bosomworth] have part of these presents designed for them." Predictably, the Indians answered "no," adding that "their eyes had been opened" to the Bosomworths' scheming. Malatchi relinquished the paper he had brandished before the magistrates, and the magistrates promptly burned it.

At seven o'clock that evening, the magistrates gathered with Malatchi and other Indians at a tavern, which was to be the setting for Mary's second dramatic outburst. The Indians and Magistrates shared drinks, and all appeared well until Mary rushed into the tavern "in the most violent outrageous and unseemly manner," presumably because she had had too much to drink. Advised to return home, Mary responded with another verbal tirade in which she repeated her claim as the Creek "empress and queen." The magistrates threatened arrest and made good on their word by having peace officers drag Mary to the guardhouse. Some of the Indians slipped out of the tavern fearing for their lives. Meanwhile, Thomas approached Mary as she was being escorted to prison, verbally assaulting the guards with "many oaths and curses" that issued uncharacteristically from the minister's mouth. Thomas admitted his wife's "ill conduct," but he justified it by saying that Oglethorpe had "ruined her" and everyone else with his utopian schemes. The whole Georgia enterprise, he claimed, "was a bubble," adding that land titles were worth no more than the snap of a finger.

Mary spent the rest of that night in jail. The next morning, Thomas appealed for clemency, promising that in the future Mary would "behave as a prudent woman ought." The magistrates released Mary and delivered a strong rebuke that elicited from her (as Stephens claimed) a confession. Later that afternoon, the Indians received the remainder of their presents, and a humbled Malatchi delivered another submissive speech. That evening, another dinner was served, and the Indians departed Savannah at noon the next day, August 19. Two hours later, Abraham Bosomworth arrived bearing his commission from the South Carolina governor as distribution agent.[12]

The entire Savannah incident occupied roughly three weeks of Mary's sixty-plus-year life. Yet, the scathing reports of her behavior generated the image of Mary as a madwoman who was unable to control her emotions, her tongue, or her taste for alcohol, an image that historians have only affirmed. But how might Mary have seen things? To answer that question we must offer some explanation as to why an otherwise good woman could have lost control of herself, even to the point of pursuing self-interest to the detriment of her unlettered Indian relatives.

First, we must acknowledge the magnitude of the Bosomworths' debts and missing income and recognize that by 1749 the threat of losing their entire estate was not an idle one. The numbers are telling. Before she had ever laid eyes on Thomas Bosomworth, Mary probably owed in excess of one thousand pounds to various creditors and had forfeited several hundred more that had been invested in the destroyed Mount Venture property. After marrying Bosomworth, Mary's descent into debt continued when her husband began borrowing money. In 1746 alone, Thomas incurred between 600 and 700 pounds of debt, and Alexander Heron owed Mary roughly 650 pounds, which he could not pay. So, even a modest calculation of Mary's debt indicates that she owed in excess of 3,000 pounds. When one accounts for her uncompensated work as an interpreter, and the amount presumably owed to her in crop bounties, Mary was not entirely off the mark by claiming losses in excess of 5,700 pounds.[13] When one considers the relatively good position from which Mary started in 1733, Thomas's comment that Mary was "laboring under every circumstance of distress" becomes all the more understandable.[14]

Exacerbating that financial distress was social stigmatization, which by 1749 had left her isolated from most other colonists. Perhaps the explanation is simple: that she brought it on herself by claiming more land than the rules allowed and by luring hostile Indians into town.[15] But it is also plausible that Mary endured social stigmatization because of the class bias of the magistrates, who resented her insolence and her brazen attempts to elevate herself through property acquisition.[16] It is equally plausible that others stigmatized Mary because she flaunted English (and perhaps Creek) gender norms by refusing to act submissively and by challenging male prerogatives in the public sphere.

It is noteworthy, for example, that Stephens, in his harangue against the Indians during the August 12 meeting, exploited the misogyny of Creek men in order to isolate Mary and expose her as a pretender to imperial authority. While Creek and English conceptions of gender differed significantly, historically it is also the case that European and Indian men forged common diplomatic ground via their shared notions of female subordination.[17] Shrewdly, Stephens managed to accomplish this by asking Malatchi the "impolitic" question of whether he or Mary was the chief. Asked to think of it this way, Malatchi momentarily abandoned the urge to call her "my sister" and chafed at having his political authority usurped by "an old woman." Stephens even managed to appeal to Thomas Bosomworth's gender sensibilities, when he elicited his promise to make her behave "as a good wife ought"—in a word, submissively.

The social stigmatization that Mary experienced was also a function of her race, as is made evident in Thomas's account of the Savannah incident, which includes details William Stephens conveniently omitted. One gets a sense of the colonists' general dislike of Indians, for example, when Thomas describes how on the night of August 17 (that of Mary's second arrest), a mob formed around the guardhouse where she was detained, crying, "Damn them, shoot them all."[18] The most noteworthy exchange concerning Mary took place the night of her infamous foot-stomping speech. Amid the verbal scuffling, the magistrate Henry Parker accosted Thomas, Mary, and the Indians with a series of questions that betrayed his discomfort with Mary's racial ambiguity. First, he directed his questions at Thomas: Has she been baptized? Has she received the sacrament [of the church]? Has she stood as godmother to children? Thomas correctly responded in the affirmative to each, but the line of interrogation implies that Parker was calling into question Mary's credentials as a Christian, which she had artfully used for many years to parry accusations of being a "heathen." After Thomas affirmed Mary's Christian faith, Parker concluded that those "spiritual advantages" deprived her of her "natural right" as an Indian, meaning that, to Parker, one could not be both a Christian and an Indian.

Parker then put it to the Indians bluntly, "Is Mary an Indian or a white person?" The Indians replied that they had always looked upon her "as one of themselves." Parker then directed the same question at Mary, who replied that she had "always acknowledged herself as an Indian." "Madam," Parker retorted, "if I had told you so you would have spit in my face."[19] Parker's final comment is telling for the way it hints at how Mary tried to downplay her Indian heritage, as if being called an "Indian" was some kind of insult. In effect, Parker was asking Mary to choose sides, making it difficult, if not impossible, for her to sustain the cultural balancing act she had pulled off so effectively for years.

If she had "always acknowledged herself as an Indian," then why did Mary try to deceive Malatchi and other Creeks? Malatchi knew more about Mary's legal disputes than did any other Creek Indian, and generally he understood the tenor of the various papers he signed. But Mary also withheld information from him, as she did by not explaining that the August 12 "Recognition" had usurped his authority as "chief" by naming her "empress." If Malatchi was at times only dimly aware of Mary's designs, then other Creek headmen were even less so. Their unwillingness to give up a portion of the presents to Mary suggests she had never revealed that her share was to be subtracted from theirs. Thus the Indians' accusation that the Bosomworths had "deceived" them has merit. Moreover, on various occasions other Creeks had disavowed Malatchi's authority, which by association called Mary's into question.[20]

How, then, could Mary ever claim to be "empress" of the Creeks? The assertion is preposterous on many levels. Mary knew the Creek political system too well to believe the Creeks would accept the idea of being governed by a single figurehead, much less a woman. One might guess that she intended it as a threat to back up her self-presumed ability to "command a thousand fighting men." Perhaps it was also a way of emphasizing her Indian heritage at the expense of her English one. At the very least, it was consistent with her husband's shrewd legal strategy, which invested Mary with extensive powers to negotiate on the Creeks' behalf on both sides of the "great water," thus empowering her to transact business in England, where she had intended to go for quite some time.

Whatever Mary's intention, it is the Creeks' understanding of the document that is arguably most important, as it indicates the specific role they ascribed to Mary—"old beloved woman." To the Creeks, a "beloved woman" was an honorary title assigned to a class of women, usually of advanced age (Mary was now approaching fifty, "old" in eighteenth-century terms). It was the feminine parallel to the male rank of *isti atcagagi*, or "beloved men," which was reserved for aged men known for their wisdom and achievements, who counseled town *micos* in the exercise of governance. Although it was rare for women to receive the distinction, it was not unheard of.[21] In all likelihood, the Creek men who signed that document did so in recognition of Mary's linguistic skills and of her general knowledge of the ways of the world beyond the Creek nation. In other words, the title was a good fit for Mary's unique abilities, which Malatchi once recognized by saying "she has more sense than we [the Indians]."[22] In their eyes at least, she was a peacemaker and not the madwoman white antagonists made her out to be.

Aftermath: More Give-and-Take

Just two days after the Creeks departed from Savannah, Thomas Bosomworth was arrested for debt, a circumstance that helps to explain the couple's desperation during the tumultuous summer of 1749. Three years earlier, Thomas had borrowed 400 pounds from three different individuals—Jonathan Bryan of South Carolina and Grey Elliot and John Macpherson of Georgia. These men initiated four separate debt lawsuits against him the moment it became clear that no Indian presents were forthcoming. The Bosomworths could not even come up with enough bail money to free Thomas, who was forced to spend a few days in jail. Writing from his cell, Thomas pleaded with the President and Assistants for mercy, reminding them that the colony had originally been intended as a philanthropic project to benefit poor debtors. He didn't try to justify his or his wife's behavior, but again submitted abstracts of old letters from Oglethorpe and William Horton to remind the magistrates of Mary's past service to the colony, which he hoped would "deface and blot out" Mary's recent "rash unguarded expressions." His efforts had little effect, but Thomas's deferential tone seems to have won his release, as the magistrates decided not to "[pursue] the most rigorous steps" against the couple, perhaps to avert further confrontations with the Indians.[23]

Hounded by creditors and almost universally hated in Savannah, Mary and Thomas wisely decided to lay low for a while. As their debts made it impossible for them to acquire goods, the couple was forced to abandon their trading post at the Forks. Mary probably spent that fall collecting her belongings there and getting situated on St. Catherine's Island. In the meantime Thomas sought out the friendlier confines of Charles Town and spent four months there beginning in September. He was therefore likely on hand to witness the wedding, on November 2, of his brother Abraham to Sarah Seabrooke, heiress to a large estate in South Carolina. Thomas lingered in the South Carolina capital for at least a month after the wedding, probably in an attempt to find new sources of credit. Luckily he did, as one of Mary's former neighbors at Frederica, the surgeon Frederick Hobzendorf, was in town, and Thomas somehow got him to agree to a 400-pound loan, dated December 8 (the precise amount Thomas owed to Habersham, Elliot, and Bryan).[24] To raise a bit of extra income, sometime in December Thomas began granting timber leases to "sundry individuals," and, as expected, the magistrates issued a public advertisement prohibiting the cutting of timber by virtue of the "pretended" leases. Thwarted again, Thomas and Mary resumed their quiet lifestyle and little would be heard of them for the next seven months.[25]

As with the other parties involved, the Creek Indians continued to experience the ripple effects of the Savannah incident, though it seems that different individuals drew different conclusions depending upon their closeness to the Bosomworths and whether they experienced the tumult in Savannah firsthand. For one thing, the magistrates' decision to keep the militia on guard constantly seems to have backfired, as its acts of aggression and verbal taunting caused many Indians, among them women and children, to fear being killed.[26] Malatchi in particular appears to have been "disgusted" with the proceedings, causing him to plunder two farmsteads and spread "bad talks" about the Georgians on his way home from Savannah.[27] It is doubtful, though, that Malatchi's opinions about the "white people" were widely shared, at least not in their intensity. That fall the Georgia and South Carolina governments received visits from several friendly parties of Creeks, who accepted presents and disavowed Malatchi's authority to give away their land.[28]

By midsummer 1750, however, colonial officials were again hearing disturbing reports of hostile Indian activity, much of it concerning French efforts to court Malatchi and his Creek followers.[29] To Georgia officials it must have been an eerie coincidence that Mary Bosomworth was at the same time making plans to relocate to the Creek nation, or so it appeared. On July 29, two traders reported that Mary was "daily expected" at Tuckebatchee with her stock of cattle. As it turned out, Mary's destination was instead Coweta, where she arrived in late July accompanied by her brother-in-law Adam Bosomworth and her servant Joseph Piercy. Rather than her cattle, Mary brought three documents that Thomas had prepared in advance. Basically, they were windier versions of the deeds the Creeks had previously signed, one of which granted Mary and Thomas title to the three islands and another title to the Yamacraw tract. The third document confirmed Creek recognition of Mary as the nation's "princess." Presumably, Mary made their contents known to Malatchi and a few other headmen. But she appears to have kept that information largely confidential, and instead sold the Creeks on the idea that the papers would enable her to represent them in England, much as Abraham Bosomworth had done two years before.[30]

Although Mary and Thomas had succeeded in staying largely out of sight, they were certainly not out of mind for Georgia officials, who kept a close watch on them and took various measures to bring them to heel.[31] First, the magistrates installed two of their avowed enemies—Patrick Graham and Henry Parker—in influential positions, as distribution agent and secretary for Indian affairs, respectively.[32] Working from London, on July 16 the Trustees initiated a process by which to acquire the Yamacraw tract, recommending a gift of "extraordinary presents" to gain the Indians' consent.[33] Back in Georgia, the colony's inaugural House of Assembly convened in January 1751, and one of their first matters of business was to draw up a "Representation" against Thomas and Mary citing their extravagant land claims and threatening behavior in Savannah as evidence for treason. As the government proceeded against the Bosomworths, private individuals also got into the act. That fall, the mercantile firm of Harris & Habersham and a widow named Ann Harris filed three debt lawsuits against the couple, leading to the seizure of some deerskins and two of their boats at St. Simons Island.[34]

In spite of the hostility directed toward them, the Bosomworths would not relent in pressing their claims. One matter of unfinished business involved their projected voyage to England. To raise money for that voyage (and perhaps to keep their creditors at bay) Mary and Thomas sold off their remaining properties in Savannah in March 1751. First, the couple relinquished their town lot, which they sold to the victualer John Teasdale for eighty pounds. On March 12 Mary and Thomas sold the Cowpen to Mary's long-time friend and former servant, William Francis, who died in possession of the tract that became more commonly known as "The Grange."[35] Selling the Cowpen, in particular, must have been a sad occasion for Mary, who invoked the names of her deceased first husband, John Musgrove, and her deceased sons, James and Edward, when composing the deed to Francis. Also sobering was the fact that the Cowpen netted the Bosomworths a mere sixty-one pounds, hardly a princely sum for a tract of land that had once been productive and economically promising.

The Bosomworths also took the opportunity to needle the government with another round of petitions demanding some of what remained of the royal Indian presents. Neither the board nor the recently constituted House was receptive, particularly after the Bosomworths' activity had been represented as treasonous. House members in particular seemed exasperated. "We can see no end to what Mr. Bosomworth and his advisers mean by this," wrote several House members, adding that to deal with them leniently would only encourage the Bosomworths to disturb the peace again. The time had come, they argued, "to use extremeties."[36]

In response to the damning evidence compiled against the Bosomworths, the Trustees recommended sending a "proper person" to Augusta to hold a conference with the Creeks in order to purchase the Yamacraw tract and the three islands.[37] By then, Georgia officials had already taken matters into their own hands, spurred by the trader George Galphin's startling recommendation: "if you will send me an instrument of writing to disannul the one [Mary] has got done, then I am sure I can get more headmen than she had to sign hers."[38] The magistrates eventually accepted Galphin's advice, but instead, on April 21, 1751, named Patrick Graham as their agent to the Creeks.

Graham's instructions were to counter Mary's influence among the Lower Creeks by courting the Upper Creeks who lived on the Coosa and Talapoosa Rivers. Graham was to give the headmen "a large quantity of valuable presents" and then to find a "prudent means" to get them to relinquish the three disputed islands and the Yamacraw tract. If he succeeded in these aims, he was to proceed to the Lower Creeks to do the same and to remove any "jealousies."[39] Bearing these instructions Graham departed Georgia in early May and arrived in Okchay later that month.

In Okchay, Graham castigated the Bosomworths for their "foolish and idle" claims, asking the Upper Creeks "if it would not be unreasonable" for them to convey the disputed land to their friend and brother, the king of Great Britain. Graham distributed presents, and twenty-five Upper Creeks signed a deed conveying the lands to the Trustees.[40] The Graham deed later became a sticking point when Upper Creek leaders protested that they did not know what they were signing, but for the moment it appeared that Graham had accomplished what the board had sent him to do. Following orders, Graham went to Coweta on June 3 to get the Lower Creeks to consent to the action the Upper Creeks had taken. He received a generally favorable reception there and managed to get the Lower Creeks to deny their conveyance of land to Mary. When he asked to purchase the land from them for the Trustees, however, Graham met with stiff resistance. Reflecting their usufructuary conception of land rights, the Indians declared that they had no objection to lending the Trustees the land for use "during pleasure," but they refused to make an absolute cession.[41]

Although Graham returned to Savannah with his mission only partially accomplished, his work did much to convince Georgia officials that they had finally turned the tide against the Bosomworths. The deed he obtained from the Upper Creeks, after all, had more than three times the number of Indian signatures as the recent Bosomworth deeds, and even the Lower Creeks refused to confirm the cessions they had supposedly made to Mary.[42] The "next step," the Trustees discerned, was to use presents to induce the Lower Creeks to make an "absolute cession" of the disputed lands. Little did they know just how difficult Mary and Thomas would make it for them to take that next giant step.[43]

The Creek Agency

Mary's agency to the Creek Indians in the fall of 1752 was one of the signature achievements in her eventful life. While she was not installed in an official capacity (the commission was made out in Thomas's name), Mary's knowledge of the inner workings of the Creek kinship system enabled her to help orchestrate the execution of a Creek warrior named Acorn Whistler for the murder of several Cherokee men outside of Charles Town. While there was ample evidence that Acorn Whistler was an innocent man, Mary was able to persuade his Creek relatives of the necessity of his death and convince South Carolina officials to accept it as satisfaction for the murders. In so doing, Mary diverted attention away from her Lower Creek kinsmen who perpetrated the crime and earned praise from the South Carolina governor James Glen. By playing the South Carolina government against that of Georgia, the Creek agency effectively revived the Bosomworths' case.

To understand the circumstances that led to the Creek agency, it is important to remember that a state of war existed between the Creeks and Cherokees. The Cherokees had made a habit of paying unexpected visits to Governor Glen, and these visits attracted Creek war parties bent upon picking off stray Cherokees on their return trip. Among these war parties was a band of eleven Upper Creeks led by one Acorn Whistler, who along with twenty-six Lower Creeks descended uninvited upon Charles Town in late March. A group of Cherokees arrived a few days later to pay Governor Glen a surprise visit, and Glen made the best of the situation by pacifying both sides with presents and kind words. All seemed to be going well until April 1, when Glen dismissed both delegations and sent them home. On the path leading away from Charles Town, a party of Creeks met up with the Cherokees, feigned peace overtures, and killed them in cold blood (estimates range between six and ten dead). A manhunt for the perpetrators ensued, as Acorn Whistler was held in Charles Town for questioning. Acorn Whistler denied being involved in the murders and blamed the Lower Creeks, who were rumored to have been heading south with one Cherokee prisoner still in their possession. But Acorn Whistler gave shifty and inconsistent answers that left just enough doubt in people's minds as to whether the perpetrators were Upper or Lower Creeks.[44]

Normally, the killing of Indians by other Indians would have aroused little concern in Glen or any other colonial governor, who tended to intervene only when warfare posed a direct threat to the colonies. This situation was different, however, in that the murders occurred within the colonial settlements and the Cherokees had been under the protection of the South Carolina government. Glen also probably took the matter personally, as the Cherokees were murdered a mere half mile from his home. The governor therefore resolved to take some kind of action, arguing that to do otherwise would dishonor his colony's reputation and, as he put it, "render ourselves cheap and contemptible to all Indians." Specifically, Glen intended to target Malatchi and the Lower Creeks, whom he regarded as the perpetrators of the crime, indicating as much in every verbal and written address he issued that year between April and June. Glen tried to diffuse the situation first by drafting a letter of condolence to the Cherokees, which was soon followed by a letter to his "friends and brothers" the Upper Creeks that exonerated Acorn Whistler.[45] As for the Lower Creeks, Glen wanted satisfaction for the murders and the restoration of the Cherokee prisoner believed to be still in their possession.[46]

As it turned out, Glen never sent these dispatches, because, in his estimation, a situation this serious required the services of an agent who could pressure the Creeks in person to give in to these demands. Glen first floated the idea before the council on April 28, and sent a message to the assembly requesting funding for the proposed agency to the Creeks.[47] The Assembly, which tended to be parsimonious anyway, refused on the grounds that pressing the Creeks in this manner might "bring on a war," and that it was "too late to remedy" the situation.[48] Glen and the assembly continued to spar over the proposed agency for another two weeks, and the assembly rejected the plan twice more before adjourning on May 16.[49] Then, a letter arrived on May 25 indicating that a party of Lower Creeks had plundered several traders residing among the Cherokees.[50] Glen and the council revisited the matter of the Creek agency and determined that it "be still pursued." With the assembly in recess, Glen invoked his executive authority and recommended having the Commissioner for Indian Affairs, William Pinckney, make a personal appearance in Creek country.[51] As Pinckney's health and fitness for the mission seems to have been in question, Glen recommended sending someone else "in his place" if he was unable to serve.[52]

Enter Mary Bosomworth. While the relationship between the Creek Indians and the South Carolina government spiraled toward conflict, Mary and Thomas were hastily making preparations for their trip to England.

This involved not only scraping together enough money for the voyage, but also padding the paper trail in order to make a favorable impression on high-ranking British officials.[53] Given that the Bosomworths had publicly broadcast their intention to go to England for years, it is no surprise that news of their plans preceded them to Charles Town. By what route this information traveled is impossible to know, but it appears that news circulated among Thomas's creditors, including Frederick Hobzendorf, the former surgeon at Frederica who had loaned Thomas 400 pounds three years earlier in 1749, a loan that remained uncollected. Around May 12, Hobzendorf seems to have received vague information that some of Thomas's property was being held in town and obtained an order to seize any of Thomas's "monies, goods, chattels, debts, and books of account" that might turn up. Perhaps unaware that Hobzendorf had initiated a lawsuit against him, Thomas arrived in Charles Town around May 27 and left ten bundles of deerskins with the widow Mary Yarworth. When a constable finally caught up with widow Yarworth on May 29 and discovered the ten bundles of deerskins on her property, a warrant was then issued to Yarworth to appear in court as an accomplice. At that point Thomas must have known that he would also be summoned to answer Hobzendorf's charges.[54]

Fortuitously, news of the Bosomworths' arrival reached the ears of James Glen, who still had not found a suitable or willing Creek agent. On May 27 Glen informed the council that the commissioner of Indian affairs had refused the assignment and then raised the possibility of sending Mary Bosomworth, noting that she "is in town." Although he had probably never met Mary in person, Glen knew of her and was already familiar with Mary's brother-in-law, Abraham. Sensing that Mary "might be useful," Glen nevertheless refused to consider investing Mary with the authority as agent, presumably because she was female. Instead, Glen recommended that she serve as an "assistant" to his preferred candidate, the Colleton planter Henry Hyrne.[55]

This proposal must have been floated to Mary by word of mouth, prompting her to write Glen on June 1 and volunteer for the mission. While couched in self-sacrificial terms, Mary nevertheless made it known that her acceptance was conditional upon certain demands being met. For one thing, Mary insisted that Thomas accompany her, arguing that his "advice and cooperation" would be "absolutely necessary for my carrying these matters into execution." Thomas may in fact have been useful to her, but Mary's main concern was the "unhappy state of affairs" relating to the Hobzendorf lawsuit, for which she requested a writ of protection granting Thomas temporary immunity from any legal action.[56]

Mary and Governor Glen spent the next two weeks haggling over the terms of her employment. On June 2 Mary was called into the council chamber and listened patiently as Governor Glen recounted recent Lower Creek atrocities and raised the possibility of having Mary persuade the Creeks to give satisfaction for them. In return, Glen offered to make sure that she would be "well recommended by this government when she went to Great Britain," along with a monetary reward, conditional upon her "[success] in the services proposed." Although the terms remained vague, Mary's interest was clearly piqued, and she asked the governor for a written proposal. Impatient, Thomas wrote to Glen later that night asking to know more about the "particulars" of Mary's assignment: What services was she to perform? On whose authority? How was "success" to be defined? What reward was she to expect from the government? Upon considering those pointed questions the council affirmed that Mary was to be employed principally as the agent's interpreter but vaguely hinted again that a greater reward might be forthcoming if she succeeded in forcing the Creeks to submit to government demands.

Negotiations appear to have stalled for a week, after which Mary and Henry Hyrne appeared before the council. Mary spoke first and repeated her demand that Thomas accompany her. Correctly anticipating that Hyrne was about to refuse the position of Creek agent, Glen agreed to have a writ of protection drawn up for Thomas and advanced the Bosomworths one hundred pounds.[57] On June 16 the council approved Thomas's appointment, guaranteeing him one hundred guineas (roughly 700 pounds in local paper currency) and another hundred if he succeeded in getting the Creeks to submit to the governor's demands. A week later the council drew up a commission and instructions for Thomas, and on July 3 the couple set off for Coweta.[58]

The council's instructions to Thomas must inform any analysis of the turn of events set forth in the lengthy journal Thomas kept during his agency. First, it is clear that Mary's relationship to "some of the head men" was considered pivotal, as the council specifically cited her "interest and influence" as the government's primary source of leverage over the Creeks. In fact, the instructions may even reflect Mary's input in the negotiating strategy, which was to have the Bosomworths first consult privately with her kinsmen, Chigelly and Malatchi, and only then publicize the government's demands. Importantly, the Bosomworths' compensation was not guaranteed, as Thomas's 700-pound salary was to be paid only "at your return." The government agreed to double it, but only upon the condition that their agency was a "success" as defined by Glen and members of the council. They set the bar prohibitively high by requiring the Creeks to (1) return the Cherokee prisoner; (2) execute "some of the most considerable" offenders; (3) restore the goods taken from the Cherokee traders; and (4) agree to peace terms with the Cherokees. In order to receive their full compensation, then, the Bosomworths had to provide proof that each of these requirements had been met, a burden that explains the length and detail of Thomas's journal and the numerous affidavits he attached attesting to its accuracy.

Importantly, the instructions provide unequivocal evidence that the government considered the Lower, rather than the Upper, Creeks guilty of the recent attacks against the Cherokees and their traders. The council specifically named "26 fellows of the Ousetchee town" as the perpetrators, adding that they had slipped home unnoticed by evading the garrison at Fort Moore and still had the Cherokee prisoner in their possession. In the event that the Lower Creeks would not give in to their demands, the council directed the Bosomworths to Oakfuskee, where they were to plead with the Upper Creeks to "procure satisfaction" from the Lower Creeks. If that failed, they were to institute a trade embargo against the Lower Creeks. This meant that Mary was being asked to confirm the Lower Creeks' and Malatchi's guilt, have some of her own relatives executed, and cut off their trade in the event that they did not succeed.[59] As will be demonstrated shortly, Mary instead shielded her kinsmen and artfully diverted blame away from the Lower Creeks by fingering Acorn Whistler as their scapegoat.

The Bosomworth agency got off to a rocky start. Much of their difficulty stemmed from damaging rumors that several Creek traders spread, namely, that Acorn Whistler had recently spent time at the Bosomworths' home and that the couple had some indirect role in the recent Cherokee murders. While Mary and Thomas dismissed these rumors as "entirely false," they were evidently concerned enough for their reputations to pen a brief letter to Glen denying having seen Acorn Whistler "for some years past."[60] Along with these blows to their character came blows to their physical well-being. As they approached Augusta Mary contracted a "violent fever" and had to recuperate there for three days before continuing on.[61] Her health would remain precarious for the duration of the agency.

After three weeks of travel, on July 24 Mary and Thomas arrived to a "joyous reception" in Coweta and took up lodging in Malatchi's home. Proceedings between them were delayed, however, due to Malatchi's absence and the annual *poskita* ceremonies in which the Cowetas were engaged. The Bosomworths finally got down to business on August 6, when Thomas related the South Carolina government's demands privately to Chigelly and Malatchi. As Thomas spoke, Malatchi and Chigelly became visibly concerned and admitted that they were having a difficult time comprehending the nature of the offense. Chigelly offered that he would have "readily agreed" to punish the offenders had they killed some "white people," but "to kill their own people for killing their enemies" was something he could not understand. Thomas tried to clarify the situation by putting it in native terms: the government wasn't demanding satisfaction simply for killing the Cherokees but rather for "staining the white beloved town [Charles Town] with the Blood of our friends." Open defiance of the English would not be tolerated, and Thomas threatened that failure to punish the offenders "could not be looked upon in any other light but as an open declaration of war against us." By giving in to Glen's demands, however, the Creeks could prove their friendship and maintain peace.

While the task of spilling the bad news to Chigelly and Malatchi was Thomas's responsibility, most of the important negotiating fell upon Mary's shoulders, and it is likely that talks between the English and the Creeks would have remained at an impasse without her contributions. Most important, of course, were Mary's kinship ties, which she invoked at every turn to enhance her authority as a negotiator, give added legitimacy to the agency itself, and appeal to the Creeks' sense of self-interest. Moreover, Mary made critical strategic decisions over the course of their agency and probably saved Thomas from several serious blunders by overruling him. As such, Mary's input was vital for reasons beyond her knowledge of the Muskogee language, and the agency of 1752, particularly at this vital early stage, was more Mary's moment than Thomas's.

Chigelly, for one, needed no prompting to recognize Mary's usefulness during the private talks held between him, Malatchi, and the Bosomworths on August 6. After listening to Thomas's harangue, Chigelly expressed satisfaction that Mary had accompanied him, claiming "the offenders were her relations as well as theirs." Because she was related to them by blood, Chigelly recognized that she had "as much to say in the affair" as they did, even though he regarded the proposed method of punishment "a very hard sentence." Thus invited to weigh in, Mary followed Chigelly's lead by reframing the issue as an internal matter for the Creeks to decide rather than one imposed externally by an English agent. She achieved this by reminding Chigelly and Malatchi that she had "as much regard for her friends, and relations, and the welfare of the whole nation" as they did, and appealed to Creek self-interest by demonstrating that executing one or two of the offenders would spare the rest of the nation from South Carolina's wrath. As she reasoned with her kinsmen Mary also played to their emotions. In addition to its lengthiness, Mary's speech, by Thomas's description, was "very feeling and affectionate," and he noted the tears that welled up in her eyes as she spoke. With such earnestness on display, how could Chigelly and Malatchi think that Mary had anything but their best interests in mind and was giving them useful advice?

Mary's tearful plea seems to have worked. While skeptical, Chigelly and Malatchi agreed to consult with the other headmen and give an answer to the Bosomworths in four days. Forgetting that Southeastern Indian leaders tended to deliberate carefully and slowly, Thomas impatiently asked Mary to exert pressure on the Creeks to give them a "positive answer one way or other" so that they could proceed to Oakfuskee. Mary, who had a better understanding of the situation, urged patience, adding that she "did not think proper to push the point any further at present." "All our hopes of success," she reminded Thomas, were "entirely founded on the interest and influence" of Malatchi and Chigelly. To leave Coweta prematurely would "naturally disgust them and would be a very great obstacle towards obtaining the satisfaction demanded." The Upper Creeks, she surmised, would do nothing contrary to the wishes of the Lower Creeks. Wisely, Thomas heeded Mary's advice and the couple remained in Coweta awaiting their reply.

As promised, Chigelly called headmen to the square four days later and acquainted them with everything Mary and Thomas had mentioned to him privately. After an all-night deliberation, the headmen reassembled in the Coweta square on August 11, only to inform the Bosomworths that they "could not determine what answer was best to be given to the demand that was made." Thomas related that he used "all the arguments in my power" to get them to comply, but to no effect, and the deliberations yet again seemed to be at an impasse.

At that point, however, Mary stepped forward to deliver "a very long and publick speech" that proved to be far more effective than anything Thomas could have mustered. Mary's oration is likewise noteworthy because rarely, if ever, did Creek women speak publicly before leading headmen and warriors, indicating that this was a privilege granted only to the occasional "great beloved woman." By invoking kinship in her prefatory remarks, Mary addressed the Indians more as a clan matriarch than as a representative of the South Carolina government. She began by reminding them that she had "as many friends and relatives in the nation as any of them" and thus had their welfare equally in mind. Sternly, she repeated Thomas's warnings that the South Carolina government had made its decision and that the entire Creek nation would surely suffer if they did not punish the offenders. Some of them, she pointed out, "were her own relations," adding that she would not speak against them "if she was not convinced that it was for the good of the whole nation." Indecision was not an option, so Mary shrewdly invoked her femininity to prick the touchy masculine sensibilities of her Creek kinsmen, stating that "it was very weak and childish for them to declare that they did not know what was best to be done." Even a woman like herself could figure out what to do.

After verbally emasculating the headmen, Mary singled out for chastisement a man named Hiacpellechi, one of her "relations" from Osuche. She asked Hiacpellechi to "tell the truth" about what happened, and Hiacpellechi admitted his complicity in the murders but then fingered Acorn Whistler as the "cause of all the mischief that was done." Hiacpellechi explained that his party of twenty-six Lower Creeks had been abroad in pursuit of their enemies with "no manner of intention of going to Charles Town," but somewhere on the path they met up with Acorn Whistler, who diverted them to the capital. Once there, Acorn Whistler devised a plan by which the Lower Creeks were to "feign a peace" with the Cherokees and then kill them. The Lower Creeks, he pleaded, were simply following the orders of an esteemed warrior.

Although he was in all probability not guilty of these deeds, Acorn Whistler proved an advantageous scapegoat for everyone with an interest in this crisis—everyone except, obviously, Acorn Whistler. Governor Glen, for one, was deeply suspicious of Acorn Whistler the day after the murders, and Mary surmised that he might be willing to accept his death as a means of upholding the colony's honor and of demonstrating his effectiveness as governor. The interests of the Bosomworths and Malatchi were also deeply intertwined. Not only did the success of the Bosom-worths' mission hinge upon their ability to have someone executed, but Mary's land claims also rested in large part upon Malatchi's reputation. As it stood, Governor Glen and the Georgia magistrates deeply mistrusted Malatchi because of his connections to the French, the 1749 disturbances in Savannah, and the recent Cherokee murders. Rehabilitating Malatchi, then, was necessary if British officials were ever to acknowledge the valid-ity of the many deeds and declarations he had endorsed in Mary's behalf. If Malatchi could be given at least some of the credit for having Acorn Whis-tler punished, then perhaps Governor Glen would form a good opinion of him. And, while Malatchi had the most to gain individually, the entire body of Lower Creeks would be more than satisfied to shift blame upon the Upper Creeks and avoid executing their own people.

Ultimately, determining what to do was Malatchi's decision. Although he often followed Mary's counsel, Malatchi was not at first predisposed to executing anybody, thinking it "a very hard demand." At Mary's insis-tence, Malatchi thought further about the matter and convened with two of Acorn Whistler's "very near relations" who happened to be in Coweta. Somewhat surprisingly, the two men consented to the execution. This evi-dently jogged Malatchi's memory, as he recalled a recent conversation he had had with Acorn Whistler in which Whistler threatened war against the English. Perhaps Acorn Whistler's death would remove the strain between the Creeks and South Carolina. Following that logic, Malatchi agreed that Acorn Whistler should make the ultimate sacrifice for the good of the nation.

As Thomas recalled shortly thereafter, "the reasonableness and justice of this proposal was agreed to, but the difficulty lay in the execution." The first problem to be solved was determining who would carry out the act of execution. As the tradition of blood vengeance required Acorn Whis-tler's clan-kin to retaliate, his death posed a real threat of cyclical inter-clan bloodshed. Another difficulty involved how the execution might be justified to Acorn Whistler's relatives, as Malatchi knew that they would protest and perhaps retaliate if they knew he had been killed at the behest of the English. The solution, then, was to work within the clan system by having one of Acorn Whistler's relatives carry out the punishment, so as to make it appear that other clans had nothing to do with his death. Malatchi likewise recommended not immediately divulging the real reason for his execution; better to explain it as a "little private resentment," wait until tempers cooled, and then divulge that information. So, in the end Malatchi settled on a plan whereby Acorn Whistler's nephew would do the deed and plead self-defense on the grounds of a trumped-up charge that "his uncle was mad and wanted to kill him." On August 12 the young man was sent away, while the Bosomworths and Lower Creek leaders waited impatiently to receive word of Acorn Whistler's execution.

As the preceding discussion indicates, Mary's kinship connections played a decisive role in convincing the Lower Creeks to execute Acorn Whistler. Blood ties alone, however, only partly explain Mary's dexterous handling of the delicate matters that arose during the course of the agency. Knowledge of the Creek political terrain, long-standing personal grudges, the habits of traders and packhorsemen, and even the contours of local information networks constitute what might be described as "frontier acumen," which Mary possessed in greater quantities than her husband. At critical junctures, self-preservation and the success of the mission hinged upon Mary's ability to summon this frontier acumen and make the right decision at the right time. That Thomas regularly deferred to Mary's judgment illustrates just how important her accumulated life experiences were to the mission.

Take, for example, Mary's handling of the startling news she received on August 19, when she met a runner in the town of Hitchiti who informed her that "the business was done," meaning that Acorn Whistler had been killed. Mary realized immediately the need for secrecy, in order to conceal the circumstances of his death and thereby avoid the clan retribution that she and Malatchi feared. The need for secrecy was compounded by the steady flow of liquor in Hitchiti. A rum peddler and frequent witness to the drinking habits of Indians and traders alike, Mary was painfully aware that strong drink meant loose lips and uncontrollable rage. To divulge sensitive information when many of the headmen and traders were out of their wits on alcohol was to risk serious physical harm. Wisely accounting for these circumstances, Mary shushed the runner who delivered the news and told him "not to speak any more" about the affair, "either to white people or Indians." Mary kept the news of Acorn Whistler's death close to her chest for the entire day, confiding only in the trader Lachlan McIntosh and an unnamed "trusty messenger" sent to convey the information to the Cussita King. Meanwhile, Mary refrained from divulging any information to Chigelly and Malatchi, who were in the midst of a drinking binge. In fact, Mary left Hitchiti to attend to other business before they came out of their stupor, and the pair wound up learning of Acorn Whistler's execution a couple of days later.

Another important decision involved how and when to confront Acorn Whistler's Upper Creek relatives about the circumstances of his death. Timing was everything, as the original plan called for masking his execution as a private act of vengeance, and only disclosing the South Carolina government's role in it after tempers had cooled. As usual, Thomas rashly proposed heading to the Upper Creeks to confront Acorn Whistler's relatives just two days after they had received word of his death. Once again Mary overruled him. As the Indians "undertook management of the affair," Mary discerned that it was best to let them remain in charge of the situation and wait "till we heard further." Thomas humbly deferred to Mary's wisdom, and the couple instead passed their time in Apalachicola collecting stolen horses and reprimanding a trader for spreading lies about them.

To avoid the appearance of English heavy-handedness, Mary understood the importance of minimizing Thomas's role and letting the Indians control the situation. The proposed excursion to the Upper Creeks, then, would not occur until Lower Creek leaders believed the time was right. On August 29 Malatchi met with the Cussita King and the two decided to send Isspuffnee, a Coweta "beloved man" and "very near relation" of Acorn Whistler's, to deliver the bad news. The next day a messenger arrived announcing that the executioner, Acorn Whistler's nephew, had also been killed to preserve the secrecy of the mission. This information seemed to lend greater urgency to the situation, so Malatchi convened another meeting on August 31 to finalize their plans. In consultation with the Bosomworths, Malatchi decided that they should travel to the Upper Creeks with Chigelly and Isspuffnee. The task would be to convince the Upper Creeks of the "reasonableness of this action and the absolute necessity of publicly declaring the true cause" of Acorn Whistler's death.

Thomas's instructions from Governor Glen called for him to conduct business with the Upper Creeks in the town of Oakfuskee, which had a long history of diplomacy with the South Carolina colony. At the time the Bosomworths and their Lower Creek companions left Coweta for the Upper Creeks on September 1, Thomas seemed to have intended to honor the governor's instructions. However, after receiving a warm welcome in Tuckabatchee, Mary decided "it would be much better to give the talk out in this town than to proceed to the Oakfuskees." Once again, Mary rather than Thomas seemed to be calling the shots. She explained to Thomas that Acorn Whistler's death was "a very ticklish point" and discerned that it would be necessary "to have some friends to stand by us" should something bad happen. Tuckabatchee and Coweta, she knew, had long considered themselves "friend towns," and clan ties further bound the two peoples, Mary included. Thomas, afraid to breach his instructions in any way, protested mildly to Mary, who finally convinced him to stay by citing fatigue and arguing that "nothing could be done at the Oakfuskees, which could not as well or more effectually be done here." Somewhat reluctantly, then, Thomas began writing letters to Upper Creek headmen and traders, asking them to appear in Tuckabatchee in six days to hear his talk.

Representatives from the Upper Creek towns began arriving in Tuckabatchee around September 20, and the following day they gathered in the town square to hear what Thomas had to say. Bosomworth presented his credentials, reminded the Creeks of their treaty obligations by ticking off numerous violations, and then offered words in defense of Acorn Whistler's execution. On paper, Thomas's oration appears to have been ably presented. At the same time, however, he seems to have missed his mark with the audience, for he rarely used Creek idiomatic expressions and generated no give-and-take with the assembled Upper Creek headmen. That is probably why Mary had to step in after Thomas had finished speaking and hand over the proceedings to the Atasi King, who she introduced as the "one man here present ... who knows the truth." At that point the Atasi King explained that he was a relative of Acorn Whistler and had assented to the execution. The rest of the Upper Creek leaders followed suit and thanked Acorn Whistler's relations for setting matters straight. The Bosomworths met with the headmen again the following day, coaxing from them a tentative agreement to cease hostilities against the Cherokees, one of their agency's principal goals.

If there was any doubt that self-interest motivated the Bosomworths, then the hidden agenda of September 23 confirms that the couple had more on their minds than intercultural harmony when they volunteered for the Creek mission. That day was to have been set aside to ratify a written copy of the Tuckabatchee proceedings, and Thomas's terse journal entry for September 23 employs uncharacteristically passive verb constructions to give the impression that the day was uneventful: "the above proceedings were read, and interpreted, paragraph by paragraph, and acknowledged and declared by all the head men to be the true interest and meaning of the speeches made, and the answers given by them."

What Thomas did not reveal was that he had the Upper Creeks sign a written instrument repudiating the Graham deed of May 1751. In the "Repudiation," fifteen Upper Creek leaders—the same men who had ratified Thomas's journal entries—vowed that they "never did (with our knowledge or consent)" convey the three islands and Yamacraw tract to the Georgia government and insisted that those lands ought to belong to Mary "in justice to our beloved woman Coosaponakeesa." The Georgia Trustees' title to those lands, they declared, was "fraudulent," because Malatchi had previously conveyed them to Mary. As the Georgia government considered the Graham deed a lynchpin in their case against the Bosomworths, the "Repudiation" struck a major blow by nullifying it.[62]

Following the momentous events in Tuckabatchee, Mary's direct participation in Thomas's affairs lessened dramatically, owing most likely to her fall from a horse on her way back to Coweta. Hobbling into town "very much hurt" on September 26, Mary convalesced in Coweta throughout the fall, winter, and much of spring.[63] During that time her activity seems to have been limited due to the injury; she does not surface again in Thomas's journal until early November.[64] Meanwhile, Thomas wrested a tentative agreement from the Lower Creeks to end their war with the Cherokees and began making arrangements for an expected Creek meeting with the South Carolina governor. Throughout November and December, Thomas took affidavits from traders and other witnesses attesting to the veracity of his now-lengthy journal, parts of which he had already sent along to Governor Glen.[65]

On December 8 the Bosomworths' messenger Lachlan McIntosh arrived from Charles Town with two letters from Governor Glen, one directed at the Creeks and the other at Thomas Bosomworth. In his letter to the Creeks, Glen lavished praise upon their leaders for executing Acorn Whistler and singled out Malatchi as a "worthy defendant of the renowned Brims and the heir of all of his virtues." In addition to these laudatory remarks, Glen extended to Malatchi an invitation to meet with him next spring to ratify the peace agreement with the Cherokees. To Bosomworth, Glen indicated that the council was "well pleased" with Mary's efforts and ordered Thomas immediately to return "as you have now finished the business."[66] Thus summoned by the governor, Thomas prepared to go to Charles Town while Mary continued her convalescence in Coweta. Although the Bosomworths' business in the Creek nation was finished for the time being, the couple soon realized that settling their claims would require much more work in Charles Town, London, and Savannah.

8 🖎 *"Your Memorialist"*

Your Memorialist is of Indian Extract, descended by the Maternal
Line from the Sister of the old Emperor of the Creek nations, a
numerous, bold, and warlike People, who have always maintained
their own Possessions and Independency against all Opposers by
War and ever since the first Settlement of the Colony of Georgia,
always proved themselves faithfull Allies and a strong Barrier to his
Majesty's Southern Frontiers.

Coosaponakeesa, 1754

That Your Memorialist always Gloried in having it in her power
when in her Native Country to be of Service to his Majesty's
Subjects & in return Your Memorialist might perish in the Streets
of Your great Metropolis, if the King of Kings had not most wisely
ordained.

Coosaponakeesa, 1755

I, Mary the wife of the within named Thomas Bosomworth . . . do
declare [and] renounce all Title or Claim of Dower that I might
claim or be intitled to after the Death of said Husband to or out of
the Lands or Hereditements hereby conveyed.

Mary Bosomworth, 1760

JUDGED IN RELATION TO Governor Glen's instructions, or perhaps in
relation to any standard, the Bosomworth agency to the Creeks was an
unqualified success. Acorn Whistler was dead, peace between the Creeks
and Cherokees was imminent, and Governor Glen appeared satisfied
with the Bosomworths' conduct and the results. But upon returning to
Charles Town, Thomas and Mary again found themselves haggling for
denied income due to the assembly's repeated refusal to honor the governor's commitments. After spending a year in the colony petitioning, Mary

and Thomas ended up getting only a portion of what they had asked for, but the final sum proved sufficient to launch them on their long-delayed voyage to London.

In 1754, Mary and Thomas finally reached Britain's "great metropolis," where they spent the better part of a year lobbying the highest offices of the home government. Their petitions, however, were met with skepticism and delay, as British officials referred their case back to Georgia. After their return home in 1755, the beleaguered couple spent the next four years haggling with the colony's governors, and, by dint of Thomas's perseverance, reached a compromise that netted them St. Catherine's Island and in excess of two thousand pounds. With clear title and perhaps even a cleared name, Mary was finally in a position to enjoy the twilight of her life with peace of mind. The pity of it all is that Mary did not long enjoy the benefits of her hard-won gains; she died on the island around 1764, gone and seemingly forgotten.

Epic in terms of the amount of ink spilled, distance traveled, and time, energy, and money spent, Mary's quests at the end of her life affirm the complexity of life for bicultural individuals living in the eighteenth-century in the British Empire. As the historian Joshua Piker reminds us, Mary was the product of a distinctly colonial world where ambitious nobodies could rise to prominence by crafting "novel but effective forms of power." "In the right context," Piker adds, "being colonial could mean inhabiting a very advantageous position, a position with access to both an established center of power and an emerging world of transformative possibility." Mary's Creek ancestry and kinship ties represented one such potential advantage, particularly in London, where some of her grandiose claims might have been taken at face value out of ignorance. Knowing this, Mary repeatedly invoked her invented Creek name, Coosaponakeesa, and the title of Creek "princess" in an attempt to leverage Creek power when pressing her case before British authorities. The problem, however, was that Mary's power was mostly illusory; if received skeptically in London, Mary's claim as "princess" of the Creeks held no weight on the Chattahoochee River, and even her kinsman Malatchi had once scoffed at being equated politically with an "old woman." Moreover, the need to transform Indian land grants into English title, combined with her poverty, required Mary to humble herself before the authorities as a memorialist who had been of great "service to His Majesty's subjects." Ironically, in her last action before the state, the "Creek Princess" had to sign away dower rights to relinquished property, thus reverting to a feme covert like any other English wife. She was not, of course, a typical English wife but an anomaly in a rising plantation society that drew ever sharpening distinctions between Englishman and Indian. That she died without eulogy or public acknowledgment suggests that there was no longer a place in Georgia for an anomaly like Mary Bosomworth.

Charles Town

After leaving Coweta in late December, Thomas met with the governor in Charles Town on January 8, thus marking the end of his official duties.[1] With the Creek agency behind him, Thomas's next task was to demonstrate his fulfillment of the standards for "success" the council had set. First, he presented the remainder of his journal, along with a submissive letter to Governor Glen explaining that everything in it was "plain fact."[2] Thinking the journal might not be enough, Thomas then wrote a windy appendix focusing on the many "obstacles" he had had to overcome during the course of his agency, and submitted it along with eleven sworn statements confirming various details in his journal. In all, the copious paperwork seemed to make the necessary point: that each of the council's instructions had been adhered to in the spirit, if not by the letter, of the law.[3]

While the governor and council were predisposed to view Thomas's submissions favorably, the assembly was not, having never consented to the Creek agency in the first place. As the assembly held the purse strings, though, Thomas had little choice but to take up matters with them. Prematurely, perhaps, back in November, Thomas had sent to the assembly an account for his services totaling a whopping 2,695 pounds, hoping that they would speedily provide for him in that year's tax bill.[4] Instead, the assembly sat on his account and took no action until February, when it received Thomas's journal and other paperwork. On February 24, a subcommittee assigned to Thomas's case opined that the Creek agency had been "contrary to their opinion" and that Thomas's request "should not be allowed in the estimate" for the current tax bill.[5] Glen appealed to the assembly again a few days later, but the assembly ended up excluding Thomas's requested funds and adjourned.[6]

Increasingly distraught, Thomas raised the issue of his compensation again when the assembly reconvened in April. Hoping to use the governor and council as leverage, Thomas submitted a plaintive memorial practically begging them to pressure the assembly for "speedy relief." The council did as Thomas requested but made the tactical decision to request a more modest sum of 475 pounds as payment for presents the Bosomworths distributed to the Creeks from their own stockpiles.[7] The assembly called Thomas before them on April 18 and demanded more paperwork.[8] Wasting no time, Thomas petitioned the governor and council a day later, again asking them to intercede in his behalf. This time, his tone was even more desperate. Thomas explained "there is now an action [that] lyes in the court of common pleas against a poor widow" [Mary Yarworth], who was party to the Hobzendorf lawsuit, and pleaded for "immediate cash" to avert the "utter ruin of an innocent person." Thomas's situation meanwhile was "as gloomy as imagination can form to complement human misery."[9] Seeming to pity Bosomworth, the council made one final plea for his relief, which the assembly again refused to consider until the fall.[10]

While Thomas was in Charles Town desperately trying to avoid insolvency, Mary spent seven months in Coweta—possibly the most time she had spent there continuously since early adulthood. From there, Mary was perhaps unaware of the difficulties her husband was having in Charles Town and must have been cautiously optimistic when she received a letter from Governor Glen in late March in which he promised to "take every opportunity of acknowledging" them to officials in London.[11] By April plans were set in motion for the Creeks to visit South Carolina, and Mary was undoubtedly with them en route by early May.[12] Finally, on May 23 Mary's party of thirty Lower Creeks, joined by seventy more from the Upper towns, arrived in the capital, thus setting the stage for talks between the Indians and Governor Glen that had been anticipated since the fall.[13]

Historically speaking, Governor Glen's conference with the Creek Indians in 1753 ranks as one of the notable diplomatic episodes in the colonial South. The stakes were high. One necessary task was to diffuse any lingering resentment over Acorn Whistler's execution, which Governor Glen and Malatchi seem to have accomplished on the first day of the proceedings. This in turn enabled Glen and Malatchi to mend their relationship, as is evidenced by the frequency with which Glen singled out Malatchi for praise and compared him to his esteemed "father," Brims. More importantly, Glen was able to accomplish what had seemed impossible just the year before by having the Creeks ratify peace with the Cherokees. Unlike past truces, this one proved durable and deep, to the point where some Creeks and Cherokees even intermarried, lived together, and coordinated diplomacy. Finally, the conference of 1753 was also well publicized, as transcripts of the proceedings found their way into newspapers not only in South Carolina, but also in Philadelphia, Boston, New York, and London.[14]

From the Bosomworths' perspective, however, the importance of the conference lay in the opportunity it gave Mary to interject, using Malatchi as her medium, the issue of her outstanding land claims. While Mary refrained from interpreting, perhaps to give the appearance of impartiality, she was present at the conference, and during moments of recess was able to coach Malatchi and make sure he raised the subject matter of interest to her. This is not to say that Malatchi lacked a will of his own, but rather that he and Mary shared a common interest in stifling settler encroachment onto lands they both considered to be, in one way or another, theirs.

Mary's not-so-invisible hand began to manifest itself on day two of the proceedings. Malatchi transitioned to the subject of Mary's land claims first by comparing Charles Town, a town of "old standing" and long friendship with the Creeks, to the "other town in the colony of Georgia [Savannah]," which, he complained, had been "encroaching upon our lands reserved by treaty." Malatchi informed Glen that Mary had been their interpreter ever since the arrival of the first Georgia settlers, tacitly reminding him that Mary had an existing claim to land there. Malatchi then brought up the issue of the so-called Graham deed and invited other headmen to nullify it. Out of deference to Malatchi, no one interjected, and Malatchi was able to hold the floor and continue to insist that Mary was an Indian and "entitled to all the rights and privileges of an Indian," including land ownership. Significantly, Malatchi referred to Mary as "my sister" on two separate occasions, thereby confirming the blood ties between the two, which William Stephens had called into question years before.[15]

Glen listened patiently to Malatchi and responded in earnest that as Georgia was a "distinct province," he was powerless to decide "such controversies" outside of his jurisdiction.[16] The matter of Mary's land claims lay dormant until Malatchi brought them up again on the third day of the conference, repeating many stock assertions about Georgia's malfeasance and Mary's past service. What Malatchi appears to have wanted most, however, was for the Upper Creeks to make an explicit public statement rejecting the "pretended" Graham deed. Several men in the room had signed both the 1751 Graham deed and the Bosomworths' "Repudiation" of it in September 1752. Therefore, a public denial was needed to support the argument that Graham had duped the Upper Creeks into signing something they neither undersood nor supported. Malatchi informed Glen that he had "enquired of all the head men" whether or not they had signed such a grant and that everyone he had spoken to privately had denied it. Then, addressing the Creek headmen in the room, Malatchi asked them publicly to "declare before your Excellency whether they assented to any grant or not." Unwilling to dredge up the Georgia controversy again, at that point Glen politely cut Malatchi off.[17] Talks continued for another day, during which Malatchi sparred with the Upper Creeks over trade policy, further ingratiating himself to Glen. After presents were distributed on June 3, the Creek leaders departed from Charles Town, and the conference of 1753 came to an unceremonious end.[18]

In retrospect, it would appear that Malatchi's performance before the South Carolina governor was modestly successful. At the very least, Malatchi seems to have won over James Glen, which cleared the odium associated with his name and Mary's. By invoking the issue of the disputed Georgia lands twice at the conference, Malatchi managed to have his sentiments entered into the public record and elicited a promise from Glen to intervene in Mary's behalf. Glen made good on his word. On July 30, Glen wrote a lengthy letter to the board of trade indicating that the Bosomworth controversy required its "particular notice" and informing them that Malatchi and others had pressed the issue "much more in private" than was even indicated in their public talks. In mentioning these private consultations, Glen revealed that many of the Upper Creeks who had purportedly signed the Graham deed "absolutely disavow[ed]" conveying lands to the Georgia Trustees, thus calling into question the deed's legitimacy.[19]

For good reason, then, Mary and Thomas came to regard South Carolina as friendly territory. Despite their ongoing trouble with the assembly, certain institutions of government proved useful to them, particularly the Secretary of State's office, where documents relating to property transactions were recorded. Up to that point, most of the documents the Bosomworths had compiled in defense of their case remained in their possession; they had, in fact, for years carried around several critical items that were controversial and of dubious legality in the minds of the Georgia magistrates. As such, even before the Creek conference began, Thomas had recorded Malatchi's 1748 Deed for the three coastal islands, along with the August 2, 1750 "Confirmation Deeds" and the recent Upper Creek "Repudiation" of the Graham deed.[20] After the conference, Mary and Thomas picked up where Thomas had left off by recording, among other things, Thomas Christie's important minutes of the 1738 meeting with Oglethorpe.[21] By entering these documents into the public record, Thomas managed to endow them with at least a semblance of legal standing, which was necessary if they were ever to present their case to officials in London.

Meanwhile, Mary lobbied the government in order to reclaim the Colleton County lands she and John Musgrove had abandoned back in 1732. After having her attorney, Charles Pinckney, and the colony surveyor George Hunter conduct an initial search for John's old paperwork, Mary learned that there was sufficient evidence to back up her claims. Accordingly, on June 30 Mary filed a petition with the governor and council recounting John Musgrove's original purchase of 650 acres in Colleton County in 1716. In it, she affirmed how John had taken all the necessary steps to secure title to those lands and explained that their attorney, Daniel Green, had neglected to follow through by having the royal grants sent to him in Georgia. Her request was simply to have John's old grants made out in her name. While seemingly receptive to Mary's request, the council postponed making a final decision until more proof could be obtained.[22]

By this point in her life Mary was accustomed to having men in high places deny her petitions. This time, however, the governor and council kept an open mind, and Mary likewise worked hard to provide the evidence that was requested of her. First, on July 4 Mary had the executor of Daniel Green's estate, Jacob Motte, inspect the family's papers to see if any documents pertaining to the Musgrove lands could be found. The search turned up nothing, so Mary improvised by beating the bushes around Charles Town to find longtime residents who knew something about her past. That search produced none other than Elizabeth Clark Hunt, former wife of the now deceased trader Alexander Clark and longtime resident of St. Bartholomew's Parish. Mary had Elizabeth draw up a written statement that confirmed much of what Mary had said about her land claims. Hunt first vouched that she had known Mary since girlhood and remembered John making the purchase of land around the time the Musgroves wed. Hunt confirmed that the lands had remained in their possession until their departure for Georgia and were commonly known as "Musgrove's lands" for several years thereafter.[23]

Sensing that her first petition had not quite made the point, on August 7 Mary drew up another petition, which was similar in focus but lengthier, offering more of the details that she "full well remembered." Mary's second petition seemed to have hit the mark; perhaps the minute details she provided and the name dropping she engaged in validated her story.[24] Moreover, the land records unquestionably proved much of what Mary had said, so on August 8 Governor Glen and the council awarded her the two tracts totaling 440 acres and issued a warrant to have another tract of 210 acres surveyed to make up the difference.[25] Very quickly, and with relatively little fuss, Mary again was a landowner in Colleton County, and the couple's prospects looked better than they had for quite some time.

However beneficial title to land in South Carolina might have been, the Bosomworths had yet to obtain compensation for the Creek agency and Thomas still had a debt lawsuit hanging over his head. As the assembly was scheduled to convene again in late August, Thomas decided one last time to appeal for the money and petitioned the governor and council to intervene in his behalf. As before, the assembly refused to take action, and again brushed them off until a future legislative session.[26] By September 3 Thomas had given up on the assembly, so he penned a plaintive letter to Glen asking the governor to plead their case in Great Britain, which Thomas described as "our last resource."[27] Glen had previously raised the issue with the board of trade, so the governor sent a letter to the magistrates of Georgia urging them to find "some remedy."[28] Glen's letter seems to have fallen on deaf ears, however, as high officials in Georgia believed that the Bosomworth agency was little more than a ploy to obtain support from the neighboring province.[29] Predictably, the Georgians ignored Glen's letter, never bothering even to respond.

What happened to the Bosomworths next is difficult to determine, as the paper trail leaves few clues of their activity. Having left their plantation on St. Catherine's Island under the care of Adam Bosomworth, it appears that the couple remained in South Carolina for almost another year, seeking compensation for the Creek agency and finalizing plans for their voyage to London.[30] Thomas miraculously evaded Hobzendorf's lawsuit, thanks to Governor Glen's repeated re-issuance of writs of protection, the last of which came in January 1754.[31] During that time, Mary and Thomas may have even begun making improvements to their newly acquired South Carolina properties, as there is evidence to suggest that the couple planted grass on one of the Colleton County tracts. Their attempts to settle there again, however, brought them into conflict with the Colleton landowner Joseph Glover, who in mid-September allegedly arrived armed and on horseback on Mary's property, dismounted, and then trampled underfoot their freshly sown grass. In retaliation, on November 13 Thomas filed a lawsuit against Glover for trespass, requesting damages totaling 500 pounds. The Court of Common Pleas heard their case the following April but appears to have rendered no judgment, leaving the Bosomworths still short on funds.[32]

Litigious by nature, Thomas filed one more lawsuit while in South Carolina, this time seeking the long-awaited compensation for the Creek agency. The lawsuit appears to have originated with an unfounded rumor that the assembly, in its 1754 tax bill, had finally agreed to pay the Bosomworths in excess of 2,200 pounds. When no compensation appeared forthcoming, Thomas on June 7 confronted the provincial treasurer, Jacob Motte, demanding his money. Motte refused to honor the request, prompting Thomas to file a lawsuit against him for 3,000 pounds, including damages. The case eventually made it to court, and Motte pled not guilty, arguing that Thomas's charge "had no basis in law." The plaintiff, however, failed to appear, so the court gave Bosomworth another year to appear and offer his side of the story.[33] In the end, the lawsuit proved meaningless, as Thomas and Mary by then were in London, where the next phase of their protracted case was underway.

London

Mary and Thomas's voyage to London in 1754 was long in the making. Finally, after experiencing two years of frustration in South Carolina, the couple somehow managed to scrape together enough money for passage on a ship. They made their break sometime after July 2, arriving in London before mid-October. After eight months of petitioning and pleading face-to-face with members of the board of trade, Mary had to face the fact that that august body had done little more than refer her case back to Georgia. Given their past brushes with Georgia officials, Mary and Thomas must have felt the board's resolution offered them little hope, and they must have wondered if it had all been worth it.

Speaking with his friend James Boswell in 1777, the poet and scholar Samuel Johnson once quipped "when a man is tired of London, he is tired of life; for there is in London all that life can afford." From the perspective of London's elite, Johnson's observations seem justified, as the city had emerged as the administrative, economic, and cultural center of a vast empire spanning the globe. Estimated at well over half a million, the greater London area was home to one tenth of the English population, and the city had burst well beyond the confines of its ancient city walls and nearby Westminster.[34] Buildings erected in that century reflected the nation's accruing wealth, and the city—parts of it, anyway—had become a physically attractive place. By 1750, fifty-one stately houses had sprung up around Grosvenor Square, sixteen of which were occupied by peers of the realm, including three earls and a lord.[35] Pleasing to the eye, London offered stimulating social and cultural life, as Londoners could frequent its many coffee houses and taverns or take in a show in the West End at the Theater Royal or Covent Garden. Intellectual life was also thriving; during Mary's stay in London, Samuel Johnson published his magnum opus, the *Dictionary of the English Language*.[36]

But while the chronicles of Johnson's life draw attention to the city's Georgian splendor, there was another London—that of pickpockets and prostitutes, of highwaymen and hangmen, of wrenching poverty and madness—that was overcrowded, filthy, and generally appalling by modern standards. This was the world of London's slums, such as those in St. Giles Parish, where boarders huddled five to a room and old, rickety houses routinely collapsed, sometimes killing their occupants. Like shelter, food was in short supply, and what was available was nutritionally deficient, leaving the constitutions of the city's poorest residents, many of whom were destined for one of the local charity hospitals, further weakened. Hard on English bodies, life in London was perhaps even harder on the nose. Londoners were in the habit of depositing fecal matter in their own basements, while the city's many horses and the offal of slaughtered animals contributed to the oppressive stench of decaying body matter and effluvia. The River Thames naturally suffered from the city's squalid growth; it was not uncommon to find industrial waste or the bloated corpse of a pauper washing up on the river's banks. Muck and mire several inches thick covered London's streets, which the wealthy did their best to avoid.[37]

Mary leaves very little evidence of her impression of London. Londoners, however, had undoubtedly become keenly interested in North America around the time of the Bosomworths' arrival thanks to the brewing conflict with France, which, as the *Gentleman's Magazine* put it, "justly excited the attention of the publick."[38] What would be known as the French and Indian War figured prominently in the London press, which published